Lecture Notes in Computer Science   11283

Commenced Publication in 1973
Founding and Former Series Editors:
Gerhard Goos, Juris Hartmanis, and Jan van Leeuwen

More information about this series at http://www.springer.com/series/7408

Swaroop Pophale · Neena Imam
Ferrol Aderholdt · Manjunath Gorentla Venkata (Eds.)

OpenSHMEM and Related Technologies

OpenSHMEM in the Era of Extreme Heterogeneity

5th Workshop, OpenSHMEM 2018
Baltimore, MD, USA, August 21–23, 2018
Revised Selected Papers

Springer

Editors
Swaroop Pophale 🔘
Oak Ridge National Laboratory
Oak Ridge, TN, USA

Ferrol Aderholdt 🔘
Oak Ridge National Laboratory
Oak Ridge, TN, USA

Neena Imam 🔘
Oak Ridge National Laboratory
Oak Ridge, TN, USA

Manjunath Gorentla Venkata 🔘
Oak Ridge National Laboratory
Oak Ridge, TN, USA

ISSN 0302-9743   ISSN 1611-3349   (electronic)
Lecture Notes in Computer Science
ISBN 978-3-030-04917-1   ISBN 978-3-030-04918-8   (eBook)
https://doi.org/10.1007/978-3-030-04918-8

Library of Congress Control Number: 2018962483

LNCS Sublibrary: SL2 – Programming and Software Engineering

This Springer imprint is published by the registered company Springer Nature Switzerland AG
The registered company address is: Gewerbestrasse 11, 6330 Cham, Switzerland

Preface

The OpenSHMEM Workshop is the premier venue for presenting new and innovative PGAS research in the context of OpenSHMEM. OpenSHMEM 2018, held in Baltimore, Maryland, was the fifth event in the OpenSHMEM and Related Technologies workshop series. The workshop was organized by Oak Ridge National Laboratory (ORNL) and sponsored by ORNL and the Department of Defense. The workshop was attended by participants from across academia, industry, and private and federal research organizations.

This year, the workshop focused on OpenSHMEM in the Era of Extreme Heterogeneity. Extremely heterogeneous computing platforms are emerging in every domain of computing. These platforms are the result of integrating multiple types of processing units and memory components in a single computing platform. There is also emerging heterogeneity in the application workloads and user community. As the international scientific community races to achieve exascale computing, the level of heterogeneity in computing hardware, software, and applications is expected to increase. OpenSHMEM 2018 was organized to prepare the SHMEM programming model for such extremely heterogeneous environment. The workshop included two days of technical presentations followed by one day dedicated to the OpenSHMEM Specification discussions and development. This year the workshop had two keynote addresses, one from Gil Bloch from Mellanox and the second one from Will Deacon from ARM. Gil's talk was focused on InfiniBand In-Network Computing Technology and Roadmap and its impact on current data-centric vision of HPC. Will's keynote highlighted the memory consistency models and his experiences in formalizing the same for Armv8 architecture.

This proceedings volume comprises a collection of papers presented at the workshop. All papers submitted to the workshop were peer-reviewed by the Program Committee, which included members from universities, industry, and research laboratories. Each paper was reviewed by at least three reviewers. In total, 14 full papers were selected to be presented at the workshop. The technical papers provide a variety of ideas for extending the OpenSHMEM specification and they discuss a variety of concepts, including interesting use of OpenSHMEM in HOOVER – a distributed, flexible, and scalable streaming graph processor and scaling OpenSHMEM to handle massively parallel processor arrays, to name a few. The Oak Ridge Benchmark Suite provides the much-needed micro and macro benchmarks that have been missing in the OpenSHMEM eco-system. This year we are thrilled to publish the first simulation research paper that provides a software for lightweight and scalable simulation of large-scale OpenSHMEM applications. Other interesting topics included SHMEM for GPU kernels, SHMEM profiling tools, and network conduits for SHMEM.

We are sure all these concepts will be of use to the wider PGAS community.

We would like to thank everyone who contributed to the organization of the workshop. Particularly, we would like to thank the authors, Technical Committee chairs and members, reviewers, session chairs, participants, and sponsors. We are grateful for the excellent support we received from our ORNL administrative staff and Daniel Pack, who helped maintain and update our workshop website.

October 2018   Swaroop Pophale
                                                                Neena Imam

Organization

General Co-chairs

Neena Imam   Oak Ridge National Laboratory, USA
Manjunath Gorentla   Oak Ridge National Laboratory, USA
  Venkata

Technical Program Co-chairs

Manjunath Gorentla   Oak Ridge National Laboratory, USA
  Venkata
Ferrol Aderholdt   Oak Ridge National Laboratory, USA

Technical Program Committee

Ferrol Aderholdt   Oak Ridge National Laboratory, USA
Matthew Baker   Oak Ridge National Laboratory, USA
Pavan Balaji   Argonne National Laboratory, USA
Swen Boehm   Oak Ridge National Laboratory, USA
Tony Curtis   Stony Brook University, USA
James Dinan   Intel Corporation, USA
Khaled Hamidouche   AMD, USA
Naveen Namashivayam   Cray, USA
Thomas Naughton   Oak Ridge National Laboratory, USA
Dhabaleswar (DK) Panda   Ohio State University, USA
Nick Park   Department of Defense, USA
Stephen Poole   USG, USA
Swaroop Pophale   Oak Ridge National Laboratory, USA
Michael Raymond   HPE, USA
Gilad Shainer   Mellanox Technologies, USA
Pavel Shamis   ARM, USA
Sameer Shende   University of Oregon, USA
Min Si   Argonne National Laboratory, USA
Manjunath Gorentla   Oak Ridge National Laboratory, USA
  Venkata
Weikuan Yu   Florida State University, USA

Logistics

Daniel Pack (Web Chair)	Oak Ridge National Laboratory, USA
Eric Mitchel	Oak Ridge National Laboratory, USA

Sponsors

Contents

OpenSHMEM Simulators, Tools, and Benchmarks

OpenSHMEM Library Extensions and Implementations

OpenSHMEM Sets and Groups: An Approach to Worksharing and Memory Management

Ferrol Aderholdt, Swaroop Pophale$^{(\boxtimes)}$, Manjunath Gorentla Venkata, and Neena Imam

Computer Science and Mathematics Division, Oak Ridge National Laboratory, Oak Ridge, USA
pophaless@ornl.gov

Abstract. Collective operations in the OpenSHMEM programming model are defined over an active set, which is a grouping of (PEs) based on a triple of information including the starting PE, a log_2 stride, and the size of the active set. In addition to the active set, collectives require *Users* to allocate and initialize synchronization (i.e., *pSync*) and scratchpad (i.e., *pWrk*) buffers for use by the collective operations. While active sets and the user-defined buffers were previously useful based on hardware and algorithmic considerations, future systems and applications require us to re-evaluate these concepts. In this paper, we propose Sets and Groups as abstractions to create persistent, flexible groupings of PEs (i.e., Sets) and couple these groups of PEs with memory spaces (i.e., Groups), which remove the allocation and initialization burden from the *User*. To evaluate Sets and Groups, we perform multiple micro-benchmarks to determine the overhead of these abstractions and demonstrate their utility by implementing a distributed APSP application, which we evaluate using multiple synthetic and real-world graphs.

1 Introduction

Since the initial release of the OpenSHMEM Specification [5], many features have been incorporated to address the changing hardware and applications.

F. Aderholdt—This work was sponsored by the U.S. Department of Energy's Office of Advanced Scientific Computing Research. This manuscript has been authored by UT-Battelle, LLC under Contract No. DE-AC05-00OR22725 with the U.S. Department of Energy. The United States Government retains and the publisher, by accepting the article for publication, acknowledges that the United States Government retains a non-exclusive, paid-up, irrevocable, world-wide license to publish or reproduce the published form of this manuscript, or allow others to do so, for United States Government purposes. The Department of Energy will provide public access to these results of federally sponsored research in accordance with the DOE Public Access Plan (http://energy.gov/downloads/doe-public-access-plan). This research used resources of the Oak Ridge Leadership Computing Facility at the Oak Ridge National Laboratory, which is supported by the Office of Science of the U.S. Department of Energy under Contract No. DE-AC05-00OR22725.

© Springer Nature Switzerland AG 2019
S. Pophale et al. (Eds.): OpenSHMEM 2018, LNCS 11283, pp. 3–21, 2019.
https://doi.org/10.1007/978-3-030-04918-8_1

Specification 1.0 had support for point-to-point communication and synchronization, *Atomic Memory Operations* (AMO), collective operations, memory update ordering, and global locking for critical region execution. More recently, significant additions to the API have been made including implicit non-blocking point-to-point operations, all-to-all collective operations, resource contexts, and a threading model.

The OpenSHMEM Specification provides support for many collective operations such as the barrier, barrier all, sync, sync all, broadcast, collect, reductions, and all-to-all operations. Each collective other than the barrier all and sync all is defined over an **active set**. The active set is defined by the *User* with a triple of information including the starting PE index, a log_2 stride, and the size of the active set. In addition, synchronization (i.e., *pSync*) and scratchpad (i.e., *pWrk*) buffers are expected to be defined and initialized by the *User* on a per collective basis.

While the active set definition was useful due to previous hardware and algorithmic considerations, future systems and applications may suffer due to a lack of expressivity. More specifically, the requirement of a log_2-based active set limits work distribution flexibility for *Users*. For example, if the *User* needs an active set to encompass a collection of PEs as depicted in Figs. 1(a)–(c), then it is not possible with the current active set as defined by a log_2 stride. This problem is exacerbated by having to pass the active set definition triple for all collectives, which is true for the partitioning of work in irregular applications where the creation of an active set may require calculations at runtime based on optimized work partitioning. In addition, having to maintain and manage the multiple *pSync* and *pWrk* buffers can be burdensome for the *User* and limit productivity.

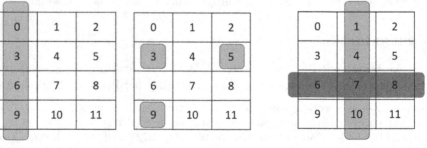

(a) Odd *stride* between PEs   (b) Disjoint PEs PEs   (c) Combination of different strides

Fig. 1. PE groupings not captured by the current *active set* definition

To overcome the limitations of active sets and simplify the interfaces of collective operations for *Users*, we are proposing two abstractions: **Sets** and **Groups**. The Sets abstraction serves to create persistent groupings of PEs using ranges and strides, which are not limited to log_2, through only local operations. This allows the *User* to create Sets locally (i.e., no communication between PEs) that may be used in multiple collectives. In addition, the Groups abstraction builds on Sets by coupling a Set with the resources required to efficiently complete collective operations such as a memory space, which removes the *pSync* and *pWrk* creation and management burden from the *User*. The contributions of this paper are as follows:

* We propose the Sets and Groups extensions to the OpenSHMEM programming model to address the drawbacks of Active Sets and collective operations semantics.
* We systematically evaluate and demonstrate the productivity advantages of using Sets and Groups by porting micro-benchmarks and application kernels to these abstractions.
* With the collective benchmark evaluation, we show the performance and scalability advantages that can be achieved for collective operations while using Sets and Groups.
* With APSP evaluation, we demonstrate the performance and productivity advantages for application kernels. Also, we show how multi-grained parallelism can be achieved, which further leads to performance advantages of up to 94% when compared to a vanilla approach.

2   Background

As mentioned in Sect. 1, the OpenSHMEM Specification [1] provides support for barrier, barrier all, sync, sync all, broadcast, collects, reductions, and all-to-all collectives. With the exception of barrier all and sync all, the collective operations need to be defined over an active set. A demonstration of collectives in OpenSHMEM through a simple OpenSHMEM program can be seen in Listing 1.1. This program is simple and makes use of barrier, broadcast, and all-to-all collective operations. Since the *pSync* array is different for both collectives it has to be initialized separately. Because broadcast on line 29 and 36 can be called simultaneously, we are required to provide separate *pSync* arrays to the library. Similarly for barrier calls on lines 31 and 38. This example motivates the need to move the synchronization and work buffer allocation and maintenance to the OpenSHMEM library implementation.

```
1  #include <stdio.h>
2  #include <shmem.h> /* Required */
3
4  long src[4], dest[4]; /* Globals are symmetric in C */
5
6  int main(void) {
7      shmem_init(); /* Required - Initializes library */
8      int npes = shmem_n_pes();
9      /* Required - Allocating symmetric synchronization arrays */
10     long * pSync1 = (long *) shmem_malloc(sizeof(long) *
       SHMEM_BARRIER_SYNC_SIZE);
11     long * pSync2 = (long *) shmem_malloc(sizeof(long) *
       SHMEM_BARRIER_SYNC_SIZE);
```

```
12   long * pSync3 = (long *) shmem_malloc(sizeof(long) *
     SHMEM_BCAST_SYNC_SIZE);
13   long * pSync4 = (long *) shmem_malloc(sizeof(long) *
     SHMEM_BCAST_SYNC_SIZE);
14   long * pSync5 = (long *) shmem_malloc(sizeof(long) *
     SHMEM_ALLTOALL_SYNC_SIZE);
15   ...
16   /* Required - Initializing symmetric synchronization arrays */
17   for (int i = 0; i < SHMEM_BARRIER_SYNC_SIZE; i++) {
18       pSync1[i] = SHMEM_SYNC_VALUE;
19       pSync2[i] = SHMEM_SYNC_VALUE;
20   }
21   for (int j = 0; j < SHMEM_BCAST_SYNC_SIZE; j++) {
22       pSync3[j] = SHMEM_SYNC_VALUE;
23       pSync4[j] = SHMEM_SYNC_VALUE;
24   }
25   for (int k = 0; k < SHMEM_ALLTOALL_SYNC_SIZE; k++) {
26       pSync5[k] = SHMEM_SYNC_VALUE;
27   }
28   ...
29   /*Only odd PEs*/
30   if (my_pe % 2) {
31       /*Some Work*/
32       shmem_broadcast64(dest, src, 4, 0, 1, 1, (npes/2), pSync3);
33       /*Some Work*/
34       shmem_barrier(1, 1, (npes/2), pSync1);
35   }
36   /*All PEs except PE 0*/
37   if (my_pe > 0) {
38       /*Some Work*/
39       shmem_broadcast64(dest, src, 4, 0, 1, 0, npes-1, pSync4);
40       /*Some Work*/
41       shmem_barrier(1, 0, npes-1, pSync2);
42   }
43   shmem_alltoall64(dest, source, 4, 0, 0, npes, pSync5);
44   shmem_barrier_all(); /* Synchronizes all PEs and completes
     pending updates */
45   /*Free allocated resources*/
46   shmem_finalize(); /* Required - Cleans environment and frees
     resources */
47   return 0;
48 }
```

Code 1.1. OpenSHMEM Active Sets, pSync, and pWrk usage

3   API Description

In this section, we will discuss our proposed APIs for creating persistent and flexible groupings of PEs. As the Groups abstraction builds upon the Sets abstraction, we will first discuss Sets and then Groups.

3.1   Sets

A Set is a group of PEs. The PEs composing the Set are indexed based on positive integers where the indexes are monotonically increasing from zero. Any PE not included in the Set will have a negative index.

Sets are created using the creation operations described in Listing 1.2. Each Set creation operation is blocking and is a local operation, which does not require communication between PEs. This is because each PE performing this operation

will generate the same Set. While Set creation is a local operation, each PE
should participate in Set creation to obtain knowledge of their existence within
the Set.

```
/* Set Creation API */
int shmem_create_set_strided (shmem_set_t * parent_set ,
                              int index_start ,
                              int index_stride ,
                              int size ,
                              shmem_set_t ** new_set );
int shmem_create_set_strided_multi (shmem_set_t * parent_set ,
                                    int nr_strides ,
                                    int strides_array [][3] ,
                                    shmem_set_t ** new_set );
int shmem_create_set_range (shmem_set_t * parent_set ,
                            int low_index ,
                            int high_index ,
                            shmem_set_t ** new_set );
int shmem_set_union (shmem_set_t * set1 ,
                     shmem_set_t * set2 ,
                     shmem_set_t ** new_set );
int shmem_set_intersection (shmem_set_t * set1 ,
                            shmem_set_t * set2 ,
                            shmem_set_t ** new_set );
int shmem_set_difference (shmem_set_t * set1 ,
                          shmem_set_t * set2 ,
                          shmem_set_t ** new_set );
int shmem_free_set (shmem_set_t * free_set );

/* Utility API */
int shmem_set_query_size (shmem_set_t * set , int * size );
int shmem_set_get_index (shmem_set_t * set , int * index );
int shmem_set_translate_index (shmem_set_t * from_set ,
                               shmem_set_t * to_set ,
                               int from_index ,
                               int * to_index );
```

Code 1.2. OpenSHMEM API for Sets

We propose the Set creation operation found in Listing 1.2. We will describe
their semantics below.

- shmem_create_set_strided: Creates a new set with the first PE represented
  by index *index_start* of the parent Set. The created Set has a size corresponding to the size parameter with a stride defined by the index_stride
  parameter.
- shmem_create_set_strided_multi: Creates   a   new   Set
  similar to shmem_create_set_strided with multiple strided subsets of PEs.
  An example of a Set created with this operation can be seen in Fig. 1(c).
- shmem_create_set_range: Creates a new Set using an inclusive range. Thus,
  contains the PEs with an index from low_index to high_index from the
  parent_set.
- shmem_set_union: Creates a new Set, which is a collection of all the unique
  PEs in set1 and set2. The PEs are translated to world PEs as the same
  world PE could exist at different indexes in different Sets.
- shmem_set_intersection: Creates a new Set, which is a collection of all the
  PEs present in both set1 and set2.

- **shmem_set_difference**: Creates a new Set, which is a collection of all the PEs in **set1** not present in **set2**. Unlike the union and intersection creation operations, the difference operation is not commutative and the order of the contributing Sets matters.

   All Sets have to be created from a parent set. The library provides two sets at the start of the program: **SHMEM_SET_WORLD** and **SHMEM_SET_EMPTY**. SHMEM_SET_WORLD consists of all the PEs executing the OpenSHMEM program. SHMEM_SET_EMPTY is used to indicate an empty set.

   In addition to creation operations, the Sets API contains querying operations to give *User*'s the ability to determine the size of the Set and a PE's index within the Set. The *User* may also translate indices between Sets.

3.2   Groups

A Group is a coupling of a valid Set with the resources required for the efficient execution of collective operations. For collectives built on the one-sided operations such as in OpenSHMEM, a memory buffer accessible by all PEs is required for synchronization and for storing intermediate results. Besides that, resources such as network injection queues, hardware collective resources, and application usage hints can be useful. We will demonstrate the utility of the Group abstraction and API for achieving productivity and performance with memory spaces. Though the Group abstraction can be useful for coupling other resources, we will not demonstrate that in this paper.

   The coupling between the memory space and the Set, gives the library a memory space that can be accessed by the PEs composing the Set while remaining opaque to the *User*. The purpose of creating this abstraction is to simplify the interfaces for collective operations by combining the persistent Set abstraction with the memory necessary to fulfill the role of the synchronization (i.e., pSync) and scratchpad (i.e., pWrk) buffers.

   Group creation is guided by a existing, valid Set or the Set of an existing Group. This allows the PEs of the Set or Group to allocate a local memory space and exchange this memory space with the other members of the forming Group. Unlike the symmetric heap, this memory space does not need to be symmetric with respect to addressing across the PEs, but it does need to have a symmetric size. Because of this exchange, Group creation is a collective operation within the Set.

```
/* Group Creation API */
int shmemx_create_group_from_set(shmemx_set_t * set,
                                 shmemx_group_t ** new_group);
int shmemx_group_split_color(shmemx_group_t * parent_group,
                             int color,
                             shmemx_group_t ** new_group);
int shmemx_group_dup(shmemx_group_t * group,
                     shmemx_group_t ** dup_group);
int shmemx_group_free(shmemx_group_t * free_group);

/* Group Utility API */
```

```
12  int shmemx_group_size(shmemx_group_t * group, int * size);
13  int shmemx_get_set_from_group(shmemx_group_t * group,
14                                shmemx_set_t ** set);
```

Code 1.3. OpenSHMEM API for Groups

The API to create, query, and free Groups is shown in Listing 1.3. For each interface, a return code is returned to the *User* indicating whether or not the operation was successful. The semantics of these operations are as follows:

- shmem_create_group_from_set: Creates a Group from an existing Set, which may include predefined Sets including SHMEM_SET_WORLD. The implementation will locally allocate memory and register this memory with the NIC. Afterwards, each PE of the Set will exchange the address information to enable future communication between PEs.
- shmem_group_split_color: Creates a new Group using a color-based split operation from an existing Group. This is similar to existing programming models [8,10]. However, unlike existing programming models, the *User* cannot define the ordering of the newly defined Group by using a key. Instead, ordering is based on the parent Group's PE ordering.
- shmem_group_dup: Duplicates an existing Group.
- shmem_group_free: Frees an allocation of a Group. This includes both the freeing of the resources associated with the Group and any internal structures used to create the Group (i.e., the Set).
- shmem_group_size: Returns to the *User* the number of PEs composing this Group.
- shmem_get_set_from_group: Returns to the *User* the Set associated with the particular Group. This is useful if the *User* needs to query information from the Set or modify the Set (i.e., add PEs) prior to creating a new Group.

3.3 Impact on Existing Collectives and Comparison with Active Sets

Sets and Groups provide useful abstractions for the *User* to create and manipulate persistent groups of PEs for collective operations. However, existing collective operations expect active sets to be provided by the *User*, which requires log_2 strides. To support the APIs presented in this paper, we have extended the collective interfaces to include Sets and Groups based equivalents.

An example of this extension can be seen with the barrier operation, which requires the *User* to define an active set (i.e., a triple defining a starting index, log_2 stride, and size) as well as allocate and initialize a synchronization buffer (i.e., pSync array). In total, this requires four parameters and its usage can be seen in Listing 1.1. For the Sets-based interface, the active set parameters are replaced by the Set, but the synchronization buffer parameter remains. For the Groups-based interface, this is further reduced to one parameter, which is the Group as it is coupling the Set and necessary resources for the collective.

To demonstrate the utility of this approach, we have adapted the earlier example in Listing 1.1 to what is seen in Listing 1.4. In the adaptation, we ignored return values to save space. While we have shortened the lines of code in the adaptation by using Sets and Groups, we have also decreased the memory requirements and the time to completion for the application. This is because OpenSHMEM requires remotely accessible data objects to be symmetric, where every PE allocates a data object with the same address and size. Thus, in the first example (i.e., Listing 1.1), every PE must perform a blocking, collective (i.e., **shmem_malloc**) to allocate space for the **pSync** buffer regardless of whether the PE will use the buffer. However, in our adaptation, only the PEs belonging to a Group will allocate a buffer.

```
1  #include <stdio.h>
2  #include <shmem.h> /* Required */
3
4  long src[4], dest[4]; /* Globals are symmetric in C */
5
6  int main(void) {
7      shmem_init(); /* Required - Initializes library */
8      int npes = shmem_n_pes();
9      shmem_set_t * set_odd, * set_gz;
10     shmem_group_t * group_odd, * group_gz, * group_world;
11
12     shmem_create_set_strided(SHMEM_SET_WORLD, 1, 2, npes / 2, &
       set_odd);
13     shmem_create_set_range(SHMEM_SET_WORLD, 1, npes - 1, &set_gz);
14
15     shmem_create_group_from_set(set_odd, &group_odd);
16     shmem_create_group_from_set(set_gz, &group_gz);
17     shmem_create_group_from_set(SHMEM_SET_WORLD, &group_world);
18     ...
19     /*Only odd PEs*/
20     if(my_pe % 2){
21         /*Some Work*/
22         shmem_group_broadcast64(dest, src, 4, 0, group_odd);
23         /*Some Work*/
24         shmem_group_barrier(group_odd);
25     }
26     /*All PEs except PE 0*/
27     if(my_pe > 0){
28         /*Some Work*/
29         shmem_group_broadcast64(dest, src, 4, 0, group_gz);
30         /*Some Work*/
31         shmem_group_barrier(group_gz);
32     }
33     shmem_group_alltoall64(dest, source, 4, group_world);
34     shmem_barrier_all(); /* Synchronizes all PEs and completes
       pending updates */
35     /*Free allocated resources*/
36     shmem_finalize(); /* Required - Cleans environment and frees
       resources */
37     return 0;
38 }
```

Code 1.4. Example Using Sets and Groups

To understand the performance implications, we performed an evaluation of the two approaches using the code in both examples (i.e., Listing 1.1 and 1.4. Because each code is functionally identical, the comparison is valid. The testbed we used for this evaluation is the Turing cluster at ORNL. The Turing cluster is a 16 node cluster with each node having two Intel Xeon E5-2660v3 processors, which have twenty logical cores each, 128 GB of RAM, and a ConnectX-4 InfiniBand interconnect. The results of the evaluation can be seen in Fig. 2.

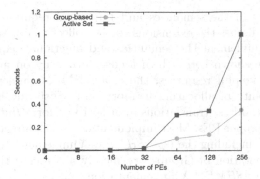

Fig. 2. Performance evaluation of Sets and Groups adaptation

The performance of the Groups adaptation is as expected and superior to the active set performance as the number of PEs increase. This is because, as mentioned earlier, the number of PEs required to perform collective allocations of the pSync arrays is limited to those belonging to the Group. Thus, as more PEs are added the time to completion of the active set version will continue to increase at a faster rate than the Groups adaptation.

4 Implementation

In this section, we will describe our implementation of both Sets and Groups. As Groups builds on Sets, we will begin with Sets and move to Groups.

4.1 Sets

Set creation is a local operation, thus all PEs need to retain some information regarding the Set membership to be able to identify other PEs that belong to the same Set. This allows the *User* to issue RMA operations between PEs of the same Set. The challenge is to collapse Set membership information in a manner that does not require huge data structures. Hence Set's memory usage is the primary design motivator. To that end, we only maintain the mathematical relationship between the members of the Set. We do not maintain any predecessor information; that is, once a Set is created, it does not retain any information regarding its parent(s). The *User* will only see a new Set that is indexed form 0 to N-1, where N is the total number of PEs in the new Set. We maintain this indexing seamlessly for the user by retaining the mapping between the PEs in the Set and their WORLD IDs.

4.2 Groups

The implementation of the Groups abstraction required two disjoint areas of adaptation to the *OpenSHMEM-X* implementation. Thus, we will first discuss the implementation of the semantics and functional requirements of Groups, and, then, we will discuss the extensions to the collective operations.

In general, to implement the semantics and functional requirements of the Groups abstraction shown here, which focuses primarily on memory resources rather than other helpful resources, the OpenSHMEM implementation needs to have the capability of allocating memory and registering it with the NIC, which also requires address translations in order to perform *Put*, *Get*, and AMO operations on the proper PEs. Most implementations can already perform these types of operations, including the *OpenSHMEM-X* implementation. Thus, for the prototype implementation of Groups, we merely abstracted that functionality within ORNL's *OpenSHMEM-X* implementation.

For the extension of the collective operations, we modified the collectives such that the original algorithmic implementation is the same, but the synchronization and intermediate results for the collectives are completed on the buffers and PEs belonging to the Group.

5 Evaluation

In this section, we will present our experimental evaluation of the proposed Sets and Groups extensions to OpenSHMEM. For these experiments, we made use of our extended OpenSHMEM-X implementation. The experiments performed were used to (i) evaluate Sets with respect to their memory usage requirements and (ii) evaluate the overhead of collectives when using Groups. Finally, we will demonstrate the effectiveness of the Sets and Groups abstractions with an irregular application kernel (i.e., APSP) using multiple synthetic and real-world graphs and compare Sets and Groups to the Teams abstraction currently implemented in Cray SHMEM.

For our evaluations, we made use of both the Eos and Titan machines located at the OLCF. Eos is composed of two 8-core Intel Xeon processors, 64 GB of memory, and the Aries interconnect. The processors form two NUMA nodes, with 8 cores and 32 GB of memory per NUMA. Titan is composed of one 16-core AMD Opteron processor, 32 GB of memory, and the *Gemini* interconnect. The Opteron processor is split uniformly across two NUMA nodes (i.e., 8 cores per NUMA), with each NUMA consisting of 16 GB of memory.

5.1 Resource Requirements

The Set creation operation can lead to one of the following three outcomes:

- *Regular Set*: All PEs in the new Set can be defined by a relationship (*start, stride, size*). This is the best case scenario and the least space consuming. Set creation operations like *strided* and *range* on such Sets result in similar *regular* sets.
- *Combination Set*: Some PEs in the new Set can be defined by a Regular Set while the rest form a disjoint *List*. For example, a Set with the WORLD PEs {0,1,2,3,4,18}. The first five PEs can be represented by relationship {*start, stride, size*} = {0,1,5} but the remaining PE does not fit.

– *List*: None of the PEs have any mathematical relationship with each other. This is a hypothetical worst case and cannot occur as it is always possible to generate a relationship between 2 PEs. We use the worst case scenario where there is a relationship between at most 2 PEs to model the theoretical worst case memory utilization by such a *List*. Example of such a Set would be a collection of WORLD PEs such as {2,5,6,17,23,29}. Here we can represent this *List* as a combination of three *Regular Sets*, namely {2,5}, {6,17}, {23,29} with *{start, stride, size}* = {2,3,2}, {6,11,2}, and {23,6,2} respectively.

Figure 3 shows the memory required in bytes for the *Regular* (best) and *List* (worst) case described above with increasing number of PEs. The results are as expected with the *strided* Sets consuming a static amount of memory regardless of the number of PEs composing the Set. This suggests that simple groupings of PEs resulting in a regular set will be able to provide efficient memory scaling as we move to jobs with a significantly large amount of PEs. While more complex groups of PEs will consume minimally more memory resources.

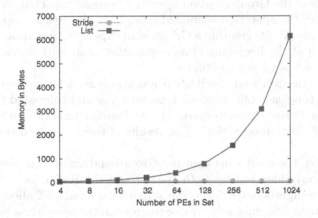

Fig. 3. Memory usage for Set information

5.2   Collective Operations

To evaluate the overhead of the Groups abstraction with respect to its performance, we will perform an experimental evaluation of the prototype implementation on the Eos testbed using micro-benchmarks to understand the overheads when compared to OpenSHMEM's active sets. Thus, we will explore the overheads of the following collective operations: (i) Group creation, (ii) Barrier, (iii) Collect, and (iv) Summation Reduction.

For Group creation, we measured the time necessary to create a group, which involves the allocation of a memory space at each PE, registration of the memory space with the NIC, and the exchange of this information with other PEs in the Set used to form the Group. The results of this experiment can be seen in Fig. 4.

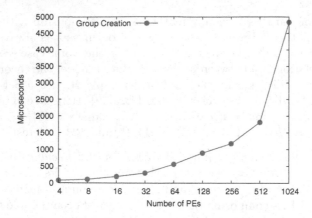

Fig. 4. The overhead of Group creation

The results of the Group creation operation were as expected. When the Set used to perform the operation contained more PEs, the creation operation consumed more time. While creating a Group is an expensive operation, performing Group creation at the beginning of an application, near initialization time, will lessen the impact of Group creation.

To measure the overhead of collective operations using Groups, we repeatedly measured the time each operation took to complete and compared these results to their vanilla active set counterpart. The evaluated operations include Barrier, Collect, and Reduction operations. The results of this evaluation can be seen in Fig. 5.

As expected, the results between the Groups and active sets versions of collectives are nearly identical for both Barrier and the Reduction. However, the Groups version slightly outperforms the active set version for Collect operations. This performance difference is likely due to noise on the network as both versions implement the same collective algorithm.

5.3   Use Case: All-Pairs Shortest Path

To evaluate the utility of Sets and Groups with an application, we chose to use an irregular algorithm such as APSP and modified it to work appropriately with OpenSHMEM and Sets and Groups. Rather than adapting an algorithm such as Floyd-Warshall to OpenSHMEM, we made use of the Bellman-Ford SSSP algorithm, which is a label-correcting algorithm and easily parallelizes in distributed environments, and iterated the source parameter over all of the vertices in the graph, which populates the distance matrix containing the distances between vertices over time. To simplify the development process, we used the synchronous Bellman-Ford algorithm described in [2].

Because the approach we used made use of all the PEs in the job, Sets, Groups, or active sets could be used with equal efficiency. However, because

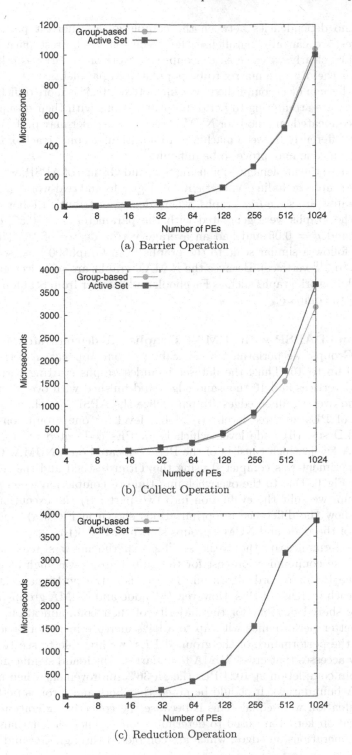

Fig. 5. The overhead of collective operations with Groups and active sets. Lower is better

there are no dependencies between the completion of shortest paths for any two sources, we can also parallelize the execution of shortest path based on sources. More clearly, we can create Groups that work on partitions of the sources allowing for the distance matrix to be populated in parallel.

While this can be accomplished by using active sets, it is more difficult for the *User* if they are attempting to perform optimizations with their group creation (i.e., PEs co-located on a node or NUMA) as the scheduler may perform process placement differently between machines. In addition, keeping track of the active set during runtime may prove to be difficult.

To evaluate the implementation using Sets and Groups of APSP, we made use of multiple graphs including synthetic R-MAT graphs and real-world graphs. The R-MAT graphs are scale-free graphs, where degree distribution follows a power law, and the graphs were generated with the parameters $a = 0.57$, $b = 0.19$, $c = 0.19$, and $d = 0.05$ and had an average vertex degree of 16. The graphs generated follow a similar scale to the graphs from Graph500 (i.e., scale=10 is equivalent to 2^{10} vertices). Because the R-MAT graphs are scale-free graphs, we used social network graphs such as Facebook and Twitter from Stanford's SNAP dataset [7] to compare.

Evaluation of APSP with R-MAT Graphs. To demonstrate the utility of Sets and Groups, we performed weak scaling of our application kernel with a scale of 10 up to 16. Thus, the dataset includes graphs starting with roughly 1 thousand vertices and 16 thousand edges and finished with over 65 thousand vertices and over 1 million edges. To parallelize the APSP kernel, we performed groupings of PEs at three levels: (i) global level, or one group consisting of the WORLD set, (ii) node level, which is all PEs co-located on a node, and (iii) NUMA level, which consists of the PEs co-located on a NUMA. Our weak scaling experiment was completed using the Titan testbed and the results can be seen in Fig. 6. Due to the overwhelming time to completion when using the global group, we split the evaluation into two parts: (i) the execution of each group to show the difference in optimizations shown in Fig. 6(a), and (ii) the execution of the node and NUMA groups shown in Fig. 6(b).

The performance of the weak scaling experiment was reasonable and expected. The communication cost for the global group was high at each iteration of the Bellman-Ford algorithm. This caused the performance to nearly double at each increase of PEs. However, the node and NUMA groups were able to leverage shared memory for the majority of their communication, resulting in much better performance with up to a 94% increase in performance. When observing the performance of the grouped PEs, we are able to see the latency of memory accesses that cross NUMA boundaries, which add significant latency to algorithm completion at 1024 PEs (i.e., a 36% improvement when not crossing NUMA boundaries). It should be noted that Sets and Groups performance in this evaluation were equal. This is because the collective operations used in this application kernel are used to determine convergence rather than perform relaxation operations on edges, which are completed through *Get* and AMOs.

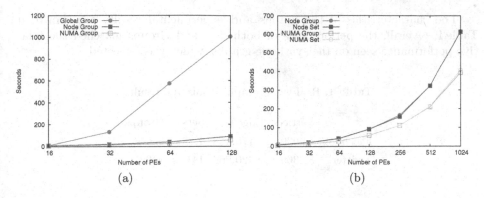

(a)   (b)

Fig. 6. Weak scaling of the APSP application kernel with graphs of scale 10 through 16

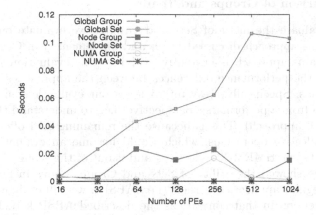

Fig. 7. Overhead associated with Group and Set creation

While the algorithmic timing showed that Groups and Sets perform equally well for the APSP application kernel, the overheads associated with Group creation as compared to Set creation are shown in Fig. 7. These measurements were gathered during the weak scaling experiment earlier. For each increase in PEs, the overhead of Set creation is the same as each creation operation is local and requires no communication. However, the Group creation operation performance is dependent on the communication between PEs of the Set. Thus, the creation of the Global Group is expensive in comparison to group creation with PEs co-located on a node or NUMA by as much as 97%.

To ensure the accuracy of our results with synthetic graphs for real-world datasets, we made use of the Facebook and Twitter graphs of Stanford's SNAP dataset [7]. As we have shown that partitioning the Group or Set creation produces efficient results with a NUMA partitioning, we made created Sets and Groups based on these partitions.

The characteristics of the graphs and experimental results are shown in Table 1. Overall, the performance of both Sets and Groups matched the relative performance seen on the synthetic graphs, which was expected.

Table 1. Real-world graph details and results

	Vertices	Edges	Sets	Groups
Facebook	4,039	176,468	2.88 s	2.88 s
Twitter	81,306	2,420,766	1417 s	1423 s

5.4   Comparison of Groups and Teams

To further evaluate the merit of Sets and Groups, we evaluate our approach with the Teams approach discussed in [9] and implemented in Cray SHMEM. While the Teams approach is currently evolving, this evaluation will give an impression of the performance differences between the approaches with actual implementations. Specifically, we want to focus our evaluation on Group and Team creation from a performance perspective (i.e., to understand the overhead offered by each approach). This is because the remaining API offered by both consists of collective operations, which would become an evaluation of Cray SHMEM and OpenSHMEM-X collectives and is out of the scope of this paper.

Because we showed the utility of Sets and Groups above in Sect. 5.3 with respect to irregular application kernels (i.e., APSP), we will evaluate the Team and Group creation in that context, as the described APSP kernel could also be implemented using Teams. More clearly, we will create Groups and Teams based on node and NUMA co-locations, which have proven to be performant for this type of application. This evaluation is completed by timing the creation operations including the time necessary to allocate and initialize the *pSync* and *pWrk* arrays used in the APSP kernel. The testbed used for this evaluation was Eos and the results of this experiment can be seen in Fig. 8.

The results were as expected. The overhead in Group creation is significantly lower than Team creation by as much as 90%. This is because Team creation with Cray SHMEM performs a collective operation involving the global set of PEs to create the Team followed by collective memory allocations through `shmem_malloc`. Meanwhile, Group creation is limited to only the PEs contained within a Set, which is limited to PEs co-located on the same node or NUMA node.

6   Related Work

The idea of asymmetric memory allocation for a persistent subset of PEs was briefly explored in [9]. The authors propose a *Team* of PEs (similar to our

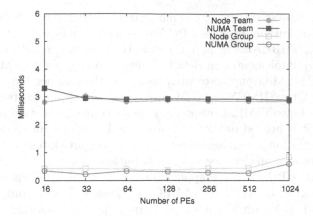

Fig. 8. Comparison of the overhead associated with Team and Group creation

Groups) as a way for expressing subsets of PEs. The main drawback of this approach is that even if no collectives are involved, the program will incur the additional cost of collective communication during team creation and of memory management associated with (implicit *pSync* and *pWrk*) only to be able to use persistent team objects. We avoid this in our approach by decoupling the Sets and Groups: Sets need be converted to Groups if and only if the *User* deems it necessary (e.g., multiple collectives over a small subset etc.). Our approach gives the user the flexibility as well as defers expensive Group creation operation to the point in the application where it is actually needed.

Message Passing Interface (MPI) has the concept of Groups and Communicators [8]. MPI_Comm_group is the equivalent of our OpenSHMEM Set. There exist similar Set Theory operations that can be used to create groups in MPI, but groups do not allow communication among the MPI ranks. A group needs a communicator to accomplish this. New communicators can be created from MPI_COMM_WORLD or by creating a communicator by passing in a group to MPI_Comm_create. The former is done via a split operation on the MPI_COMM_WORLD based on a *color* and *key* parameter. The Color decides the membership and the key decides the ordering in the new communicator. Another commonly used communicator creation operation is MPI_Comm_dup, which creates an identical but distinct new communicator. A communicator object is a combination of a context and the group of processes contained by the communicator. Internally the MPI library maintains a unique context that differentiates one communicator from another thus preventing an operation on one communicator from matching with a similar operation on another communicator.

Unified Parallel C (UPC) [6], a PGAS language, is also moving towards having better expressivity in their collectives. Version 1.3 of the specification includes collectives such as broadcast, scatter, all-gather, all-gather-all, reduce, permute etc. It currently suffers from the same shortcomings as OpenSHMEM 1.4 in its inability to express subsets of communicating THREADS (PE equivalent in UPC). In [3], the authors propose UPC Teams with a similar intent; of enabling subsets of UPC THREADS to perform collectives. Unfortunately, the work did not present any implementation details. Their approach to TEAMS is similar to the OpenSHMEM Groups presented here, but they do not have an abstraction similar to OpenSHMEM Sets. By providing a decoupling between the Sets and Groups in OpenSHMEM, we delay expensive group creation operation to the time that it is needed in the application and also prevent the unnecessary cost of group creation in embarrassingly parallel compute intensive applications where only Sets are sufficient for work distribution.

UPC++ [4], UPC for C++ applications, has included teams to allow collective communication over a set of UPC++ threads. The default team is the world team and each team has a unique team_id that is equal across the team. Team_id has an opaque handle and is specified to supports similar functionality as our Groups.

7   Conclusion and Future Work

While collective operations are commonly used in OpenSHMEM applications for communication and synchronization, the semantics of collectives are limited. This is due to the requirement of an active set, which defines a groups of PEs based a log_2 stride limiting the utility of active sets, and *User* provided memory resources, which require collective allocation across all PEs and are often difficult efficiently use.

In this paper, we presented the concept of OpenSHMEM Sets and Groups as an extension to OpenSHMEM to address these limitations. We discussed both Sets and Groups in detail in Sect. 3 and detailed the implementation of our prototype extensions in Sect. 4. We showed that Set creation is a local operation to each PE, and, as such, does not add time overheads to the critical path. In addition, we detailed that Groups are the coupling of Sets with various resources that may be required to efficiently perform collective operations. We further demonstrated this with respect to the efficient use of memory resources, application performance, and the productivity advantages of Groups in comparison to active sets in Sect. 3.3.

We have evaluated both Sets and Groups in Sect. 5 demonstrating the resource requirements, performance advantages, and utility in designing applications. In this, we showed that Set usage in the best case remains static at 64 bytes regardless of the number of PEs in the Set. We also showed the utility of Groups by implementing multi-grained parallelism in the APSP application kernel, increasing performance over a distributed approach by up to 94%. In addition, demonstrated that Group creation overheads can be minimized by up to 97% when exploiting locality between PEs.

Currently, the OpenSHMEM programming model only allows collective memory allocations over the symmetric heap through the *shmem_malloc* allocation call demonstrated in Listing 1.1. This means that all PEs must perform a collective operation with an implicit barrier to ensure completion of the allocation, which is wasteful in terms of both memory and time. Groups allows the Open-SHMEM library to perform the memory allocations only within members of the same Group removing the unnecessary constraints on memory allocation. In the future, this concept can be extended to support asymmetric memory allocations by Groups.

Acknowledgements. This research was supported by the United States Department of Defense (DoD) and Computational Research and Development Programs at Oak Ridge National Laboratory. This work was sponsored by the U.S. Department of Energy's Office of Advanced Scientific Computing Research. This research used resources of the Oak Ridge Leadership Computing Facility at the Oak Ridge National Laboratory, which is supported by the Office of Science of the U.S. Department of Energy under Contract No. DE-AC05-00OR22725.

References

1. OpenSHMEM specification 1.4. http://openshmem.org/site/sites/default/site_files/OpenSHMEM-1.4.pdf
2. Aderholdt, F., Graves, J.A., Venkata, M.G.: Parallelizing single source shortest path with OpenSHMEM. In: Gorentla Venkata, M., Imam, N., Pophale, S. (eds.) OpenSHMEM 2017. LNCS, vol. 10679, pp. 65–81. Springer, Cham (2018). https://doi.org/10.1007/978-3-319-73814-7_5
3. Almasi, G., Hargrove, P., Gabriel, I., Zheng, T.Y.: UPC collectives library 2.0. In: Proceedings of the 11th International Conference on Partitioned Global Address Space Programming Models, PGAS 2011 (2011)
4. Bachan, J., Baden, S., Bonachea, D., Hargrove, P., Hofmeyr, S., Ibrahim, K., et al.: UPC++ specification v1.0, draft 6 (2018). https://escholarship.org/uc/item/82094433
5. Chapman, B., et al.: Introducing OpenSHMEM: SHMEM for the PGAS community. In: Proceedings of the Fourth Conference on Partitioned Global Address Space Programming Model, PGAS 2010, pp. 2:1–2:3. ACM, New York (2010). https://doi.org/10.1145/2020373.2020375
6. El-Ghazawi, T., Smith, L.: UPC: unified parallel C. In: Proceedings of the 2006 ACM/IEEE Conference on Supercomputing, SC 2006. ACM, New York (2006). https://doi.org/10.1145/1188455.1188483
7. Leskovec, J., Krevl, A.: SNAP Datasets: Stanford large network dataset collection, June 2014. http://snap.stanford.edu/data
8. Message Passing Interface Forum: MPI: A message-passing interface standard, version 2.2. Specification, September 2009. http://www.mpi-forum.org/docs/mpi-2.2/mpi22-report.pdf
9. Welch, A., Pophale, S., Shamis, P., Hernandez, O., Poole, S., Chapman, B.: Extending the OpenSHMEM memory model to support user-defined spaces. In: Proceedings of the 8th International Conference on Partitioned Global Address Space Programming Models, PGAS 2014, pp. 11:1–11:10. ACM, New York (2014). https://doi.org/10.1145/2676870.2676884
10. Zheng, Y., Kamil, A., Driscoll, M.B., Shan, H., Yelick, K.: UPC++: a PGAS extension for C++. In: 28th IEEE International Parallel and Distributed Processing Symposium (IPDPS) (2014)

Design and Optimization
of OpenSHMEM 1.4 for the Intel®
Omni-Path Fabric 100 Series

David Ozog[1(✉)], Md. Wasi-ur- Rahman[2], Kayla Seager[3], and James Dinan[1]

[1] Intel Corporation, Hudson, MA, USA
david.m.ozog@intel.com
[2] Intel Corporation, Austin, TX, USA
[3] Intel Corporation, Hillsboro, OR, USA

Abstract. The OpenSHMEM 1.4 specification recently introduced support for multithreaded hybrid programming and a new communication management API. Together, these features enable users to manage communications performed by multiple threads within an OpenSHMEM process and to overlap communication and computation to hide costly latencies. In order to realize these benefits, OpenSHMEM implementations must efficiently map this broad new space of usage models to the underlying fabric. This paper presents an implementation of OpenSHMEM 1.4 for the Intel® Omni-Path Fabric 100 Series. The OpenFabrics Interfaces (OFI) libfabric is used as the low-level fabric API; we identify strategies for effectively managing shared transmission resources using libfabric, as well as for managing the communication requirements of the Omni-Path fabric. We study the performance of our implementation, identify design tradeoffs that are influenced by application behavior, and explore application-level optimizations that can be used to achieve the best performance.

1 Introduction

For the past several years, the OpenSHMEM community has released an annual update to the OpenSHMEM specification. Past versions of the OpenSHMEM specification have focused on standardizing semantics, improving portability, and enhancing existing OpenSHMEM interfaces. These past versions have set the stage for the recent OpenSHMEM 1.4 release [19], which adds multiple new features with a focus on extending OpenSHMEM to support hybrid parallel programming. In particular, OpenSHMEM 1.4 adds support for multithreaded communication as well as a new communication management interface, which provides a unique and highly efficient interface for multithreaded communication.

Lower-level fabric interfaces are also evolving to keep pace with evolving parallel programming models and system architectures. The OpenFabrics Alliance has been working to establish a new, open specification for low-level fabric software, referred to as the OpenFabrics Interfaces (OFI). The libfabric library is the

© Springer Nature Switzerland AG 2019
S. Pophale et al. (Eds.): OpenSHMEM 2018, LNCS 11283, pp. 22–40, 2019.
https://doi.org/10.1007/978-3-030-04918-8_2

core component of OFI that defines the user-facing API. It has been designed to support multithreaded communication models and to address new fabric resource management challenges introduced by modern high performance fabrics.

In our prior work, we described the implementation of the legacy OpenSH-MEM API [23] and explored the implementation of the then-proposed Open-SHMEM communication contexts API [12] on OFI using the Aries[1] network. Recently, Intel introduced support for libfabric with the Intel® Omni-Path Architecture 100 Series (OPA100) high-speed fabric. This paper extends prior work by exploring the implementation of recently added OpenSHMEM 1.4 features and by analyzing optimizations that were made in support of the OPA100 fabric.

In particular, the recently added OpenSHMEM threading and contexts features introduce several new fabric-level resource management challenges. In addition to providing thread safety, the OpenSHMEM library must now allocate and manage communication resources commensurate with the number of simultaneously communicating threads within a process. We analyze these challenges and introduce various strategies for addressing the resource requirements of multithreaded OpenSHMEM applications. We identify that differences in the usage model can lead to differences in the performance achieved by various resource management techniques. Using a cluster with the Intel® Omni-Path Fabric, we quantify these differences, measure the overall performance of our implementation, and identify opportunities for future work.

2   Background

This paper describes the implementation and optimization of the OpenSHMEM 1.4 specification [19] for the Intel® Omni-Path Architecture 100 Series Fabric [3] (OPA100). This work extends the Sandia OpenSHMEM (SOS) [8] open source [22] implementation with support for new features introduced in OpenSH-MEM 1.4, including threading support and support for OpenSHMEM communication management contexts. SOS supports the Portals 4 [2] and OpenFabrics Interfaces (OFI) [14] networking APIs. We have updated SOS to fully support OpenSHMEM 1.4 for both Portals and OFI networks; however, in this work, we focus on the implementation and optimization of OFI support in SOS.

2.1   OpenSHMEM 1.4

The OpenSHMEM 1.4 specification introduces new API features, including multithreading support; communication management "contexts"; a shmem_sync barrier operation; a shmem_calloc symmetric memory allocation operation; a shmem_test operation for nonblocking point-to-point synchronization; bitwise atomic operations; support for standard and fixed-width C integer types; and C11 type-generic interfaces. Multithreaded communication and communication

---

[1] Other names and brands may be claimed as the property of others.

management contexts, which are the focus of this work, represent a significant shift in the internal structures used to implement OpenSHMEM. Efficient support for these operations involves generalizing communication management structures to support multiple communication streams and broadening the set of communication resources available to optimize the performance of multi-stream processes.

The OpenSHMEM multithreading API is similar to the API provided by MPI [16]; it introduces a new library initialization routine, shmem_init_thread, that can be used to enable threading support when the library is initialized. Four levels of threading support are defined; in increasing order of flexibility they are SHMEM_THREAD_SINGLE, SHMEM_THREAD_FUNNELED, SHMEM_THREAD_SERIALIZED, and SHMEM_THREAD_MULTIPLE. Our work focuses on the multiple threading model, which allows multiple threads to perform OpenSHMEM communication operations simultaneously.

The communication management API added in OpenSHMEM 1.4 introduces a *context* object that is associated with every remote memory access (RMA), atomic memory operation (AMO), fence, and quiet operation. OpenSHMEM 1.4 introduces new versions of the relevant API functions, allowing the user to specify the context on which an operation is performed. For operations where a context is not specified (e.g. when the legacy API is used), the operation is performed on the predefined SHMEM_CTX_DEFAULT context. When the user performs a fence or quiet operation on a given context, the OpenSHMEM implementation is permitted to order or complete only the operations performed on the specified context. Operations performed on other contexts are not guaranteed by the OpenSHMEM specification to have been ordered or completed. Thus, contexts enable the user to express multiple independent streams of communication operations, enabling communication overlapping and pipelining optimizations at the application level and also allowing operations performed by individual threads to be isolated from each other.

Context creation and destruction are local operations involving only the OpenSHMEM process (PE) performing the operation. The context creation routine accepts an options argument that allows the user to provide hints about the usage model of the context to guide internal optimizations. OpenSHMEM 1.4 defines three such options that allow the user to specify the threading usage model of the given context. With no options set, contexts are shareable, meaning that any thread may access such a context. The SHMEM_CTX_SERIALIZED option also allows any thread to use the given context, but the application must guarantee that no two threads will attempt to use it simultaneously. The SHMEM_CTX_PRIVATE option indicates that only the thread that created the context will use it. Finally, contexts that set the SHMEM_CTX_NOSTORE option ensure the completion and ordering of memory store operations without requiring explicit quiet and fence operations from the application.

2.2   Intel® Omni-Path Architecture

The Intel® Omni-Path Host Fabric Interface (HFI) relies on host software for higher-level processing, including processing of received messages. Targeted offload capabilities are provided to accelerate typical per-packet transport layer operations and reduce software overhead. Messages are transmitted using either eager or rendezvous protocols for short and long messages, respectively. Eager receive involves delivering packets to a FIFO ring buffer in memory, which is consumed by host software. Rendezvous receive places data directly in the destination buffer, providing improved bandwidth and reducing CPU utilization. Packet arrival can be detected either by polling or using coalesced interrupts. HPC communication models such as MPI provide opportunities for inline polling during communication phases, thus reducing overheads from interrupts. For a more description of the OPA fabric, please see [3].

2.3   OpenFabrics Interfaces

The OpenFabrics Interfaces (OFI) defines a framework to expose fabric communication services to applications [14]. These services are accessed through libfabric, which defines a rich set of portable, user-level software interfaces for utilizing high-speed communication fabrics. Section 3 describes the specific set of OFI capabilities and objects used to support OpenSHMEM.

The OFI framework utilizes a *provider* component to enable libfabric support for different fabrics. In this work, we utilize the Intel® Performance Scaled Messaging 2 (PSM2) provider, which enables OFI support for OPA100. The Intel® PSM2 API [20] provides a low-level software interface to the OPA100 fabric. PSM2 utilizes an endpoint communication model, in which messages are sent and received between connected endpoints. The corresponding OPA100 transmit buffers and receive FIFO are referred to as a PSM2 context. PSM2 supports matched communication through matched queues that match on the three-tuple of sender, receiver, and tag. In addition, PSM2 supports an active messages interface in which user-defined message handlers are invoked when processing incoming messages. One-sided communication models forego the posting of receive operations; thus, the PSM2 active messages interface is used to implement the RMA interfaces in libfabric utilized by OpenSHMEM.

In the OPA100 communication model, message processing is performed by software on the host processor. This is a natural fit for models like MPI, where users must invoke communication routines to make progress on pending operations. However, for asynchronous, one-sided communication models like OpenSHMEM, the runtime system must invest additional effort to ensure that communication operations continue to advance toward completion even when the application is busy performing computation.

OFI provides an automatic progress mode that ensures passive progress in the absence of OFI function calls. The PSM2 provider supports automatic progress by creating a thread that wakes up periodically to process received messages. The progress interval of this thread is one millisecond by default and can be adjusted to as low as $1\,\mu s$ by setting the FI_PSM2_PROG_INTERVAL environment variable. Within the implementation, the PSM2 provider code calls nanosleep() between progress intervals. The POSIX nanosleep() routine is implemented via the Linux high-resolution timer API [24], which provides fine resolution timers that are not necessarily bound to the kernel's clock interrupt period (since Linux kernel version 2.6.16). Ideally, the progress thread interval should remain relatively large to maintain low overheads. Thus, ideal communication performance involves a combination of manual progress generated by the middleware during OpenSHMEM function execution and automatic progress generated by the progress thread, which we explore further in Sect. 3.2.

3   Design and Implementation

We begin with the software architecture of Sandia OpenSHMEM (SOS) OFI transport layer, shown in Fig. 1. This figure shows the combination of OFI objects used by a single PE, and this infrastructure is replicated across all PEs. Our prior work described several of these structures in detail [12,23]. Here, we focus on new developments and details relevant to the optimizations described throughout this paper. In particular, the methods for managing transmit and receive resources have changed significantly to enable new optimizations not explored in prior work.

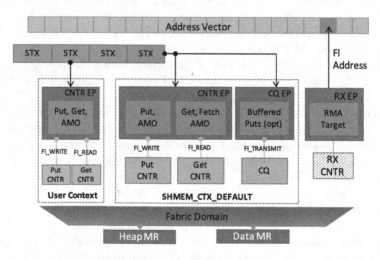

Fig. 1. Sandia OpenSHMEM v1.4.1 OFI transport layer architecture.

The diagram shown in Fig. 1 is composed of several collections of software objects: the address vector, the shared transmit context (STX) pool, the default and user-created contexts, various endpoints (EPs), and the fabric domain. At the top of the diagram, the address vector (AV) enables the libfabric layer to map integer PE indices to fabric addresses. Fabric addresses are exchanged out-of-band using the process manager and are then inserted into the AV. Below the address vector is a fixed-size collection of STX resources that is established during library initialization. Each STX corresponds to an independent transmit queue resource and is "shared" in the sense that it may be bound to multiple lib-fabric endpoints. The efficient allocation and management of STXs is a primary concern of this paper.

Below the STX pool in Fig. 1 are the SOS contexts. This figure shows the default context, denoted SHMEM_CTX_DEFAULT, and one user context. Depending on the application's usage model, many such user contexts may be created. At a minimum, contexts are comprised of a counter endpoint (CNTR EP), which manages the communication associated with initiator-side puts, gets, and AMOs. The counter endpoint uses event counters to capture completion events for operations issued on the endpoint. Event counters are lightweight but don't capture enough information to distinguish the completion of individual operations issued on the endpoint. Thus, a context optionally includes a completion queue endpoint (CQ EP), which manages buffered put operations (involving communications that copy message data to a bounce buffer, providing immediate local completion) and could be used to support proposed nonblocking operations that return explicit request handles.

Depending upon the threading model supported by the OFI provider, each context may also include a mutex that must be held prior to performing OFI operations on the context. For providers that support FI_THREAD_SAFE, this lock is unnecessary. The PSM2 provider supports the FI_THREAD_COMPLETION model as a consequence of the OPA100 HFI requiring synchronized access to send and receive hardware contexts. While this model has the disadvantage of requiring a middleware-level lock, it has the advantage that synchronization can be eliminated on private contexts, whereas any lower-level synchronization cannot be eliminated when libfabric is utilized in the thread safe mode.

The distinction between private and shared contexts (described in Sect. 2.1), the presence of multiple threads potentially having both private and shared contexts, and the finite size of the STX pool create a non-trivial resource management problem. Figure 2 illustrates a simple scenario in which multiple threads within the same PE each create two contexts. In such a scenario, the OpenSH-MEM middleware must apply an allocation heuristic to assign STXs to endpoints during each of the six separate allocation calls used to create the contexts. In the scenario shown, each thread is assigned an STX. In the resulting configuration, if the user has also set the private option on the thread's contexts, the OpenSH-MEM middleware can operate on the STX without thread synchronization.

To the right of the contexts in Fig. 1 is the receive endpoint (RX EP), which is the only endpoint with receive capabilities enabled. It is used to expose memory registered on the domain for remote access and its address is inserted into the address vector at the same location in each PE. SOS v1.4.1 currently exposes a single RX EP; however, in multi-rail or heavily multithreaded scenarios, creating

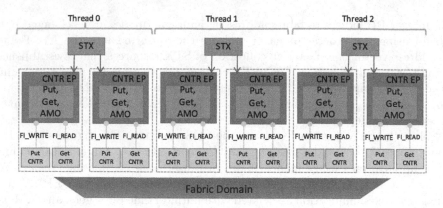

Fig. 2. OFI transport layer, showing a usage model in which multiple threads each with multiple contexts compete for STX resources.

additional RX EPs may improve receive-side throughput by increasing the set of RX resources available to communicate with an OpenSHMEM PE.

Finally, the fabric domain is a high-level object, from which all other objects are derived. It roughly refers to a physical or virtual NIC, but also dictates memory registration of the heap and data segments, defines a progress model, network capabilities, and the thread safety model.

3.1 The STX Pool and Allocation Schemes

During transport initialization, SOS allocates a pool (implemented as an array) of STX objects. This free pool consists of a collection of C structs, each containing a pointer to a libfabric object of type `fid_stx`, which refers to the actual STX resource, and a reference counter, which tracks the number of contexts using this resource. As of this writing, the size of the STX pool is set according to the environment variable `SHMEM_OFI_STX_MAX`. However, work is in progress to enable SOS to automatically detect the number of available STX resources (via the `fi_domain_attr.tx_ctx_cnt` attribute) and partition those STXs evenly across PEs sharing the same compute node.

The shared STX allocation algorithm is shown in Algorithm 1. In a thread-safe implementation, the ALLOCATE_SHARED_STX routine must be protected by a mutex before invocation, but this is omitted from Algorithm 1 for simplicity. The allocation routine accepts a *max_refs* parameter that is set through the `SHMEM_OFI_STX_THRESHOLD` environment variable. This threshold can be used to defer allocation of free STXs to the shared pool until the reference counts on all shared STXs have reached the given threshold. When it is not possible to honor this threshold (e.g. because the free pool is empty), the supplied threshold is ignored. The existence of the default context ensures that the shared pool is never empty; thus, any call to this routine eventually succeeds in allocating an STX.

A concern when allocating STXs is balancing the communication load across available resources to avoid bottlenecks. The allocator also accepts a *heuristic* argument that enables the user to select among several different STX allocation schemes. SOS currently supports two heuristics: round-robin and random, which can be selected via the SHMEM_OFI_STX_ALLOCATOR environment variable. The round-robin algorithm sequentially selects the next available STX in the pool, whereas the random algorithm selects at random from the set of available STXs. In both cases, the allocator only considers STXs whose reference count is less than the requested maximum. The maximum reference count is 1 by default; increasing this value may be useful, for example, when an application initially requires instantiating several shared contexts, but at a future point would benefit from having a reservation of STXs for private contexts.

SOS makes a best effort to assign a private STX to the calling thread when a context with the private option enabled is created. SOS tracks which threads have private access to an STX via a hash table that maps thread ids (TIDs) to an index into the STX pool. TIDs are queried using the Linux (see footnote 1) gettid system call and SOS also allows the user to supply the TID query routine for compatibility with user-level threading models. Once an STX is privatized, it

---

Algorithm 1. Shared STX allocation algorithm

Let: $F \leftarrow \{s_0, s_1, \ldots, s_N\}$ ▷ Pool of free STXs
Let: $S \leftarrow \emptyset$ ▷ Pool of shared STXs
Let: $last \leftarrow 0$ ▷ Index of last allocated STX
function ALLOCATE_SHARED_STX(max_refs, heuristic)
    $stx \leftarrow \emptyset$
    if *heuristic* = "round-robin" **then**
        for $i \leftarrow 1, size(S)$ **do**
            $j \leftarrow (last + i) \bmod size(S)$
            if $s[j].refcnt < max\_refs$ **then**
                $stx \leftarrow S[j]$
                $S[j].refcnt \mathrel{+}= 1$
                $last \leftarrow j$
                break
            end if
        end for
    else if *heuristic* = "random" **then**
        if $\exists\, s \in S : s.refcnt < max\_refs$ **then**
            repeat
                $i \leftarrow rand() \bmod size(S)$
            until $S[i].refcnt < max\_refs$
            $stx \leftarrow S[i]$
            $S[i].refcnt \mathrel{+}= 1$
        end if
    end if
    if $stx = \emptyset \wedge F \neq \emptyset$ **then**   ▷ Allocate a free STX to the shared pool and retry
        $S \leftarrow S \cup pop(F)$
        return $allocate\_shared\_stx(max\_refs, heuristic)$
    else if $stx = \emptyset$ **then**   ▷ Retry, ignoring *max_refs*
        return $allocate\_shared\_stx(\infty, heuristic)$
    end if
    return stx
end function

---

is removed from the free pool and inserted into the hash table. STX privatization eliminates thread synchronization overheads and can improve cache locality in high-throughput scenarios. However, the private or shared state of an STX is especially difficult to change while it is bound to a context without introducing threading synchronization on performance-critical paths. Thus, selecting the right resource configuration during context allocation is key to optimizing the OpenSHMEM contexts interface. When STX privatization is not possible (e.g. because the number of threads is greater than the number of available STXs), the private hint is ignored and the context is allocated on a shared STX. SOS also supports an SHMEM_OFI_STX_DISABLE_PRIVATE option, which ignores the private option during context creation. This may be useful in scenarios where the number of application threads using private contexts exceeds the number of available STXs. In such a scenario, disabling privatization may lead to better performance because it results in better load balance across available STXs.

The optimal assignment of STXs to contexts is dependent on a number of factors, including the availability of resources; the number of application threads; the pattern with which contexts are created and destroyed; and the application's communication pattern relative to its contexts. We analyze this issue in more depth and quantify the effect of different allocation strategies in Sect. 4.

3.2   Communication Progress

As discussed in Sect. 2.3, libfabric's PSM2 provider spawns a progress thread to provide automatic, passive progress; however, smaller progress intervals can cause contention between the progress thread and the application. When issuing communication operations, OFI ensures progress is made on the endpoint involved in the given operation. Past versions of SOS that supported OpenSH-MEM 1.3 utilized a single endpoint for both TX and RX. Thus, any operation generated both transmit and receive progress. With the introduction of support for multiple STXs and their corresponding endpoints, RX capabilities cannot be enabled on all endpoints. Thus, a blocking call to, e.g. shmem_quiet, is no longer guaranteed to generate RX progress.

To ensure that RX progress occurs, we have added a manual progress mode to SOS that can be enabled at compile time. Manual progress is generated by intermittently reading the event counter on the RX endpoint. In the FI_THREAD_COMPLETION model supported by the PSM2 provider, performing these probe operations requires acquiring a lock associated with the RX endpoint. To avoid blocking in probe operations, a trylock operation is used to make progress when the lock is available. Empirically, we have found that calling this probe routine in blocking OpenSHMEM routines, such as shmem_wait and shmem_quiet, can significantly improve communication performance. Generating manual progress at additional entry points into the library (e.g. when issuing nonblocking communication operations) may also be beneficial, depending on the usage model; however, we have not yet observed an instance where progress gains outweighed the overheads created by probing progress on the critical path.

4   Evaluation

We evaluate our implementation on an internal cluster at Intel, named Neptune[2]. Neptune compute nodes contain 2 sockets, each with an Intel®Xeon®Processor E5-2699 v3 (Haswell) CPU and 64 GB RAM. Each CPU has 2-way Intel® Hyper-Threading Technology with 18 cores, providing 36 physical cores and 72 hardware thread contexts per compute node. Nodes are connected via the Intel®Omni-Path 100 series fabric. The Omni-Path 100 HFI driver was configured to support 80 hardware contexts (via the hfi1 loadable kernel module) [18], rather than the default value of 36, which corresponds to the number of CPU cores per node.

The operating system on Neptune's compute nodes is CentOS 7.3.1611 (Linux kernel 3.10.0-693.el7.x86_64), and all binaries are built using Sandia OpenSHMEM version 1.4.1, libfabric version 1.6.0, and GNU GCC version 4.8.5. We use the MPICH Hydra process launcher version 3.2 to execute all jobs. Throughout the experiments below, bounce buffering was disabled in SOS, which is the default behavior when enabling multiple threads in SOS v1.4.1. Throughput data distinctly shows an injection threshold of 16 bytes, which is particularly emphasized by disabling bounce buffering.

All bandwidth experiments in this section utilize the shmem_perf_suite, which is a latency and bandwidth performance test suite included with SOS. Version 1.4.1 of SOS added multithreaded versions of the throughput benchmarks, which make use of OpenSHMEM contexts and OpenMP. The following sections focus on the multithreaded benchmark for blocking uni-directional put operations, shmem_bw_put_ctx_perf, in which several threads perform communication operations at various buffer sizes on private contexts. This benchmark can execute with any number of PEs, but we focus on node-to-node throughput between two PEs, since this measurement is most indicative of the network's remote communication capabilities. Unless otherwise indicated, all experiments measure the throughput between 2 distributed nodes connected via a single switch hop, with 1 PE per node.

Some measurements of the throughput benchmark show high variability, especially with relatively small buffer sizes below the injection threshold. For

---

[2] Intel and Xeon are trademarks of Intel Corporation in the U.S. and/or other countries.

Benchmark results were obtained prior to implementation of recent software patches and firmware updates intended to address exploits referred to as "Spectre" and "Meltdown". Implementation of these updates may make these results inapplicable to your device or system.

Software and workloads used in performance tests may have been optimized for performance only on Intel® microprocessors. Performance tests, such as SYSmark and MobileMark (see footnote 1), are measured using specific computer systems, components, software, operations and functions. Any change to any of those factors may cause the results to vary. You should consult other information and performance tests to assist you in fully evaluating your contemplated purchases, including the performance of that product when combined with other products.

For more information go to http://www.intel.com/benchmarks.

this reason, all plots include the arithmetic mean of 10 separate measurements as well as error bars showing the standard deviation. The displacement of the standard deviation is the same in both positive and negative directions from the mean; however, the negative displacement occupies a larger range in the plotted space because of the logarithmic scale.

4.1   Runtime Progress

Figure 3 shows the results of an experiment comparing manual progress (described in Sect. 3.2) with automatic progress at various polling intervals. This experiment uses the `shmem_bw_put_ctx_perf` benchmark of `shmem_perf_suite`, which measures uni-directional put bandwidth using multiple threads. However, this experiment runs only a single thread, yet initializes OpenSHMEM with a thread level of `SHMEM_THREAD_MULTIPLE`. We use this relatively simple setup to intentionally incur the overhead in the transport runtime from supporting multiple threads, while eliminating any overhead due to thread contention. In Figs. 3 (and 5), the "manual progress" line corresponds to an our proposed scheme of opportunistically calling `shmem_transport_probe()`, the "x millisecond" lines each correspond to a value of x for `FI_PSM2_PROG_INTERVAL` with `FI_PROGRESS_AUTO` set, and "default progress" corresponds to setting no environment variables related to progress whatsoever. Figure 3 is a single-pair throughput experiment with 1 PE per node, Fig. 4 shows several multi-pair experiments with values numbers of PEs per node, and Fig. 5 is a multi-pair progress experiment with 72 PEs per node. Note that despite the multi-pair setup being oversubscribed with 1 PE

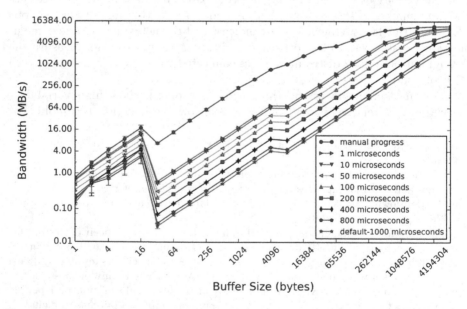

Fig. 3. Uni-directional blocking put bandwidth on Neptune with a single PE pair: comparing various automatic progress polling intervals with manual progress.

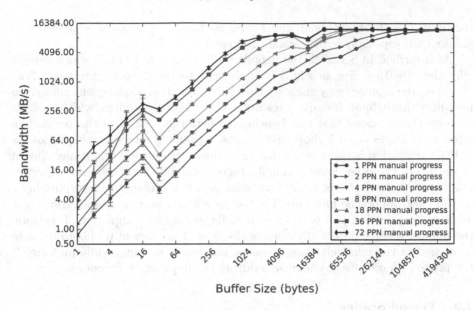

Fig. 4. Uni-directional blocking put bandwidth on Neptune with multiple PE pairs and manual progress.

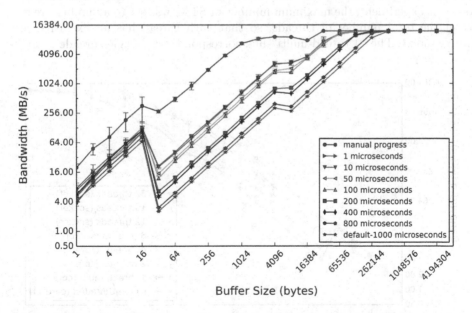

Fig. 5. Uni-directional blocking put bandwidth on Neptune with 72 PE pairs: comparing various automatic progress polling intervals with manual progress.

per node, 1 application thread, and 1 progress thread, it achieves relatively high throughput, especially with manual progress.

As described in Sect. 3.2, the default polling interval is 1 ms, which reveals why the "1000 μs" line in Fig. 3 is equivalent to the "default progress" line. However, the figure clearly suggests that this interval is not frequent enough to maximize throughput, because it results in the lowest overall bandwidth. In fact, the experiment shows that this benchmark performs best with shorter polling intervals. Figures 3 and 5 show that requesting polling intervals with as low as 1–10 μs resolution is effective on this experiment/platform without any special support. On the other hand, manual progress exhibits the best overall performance. We believe this is because manual progress probes the transport layer at the most opportune moments, i.e. during a `shmem_wait` or `shmem_quiet`, right when communication may possibly stall while waiting for completion. Therefore, the manual scheme potentially reduces the overall number of probing instances compared to the relatively more frequent automatic probing, while performing the probe at more effective moments during the application execution.

4.2 Thread Scaling

Figure 6 shows the results of an experiment that varies the number of threads in the `shmem_bw_put_ctx_perf` uni-directional put bandwidth benchmark. Throughout this experiment, the maximum number of STXs was set to a number greater than the total number of threads, so that each thread has an exclusive private context. The "1 thread-multi" line corresponds to a single-threaded execu-

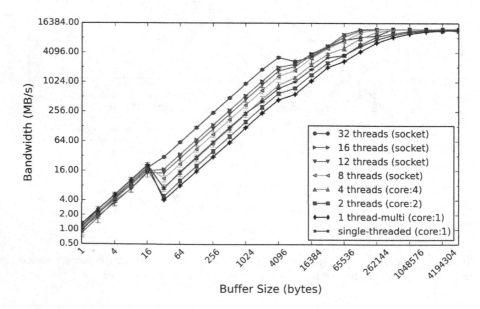

Fig. 6. Uni-directional blocking put bandwidth on Neptune: increasing the number of threads.

tion where SOS was initialized with the SHMEM_THREAD_MULTIPLE thread level. The "single-threaded" line was initialized with the SHMEM_THREAD_SINGLE thread level. The "(socket)" versus "(core)" designation refers to the processor affinity setting passed to the launcher via the --bind-to flag, which often had a significant effect on performance. All data in Fig. 6 was gathered with the --bind-to setting that achieved the best overall throughput, as determined empirically. Specifically, executing 8 or more threads with --bind-to=socket performed best (this setting binds all PEs to the same CPU socket throughout execution). On the other hand, executing 4 threads or fewer performed best with --bind-to=core:N (which binds PEs to a fixed group of N cores). It was empirically observed that the best throughput is often achieved by setting N to the number of threads, for example, by running 4 threads with --bind-to=core:4.

Figure 6 shows a notable difference in throughput between a single-threaded application initialized with SHMEM_THREAD_SINGLE and a single-threaded application initialized with SHMEM_THREAD_MULTIPLE. This difference is due to the fact that shmem_wait and shmem_wait_until poll on memory when multithreading is enabled in SOS, because any thread within a PE may satisfy the wait operation. On the other hand, an application initialized with SHMEM_THREAD_SINGLE may simply block while waiting on the RX CNTR value to make progress. However, if configuring SOS with --enable-hard-polling, which always enforces polling in shmem_wait and shmem_wait_until, then these two scenarios exhibit the exact same throughput.

While lower numbers of threads generally perform better for buffer sizes at or below the injection threshold of 16 bytes, more threads perform better with intermediate buffer sizes (32 bytes to 4 kilobytes). After 4KB, however, the communication protocol advances to an RDMA-based transport, resulting in the transitory drop in bandwidth at 8KB. This drop is more dramatic for 32 threads, likely because the overhead of multiple threads contending for local locks dominates. With relatively larger buffer sizes it is generally advantageous to execute more threads, preferably 16. After about 1 GB, running up to 16 threads results in bandwidth saturation, with the peak capability of the Intel®Omni-Path Fabric 100 series being just under 100 Gbps or 12.4 GB/s.

4.3   STX Scaling

Figures 7 and 8 show the results of an experiment that varies the number of available STXs in the shmem_bw_put_ctx_perf benchmark, while keeping the number of threads constant. All executions were run with 8 threads, and the number of available STXs was set via an environment variable. Figure 7 shows the default behavior in SOS, where user-requested private contexts receive exclusive access to an STX if one or more is available. The experiment in Fig. 8 also varies the number of STXs with 8 constant threads, but instead disables the use of private contexts via the SHMEM_OFI_STX_DISABLE_PRIVATE setting described in Sect. 3.1.

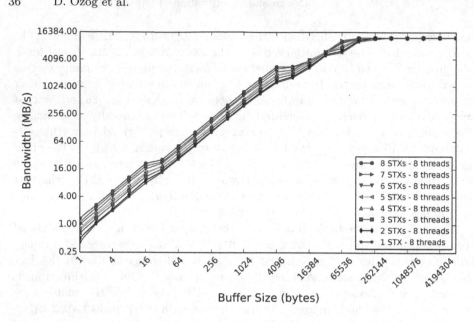

Fig. 7. Uni-directional blocking put bandwidth on Neptune: increasing the number of available STXs while keeping the number of threads constant (8 threads).

Figure 7 shows good scaling with respect to the number of STXs. Therefore, when using at least one private context per thread, as in this experiment, it is generally advantageous to utilize at least as many STXs as threads. To see why, consider a scenario where there are fewer available STXs in F than there are threads in Algorithm 1. After F is depleted, any excess contexts are assigned to a shared STX, which may result in a resource imbalance.

On the other hand, Fig. 8 suggests that the benefits of having at least 1 STX per thread are diminished when disabling private contexts. When private contexts are disabled, contexts are assigned to an STX in the pool using the round-robin allocation heuristic described in Sect. 3.1. In this scenario, when there are fewer available STXs than threads, the contexts are balanced more evenly across the available STXs. This results in less variation between lines in Fig. 8, especially when using more than a single STX.

In summary, these measurements suggest that private contexts boost throughput best when all threads have exclusive access to a private STX. However, if an OpenSHMEM application executes more threads with private contexts than there are available STXs, or utilizes other *shared* contexts that compete with private contexts for STX resources, then that application might achieve better performance by disabling private contexts.

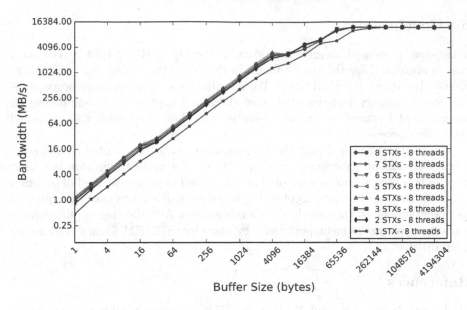

Fig. 8. Uni-directional blocking put bandwidth on Neptune: increasing the number of available STXs while keeping the number of threads constant (8 threads) and disabling private contexts.

5   Related Work

A particular focus of this work is the implementation and optimization of the OpenSHMEM 1.4 contexts API. Contexts were first proposed by Dinan et al. [11] and prototyped in Portals SHMEM [1]. Namashivayam et al. analyzed contexts in multithreaded communication scenarios and presented a comparison with Cray's thread registration extension [9,17]. This evaluation included a domain abstraction encapsulating DMAPP communication domains, which are similar to libfabric STX resources. An implementation of contexts in OpenSHMEM-X for the UCX (see footnote 1) networking layer was presented in [6]. Contexts were also previously prototyped in Sandia OpenSHMEM and evaluated on the Aries (see footnote 1) interconnect [12] using the libfabric GNI provider [10].

Thread safety in OpenSHMEM has been explored in a number of studies [15,21,25]. The proposed OpenSHMEM explicit requests interface provides several benefits similar to the contexts API, as well as several new capabilities [4,5]. A thread registration interface extension to OpenSHMEM has also been proposed [9]. AsyncSHMEM [13] was proposed as a task-based extension to OpenSHMEM that provides a task-based alternative to conventional multithreaded hybrid programming. Finally, thread safety and multithreaded communication have also been studied extensively in the context of the Message Passing Interface (MPI) [16]. In particular, MPI implementations have explored using multiple PSM2 endpoints per process to improve the performance of threaded communication [7].

6 Conclusion

This paper presented an implementation of the OpenSHMEM 1.4 specification that is optimized for the Intel® Omni-Path Fabric 100 Series using the Open-Fabrics Interfaces (OFI) libfabric. We identified communication resource management challenges introduced by new threading support and communication management features; we proposed solutions to these challenges; and measured their effectiveness.

We further identified that the optimal solution to the multithreaded communication resource mapping problem is dependent upon application behavior. Several proposed solutions are global in nature and apply across the full duration of an application. However, application behavior may change over the course of its execution. Thus, the usefulness of a more direct API allowing applications to guide resource assignment performed by the OpenSHMEM library remains an open question.

References

1. Barrett, B.W., Brigthwell, R., Hemmert, K.S., Pedretti, K., Wheeler, K., Underwood, K.D.: Enhanced support for OpenSHMEM communication in portals. In: IEEE 19th Annual Symposium on High Performance Interconnects. HotI, August 2011
2. Barrett, B.W., et al.: The Portals 4.0 network programming interface. Sandia National Laboratories, November 2012, Technical report SAND2012-10087 (2012)
3. Birrittella, M.S., et al.: Intel® Omni-path architecture: enabling scalable, high performance fabrics. In: 2015 IEEE 23rd Annual Symposium on High-Performance Interconnects, pp. 1–9, August 2015
4. Boehm, S., Pophale, S., Baker, M.B., Venkata, M.G.: Merged requests for better performance and productivity in multithreaded OpenSHMEM. In: Gorentla Venkata, M., Imam, N., Pophale, S. (eds.) OpenSHMEM 2017. LNCS, vol. 10679, pp. 35–49. Springer, Cham (2018). https://doi.org/10.1007/978-3-319-73814-7_3
5. Boehm, S., Pophale, S., Venkata, M.G.: Evaluating OpenSHMEM explicit remote memory access operations and merged requests. In: Gorentla Venkata, M., Imam, N., Pophale, S., Mintz, T.M. (eds.) OpenSHMEM 2016. LNCS, vol. 10007, pp. 18–34. Springer, Cham (2016). https://doi.org/10.1007/978-3-319-50995-2_2
6. Bouteiller, A., Pophale, S., Boehm, S., Baker, M.B., Venkata, M.G.: Evaluating contexts in OpenSHMEM-X reference implementation. In: Gorentla Venkata, M., Imam, N., Pophale, S. (eds.) OpenSHMEM 2017. LNCS, vol. 10679, pp. 50–62. Springer, Cham (2018). https://doi.org/10.1007/978-3-319-73814-7_4
7. Boyle, P., Chuvelev, M., Cossu, G., Kelly, C., Lehner, C., Meadows, L.: Accelerating HPC codes on Intel® Omni-path architecture networks: from particle physics to machine learning. arXiv preprint arXiv:1711.04883 (2017)
8. Brightwell, R., Pedretti, K.: An intra-node implementation of OpenSHMEM using virtual address space mapping. In: Proceedings of the 5th International Conference on Partitioned Global Address Space Programming Models. PGAS 2011 (2011)
9. ten Bruggencate, M., Roweth, D., Oyanagi, S.: Thread-safe SHMEM extensions. In: Poole, S., Hernandez, O., Shamis, P. (eds.) OpenSHMEM 2014. LNCS, vol. 8356, pp. 178–185. Springer, Cham (2014). https://doi.org/10.1007/978-3-319-05215-1_13

10. Choi, S.E., Pritchard, H., Shimek, J., Swaro, J., Tiffany, Z., Turrubiates, B.: An implementation of OFI libfabric in support of multithreaded PGAS solutions. In: Proceedings of 9th International Conference on Partitioned Global Address Space Programming Models. PGAS, pp. 59–69, September 2015

11. Dinan, J., Flajslik, M.: Contexts: a mechanism for high throughput communication in OpenSHMEM. In: Proceedings of the 8th International Conference on Partitioned Global Address Space Programming Models, pp. 10:1–10:9. ACM, New York (2014)

12. Grossman, M., Doyle, J., Dinan, J., Pritchard, H., Seager, K., Sarkar, V.: Implementation and evaluation of OpenSHMEM contexts using OFI libfabric. In: Gorentla Venkata, M., Imam, N., Pophale, S. (eds.) OpenSHMEM 2017. LNCS, vol. 10679, pp. 19–34. Springer, Cham (2018). https://doi.org/10.1007/978-3-319-73814-7_2

13. Grossman, M., Kumar, V., Budimlić, Z., Sarkar, V.: Integrating asynchronous task parallelism with OpenSHMEM. In: Gorentla Venkata, M., Imam, N., Pophale, S., Mintz, T.M. (eds.) OpenSHMEM 2016. LNCS, vol. 10007, pp. 3–17. Springer, Cham (2016). https://doi.org/10.1007/978-3-319-50995-2_1

14. Grun, P., et al.: A brief introduction to the OpenFabrics interfaces - a new network API for maximizing high performance application efficiency. In: 2015 IEEE 23rd Annual Symposium on High-Performance Interconnects, pp. 34–39, August 2015

15. Knaak, D., Namashivayam, N.: Proposing OpenSHMEM extensions towards a future for hybrid programming and heterogeneous computing. In: Gorentla Venkata, M., Shamis, P., Imam, N., Lopez, M.G. (eds.) OpenSHMEM 2014. LNCS, vol. 9397, pp. 53–68. Springer, Cham (2015). https://doi.org/10.1007/978-3-319-26428-8_4

16. MPI Forum: MPI: a message-passing interface standard version 3.1. Technical report, University of Tennessee, Knoxville, June 2015

17. Namashivayam, N., Knaak, D., Cernohous, B., Radcliffe, N., Pagel, M.: An evaluation of thread-safe and contexts-domains features in cray SHMEM. In: Gorentla Venkata, M., Imam, N., Pophale, S., Mintz, T.M. (eds.) OpenSHMEM 2016. LNCS, vol. 10007, pp. 163–180. Springer, Cham (2016). https://doi.org/10.1007/978-3-319-50995-2_11

18. Intel® Omni-Path Fabric Host Software User Guide Rev 9.0, April 2018. https://www.intel.com/content/dam/support/us/en/documents/network-and-i-o/fabric-products/Intel_OP_Fabric_Host_Software_UG_H76470_v9_0.pdf

19. OpenSHMEM Application Programming Interface, Version 1.4, December 2017. http://openshmem.org/site/sites/default/site_files/OpenSHMEM-1.4.pdf

20. Intel® Performance Scaled Messaging 2 (PSM2) Programmer's Guide, April 2018. https://www.intel.com/content/dam/support/us/en/documents/network-and-i-o/fabric-products/Intel_PSM2_PG_H76473_v9_0.pdf

21. Poole, S., et al.: OpenSHMEM extensions and a vision for its future direction. In: Poole, S., Hernandez, O., Shamis, P. (eds.) OpenSHMEM 2014. LNCS, vol. 8356, pp. 149–162. Springer, Cham (2014). https://doi.org/10.1007/978-3-319-05215-1_11

22. Sandia OpenSHMEM (2018). https://github.com/Sandia-OpenSHMEM/SOS

23. Seager, K., Choi, S.-E., Dinan, J., Pritchard, H., Sur, S.: Design and implementation of OpenSHMEM using OFI on the aries interconnect. In: Gorentla Venkata, M., Imam, N., Pophale, S., Mintz, T.M. (eds.) OpenSHMEM 2016. LNCS, vol. 10007, pp. 97–113. Springer, Cham (2016). https://doi.org/10.1007/978-3-319-50995-2_7

24. The high-resolution timer API, 16 January 2006. https://lwn.net/Articles/167897/
25. Weeks, H., Dosanjh, M.G.F., Bridges, P.G., Grant, R.E.: SHMEM-MT: a benchmark suite for assessing multi-threaded SHMEM performance. In: Gorentla Venkata, M., Imam, N., Pophale, S., Mintz, T.M. (eds.) OpenSHMEM 2016. LNCS, vol. 10007, pp. 227–231. Springer, Cham (2016). https://doi.org/10.1007/978-3-319-50995-2_16

Introducing Cray OpenSHMEMX - A Modular Multi-communication Layer OpenSHMEM Implementation

Naveen Namashivayam[✉], Bob Cernohous, Dan Pou, and Mark Pagel

Cray Inc., Seattle, USA
nravi@cray.com

Abstract. SHMEM has a long history as a parallel programming model. It is extensively used since 1993, starting from Cray T3D systems. For the past two decades SHMEM library implementation in Cray systems evolved through different generations. The current generation of the SHMEM implementation for Cray XC and XK systems is called Cray SHMEM. It is a proprietary SHMEM implementation from Cray Inc. In this work, we provide an in-depth analysis of need for a new SHMEM implementation and then introduce the next evolution of Cray SHMEM implementation for current and future generation Cray systems. We call this new implementation Cray OpenSHMEMX. We provide brief design overview, along with a review of functional and performance differences in Cray OpenSHMEMX comparing against the existing Cray SHMEM implementation.

1 Introduction

OpenSHMEM [10] is a Partitioned Global Address Space (PGAS) [8] library interface specification, which is the culmination of a standardization effort among many implementers and users of SHMEM programming model. SHMEM as a programming model has a long history on Cray systems with proprietary library implementations evolving over decades. The current generation of such proprietary SHMEM implementation on Cray systems is called Cray SHMEM and it is OpenSHMEM standard version-1.3 [2] compliant.

Cray OpenSHMEMX is a new proprietary SHMEM library implementation for the current and future generation Cray systems by Cray Inc.

The major part of this work covers:

- basic background and design overview on Cray OpenSHMEMX;
- analyze a list of features supported by Cray OpenSHMEMX comparing against Cray SHMEM;
- early performance regression analysis of the different Remote Memory Access (RMA) and Atomic Memory Operations (AMO) using OSU OpenSHMEM microbenchmarks [4]; and
- performance evaluation of selected features in Cray OpenSHMEMX.

© Springer Nature Switzerland AG 2019
S. Pophale et al. (Eds.): OpenSHMEM 2018, LNCS 11283, pp. 41–55, 2019.
https://doi.org/10.1007/978-3-030-04918-8_3

This work is organized as follows. Section 2 provides a brief overview for Cray SHMEM and introduces the Cray OpenSHMEMX library. Section 3 provides a brief design overview and the list of supported features in Cray OpenSHMEMX. In Sect. 4 we report the results of performance regression analysis performed using OSU microbenchmarks and in Sect. 5 we list the functional enhancements in Cray OpenSHMEMX. We discuss related work in Sect. 6 and conclude in Sect. 7.

2   Background

The current generation SHMEM library implementation for Cray Systems is Cray SHMEM. Cray SHMEM is based on an underlying communication library called DMAPP. DMAPP [21] supports logically shared, distributed memory programming model targeting Cray-developed Gemini and Aries interconnect architectures. Cray SHMEM is supported on all Cray XC and XK systems and its design is tightly coupled with DMAPP for extracting optimal performance from the underlying interconnect and processor architecture.

In anticipation of the future system architectures for exascale capable systems and beyond, they demand any OpenSHMEM implementation support for:

- multiple processor architectures and accelerators;
- different interconnects; and
- different application usage models

Hence, we extend the Cray SHMEM library implementation and the name of this new evolved Cray SHMEM library is Cray OpenSHMEMX.

3   Supported Features and Design Overview

In this section, Table 1 provides a list of features supported by Cray OpenSHMEMX comparing against Cray SHMEM. It covers the list of all the supported OpenSHMEM standard features and Cray specific features. These Cray specific features [15, 16, 22] are available as SHMEMX prefixed routines as required in the OpenSHMEM standards.

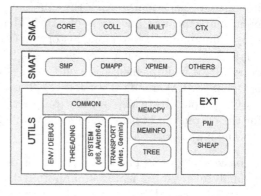

Fig. 1. Brief overview of different layers in Cray OpenSHMEMX

3.1   Design Overview

To extract maximum performance from Cray XC and XK systems, Cray SHMEM is tightly coupled with DMAPP, its underlying communication layer. Cray OpenSHMEMX is designed modular to use different communication layers and application usage models across different Cray system architectures. Figure 1 provides a brief internal overview of the multi-layered Cray OpenSHMEMX software stack. It supports four main layers - SMA, SMAT, UTILS, and EXT.

- SMA is the first layer in the library. It is the entry point for all SHMEM specific routines and it performs the following three major actions: 1. argument validation, 2. communication layer selection, and 3. multithreading selection. This layer is composed of four major components - CORE, COLL, MULT, and CTX.
  - All core SHMEM programming model features like RMA, AMO, memory ordering, and library initialization features are part of the CORE component.
  - COLL supports OpenSHMEM collectives along with Cray specific SHMEM Teams, and Team-based collective features.
  - MULT supports OpenSHMEM multithreading and Cray Thread-hot features.
  - CTX includes OpenSHMEM communication management features introduced as part of OpenSHMEM standard version 1.4 [3].

  CORE is the most independent and essential component in the library. Cray OpenSHMEMX can be build with just the features from CORE component, while other features can be added as extensions to the base CORE component.
- SMAT is the communication layer which includes support for different communication libraries. The SMP support allows us to build the library with two different communication layers one for on-node data transfer between two processes through shared memory and another for off-node data transfers through the network. Other communication layers[1] added in the SMAT layer are DMAPP and XPMEM. The SMP based library is built with DMAPP and XPMEM for off-node and on-node transfers respectively.
- UTILS layer support different utility functions like Cray optimized memcpy, support tools for interaction with different threading libraries, and system specific utilities for supporting the library on different processor architectures like X86_64 and AArch64.
- EXT layer enables the use of other external libraries like Process Management Interface [9] (PMI). Few communication libraries included in SMAT supports the symmetric heap (SHEAP) creation and maintenance internally like DMAPP. While others like XPMEM does not support symmetric heap creation. Hence, we added support for internal SHEAP maintenance in EXT layer.

---

[1] Though SMAT layer supports different communication layers, we use DMAPP and XPMEM in this work as others are experimental and not available in the current released Cray OpenSHMEMX version 8.0.1.

Table 1. List of different supported OpenSHMEM and Cray-specific SHMEMX-prefixed features in Cray SHMEM version 7.7.0 and Cray OpenSHMEMX version 8.0.1

Library features	Cray SHMEM	Cray OpenSHMEMX
OpenSHMEM (OSH) Compliance	OpenSHMEM-1.3	OpenSHMEM-1.4
- OSH-1.4 Contexts and Sync	No	Yes
- OSH-1.4 Ext Typed RMA, AMO	Yes	Yes
- OSH-1.4 shmem_test	Yes	Yes
- OSH-1.4 shmem_calloc	Yes	Yes
- OSH-1.4 Bitwise AMOs	Yes	Yes
Cray specific Teams	Yes	Yes
Cray specific Team based Collectives	Yes	Yes
Cray specific Thread-hot	Yes	Yes
Cray specific Memory Partitions	Yes	Future
Cray specific Non-blocking AMOs	Yes	Future
Cray specific put-with-signal	Yes	Yes
Cray specific Local Node Queries	Yes	Yes
Cray specific AlltoAllv	Yes	Yes
Cray specific AlltoaAllv_packed	Yes	Yes
Cray specific Fortran 2008 wrapper	No	Future

3.2 OpenSHMEM Specification Compliance

Though, recent Cray SHMEM version 7.7.0 supports few OpenSHMEM standard 1.4 specific features like extended typed RMA and AMOs, support for shmem_test and shmem_calloc routines, and bitwise AMOs, it is not completely OpenSHMEM standard 1.4 compliant. But, Cray OpenSHMEMX from version 8.0.0 is officially OpenSHMEM standard 1.4 compliant.

4   Performance Regression Analysis

In this section we report the performance regression analysis on two major OpenSHMEM features - Remote Memory Access (RMA) and Atomic Memory Operations (AMOs) using OSU Microbenchmarks. We compare the performance of the new Cray OpenSHMEMX library against the existing production ready Cray SHMEM library. Details of the test environment are tabulated in Table 2.

We used OSU Microbenchmark suite for our analysis and tested the libraries on two different processor architectures - Intel Broadwell (BDW [17]) and Intel Xeon Phi processor code named Knights Landing (KNL [20]).

Table 2. Test environment details for performance regression analysis

Component name	Version details
GCC compiler	7.3.0
Cray SHMEM	7.7.0
Cray OpenSHMEMX	8.0.1[a]
DMAPP	7.1.1
XPMEM	2.2.14
Cray linux environment (CLE)	CLE 6.0 UP06

[a]Version 8.0.1 is the most recent release of Cray OpenSHMEMX library

4.1   Analysis of OpenSHMEM Non-blocking Put

Figures 2 and 3 shows the message rate in number of messages per second for inter-node non-blocking put operations on Intel BDW and Intel KNL processors respectively. We use 2 Nodes for these tests.

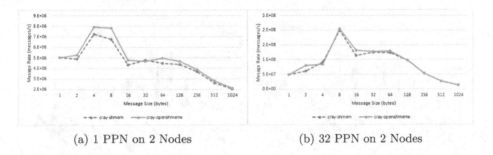

(a) 1 PPN on 2 Nodes   (b) 32 PPN on 2 Nodes

Fig. 2. Inter-node OpenSHMEM NBI put performance analysis on Intel BDW

On BDW for small message sizes less than 1024 bytes, Fig. 2 shows Cray OpenSHMEMX to performs similar to Cray SHMEM on both 1 PPN[2] and 32 PPN tests.

While on Intel KNL, Fig. 3a shows Cray OpenSHMEMX to performs similar to Cray SHMEM for 1 PPN tests but Fig. 3b shows it to perform 16% better than Cray SHMEM for 64 PPN tests. This performance improvement can be attributed to the symbol visibility optimizations and reduction in software overheads in the critical path by reducing the number of instructions. These few optimizations can have a huge effect on slow core processors like Intel KNL.

4.2   Analysis of Different OpenSHMEM Atomic Memory Operations

Similar to the tests in Sect. 4.1, we use OSU Microbenchmarks to evaluate the operation rate (million operations per second) of OpenSHMEM Fetching and

---

[2] Number of Processing Elements (PEs) Per Node.

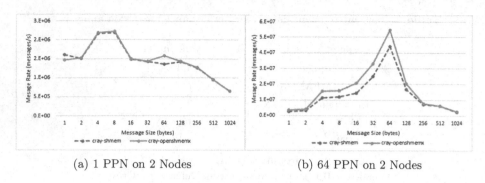

(a) 1 PPN on 2 Nodes   (b) 64 PPN on 2 Nodes

Fig. 3. Inter-node OpenSHMEM NBI put performance analysis on Intel KNL

Non-fetching AMOs. Figure 4, shows the performance of Cray OpenSHMEMX against Cray SHMEM on Intel BDW processors. We can see that the performance of the OpenSHMEM AMOs are on-par with the production ready Cray SHMEM implementation.

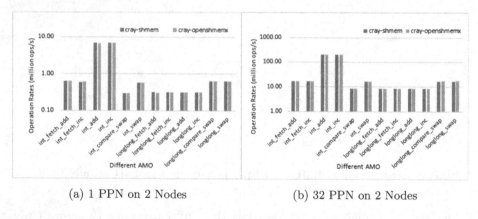

(a) 1 PPN on 2 Nodes   (b) 32 PPN on 2 Nodes

Fig. 4. Inter-node OpenSHMEM AMO performance analysis on Intel BDW. Data-type `int` is 32 bit and `long long` is 64 bit.

In brief, from Sects. 4.1 and 4.2, we can see that the performance of Cray OpenSHMEMX is similar to Cray SHMEM. This analysis is also verified on other OpenSHMEM RMA operations like blocking put and get, and non-blocking get. Similar to Cray SHMEM, the SMP build of Cray OpenSHMEMX supports XPMEM for intra-node operations and the intra-node performance analysis on RMA and AMO operations are also similar to Cray SHMEM. To be concise, these results are not shown in this work.

5   Available Features and Enhancements

In this section, we discuss the design of selected available features and enhancements in Cray OpenSHMEMX. In particular we discuss about different supported processor architectures, interoperability between OpenSHMEM communication contexts and Cray specific Thread-hot features, and Cray specific put-with-signal RMA operation. Performance results reported in this section use the same test environment as tabulated in Table 2.

5.1   Supported Processor Architectures

Table 3 provides a brief overview of different supported processor architectures. Apart from providing support for Intel Xeon (HSW [14], BDW [17], and SKL [11]) and Xeon Phi (KNL [20]) systems as Cray SHMEM, Cray OpenSHMEMX provides support for Cavium ARM based Thunder X2 [5] systems. Processor specific optimizations like optimized `memcpy` are available for intra-node data transfers.

Table 3. Overview of different supported processor architectures in Cray SHMEM and Cray OpenSHMEMX

Processor type	Cray SHMEM	Cray OpenSHMEMX
Intel Xeon (X86_64)	Yes	Yes
Intel Xeon Phi (X86_64)	Yes	Yes
Cavium Thunder X2 (AArch64)	No	Yes

Figure 5, shows the performance improvement on using processor optimized `memcpy` against the system `memcpy` on Intel KNL processor based systems. We used OSU NBI Put microbenchmark in test environment as mentioned in Table 2. On average for very small data sizes less than 1024 bytes, we can see the KNL optimized `memcpy` to perform 20% better than the system `memcpy` for both 2PPN and 68PPN tests.

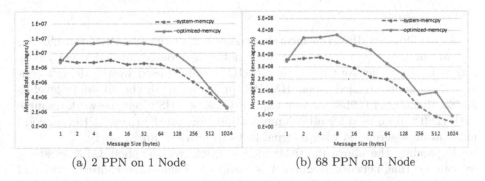

(a) 2 PPN on 1 Node   (b) 68 PPN on 1 Node

Fig. 5. Intra-node `memcpy` NBI put performance analysis on Intel KNL

5.2 Interoperability Between OpenSHMEM Contexts and Cray Thread-Hot

Communication contexts (CTX) and Thread-safety are the most important flagship features added to OpenSHMEM standard version-1.4. CTX allows users to create multiple independent streams of communication within the same application and also provide opportunities for thread isolation by eliminating synchronization overhead on multithreaded OpenSHMEM applications.

Cray OpenSHMEMX provides support for CTX routines and the synchronization routines (shmem_sync and shmem_sync_all) associated with it.

Thread-hot SHMEM (THS) [22] is another Cray specific feature available in Cray SHMEM to provide opportunities for thread isolation by eliminating synchronization overheads on multithreaded application. We evaluate the functional and performance differences between CTX and THS features in [18].

On ideal configurations, when the number of available network resources is less than or equal to the number of threads used per PE, through CTX and THS we try to provide separate network resources for each thread and maximize the network injection rate per PE. Along with this we provide isolated memory ordering per network resource and avoid synchronization overhead between threads in a multithreaded application.

In this section, we provide detailed explanation on the resource management between CTX and THS features. We use multiple hybrid OpenSHMEM and OpenMP [19] code snippets for this purpose.

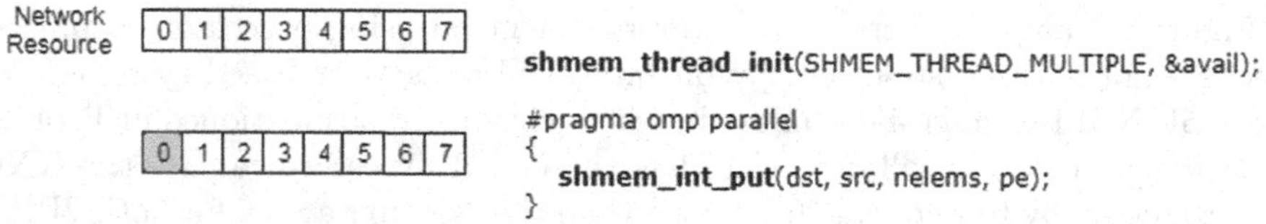

```
Network
Resource   0 1 2 3 4 5 6 7

shmem_thread_init(SHMEM_THREAD_MULTIPLE, &avail);

           0 1 2 3 4 5 6 7       #pragma omp parallel
                                 {
                                     shmem_int_put(dst, src, nelems, pe);
                                 }
```

Fig. 6. Multithreading without CTX or THS in Cray OpenSHMEMX

As per OpenSHMEM specification version 1.4, all OpenSHMEM routines are thread-safe. For example, if there are 8 network resources available per PE as shown in Fig. 6, network resource with ID 0 will be used by the default context. In a multithreaded OpenSHMEM application with thread-safety level as SHMEM_THREAD_MULTIPLE, without explicit CTX or THS usage, network resource with ID 0 will be used for all communication from all the threads. Hence, communication is serialized with internal locks to provide thread safety.

Expanding the above multithreaded example with explicit CTX creation, we can see that network resource 1 is assigned to shareable context ctx1 and network resources from 2 to 5 are assigned to private context ctx created by four threads. ctx is a thread private object and it is visible only to a single thread. When the number of private contexts exceeds the available network resource

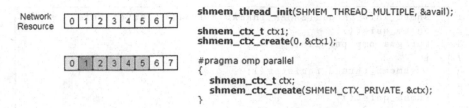

```
shmem_thread_init(SHMEM_THREAD_MULTIPLE, &avail);

shmem_ctx_t ctx1;
shmem_ctx_create(0, &ctx1);

#pragma omp parallel
{
    shmem_ctx_t ctx;
    shmem_ctx_create(SHMEM_CTX_PRIVATE, &ctx);
}
```

Fig. 7. Multithreading with explicit CTX creation in Cray OpenSHMEMX

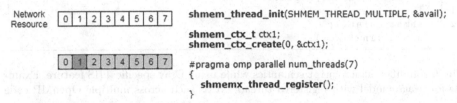

```
shmem_thread_init(SHMEM_THREAD_MULTIPLE, &avail);

shmem_ctx_t ctx1;
shmem_ctx_create(0, &ctx1);

#pragma omp parallel num_threads(7)
{
    shmemx_thread_register();
}
```

Fig. 8. Multithreading with CTX and Cray specific THS in Cray OpenSHMEMX

shmem_ctx_create returns a non-negative value. This is shown in Fig. 7. Any OpenSHMEM communication through shareable context ctx1 is serialized.

In the above example, if we perform thread registration using Cray specific THS feature instead of explicit CTX creation inside the OpenMP parallel region, we will try to provide private network resource to as many threads as possible, while the remaining threads will share the available shareable network resource. In Fig. 8, if 7 threads are registered, 6 threads are provided with private resource from 2 to 7 and the remaining thread will share the shareable network resource 1 with already created shareable context ctx. If there are no shareable network resource available, the registered thread will continue to use the default context (SHMEM_CTX_DEFAULT) for all the OpenSHMEM communications.

From the above explanation we can show that both OpenSHMEM CTX and Cray specific THS features can coexist in the same application. Destroying a previously created context or unregistering a registered thread through shmem_ctx_destroy and shmemx_thread_unregister routines respectively will release the network resource for future usage.

At present, we have the following different routines in Cray OpenSHMEMX to provide mechanisms to ensure delivery of blocking Put, AMO, memory store, and NBI Put and Get routines to symmetric data objects:

- shmem_ctx_quiet;
- shmemx_thread_quiet; and
- shmem_quiet

The shmem_ctx_quiet and shmemx_thread_quiet routines ensures delivery issued by the calling PE on the given context and the registered thread respectively.

As per OpenSHMEM specification version 1.4, shmem_quiet ensures delivery issued by the calling PE only on the default context (SHMEM_CTX_DEFAULT). In

```
1   shmem_init_thread(SHMEM_THREAD_MULTIPLE, &available);
2   shmem_quiet();
3   #pragma omp parallel
4   {
5     shmemx_thread_register();
6   }
7   shmem_quiet();
8   #pragma omp parallel
9   {
10    shmemx_thread_register();
11  }
12  shmem_quiet();
13  shmem_finalize();
```

Fig. 9. Modified shmem_quiet semantics while using Cray specific THS feature. Example for usage model with registered thread left as such across multiple OpenMP code blocks

Cray OpenSHMEMX, we have modified this semantic and ensure delivery issued by the calling PE on both the default context and the registered thread if any.

For example as shown in Fig. 9, shmem_quiet in line 2 and line 12 ensures delivery only on the default context, while shmem_quiet in line 7 ensures delivery both on the default context and the registered thread resource. This specific usage is on applications where registered threads are left registered across multiple OpenMP code blocks until unregistering in some eventual OpenMP code blocks.

The above explanation can also be interpreted for the ordering operations ensured by shmem_fence, shmem_ctx_fence, and shmemx_thread_fence routines.

OpenSHMEM Context Performance Analysis. In Fig. 10, we report the performance of CTX in Cray OpenSHMEMX using modified OSU NBI Put Microbenchmark on 2 Nodes with 1 PPN. We report the message rate by varying the number of threads used per PE with a SHMEM_CTX_PRIVATE context per thread. We can see that the message rate increases linearly by increasing the number of contexts.

Comparing OpenSHMEM Context and Cray THS Performance. In Fig. 10b, we report the performance comparison on using CTX against THS feature using modified OSU NBI Put Microbenchmark on 2 Nodes with 1 PPN. We report the message rate by varying the number of registered threads against the number of threads with a SHMEM_CTX_PRIVATE explicit context created per thread. We can see that the message rate increases linearly for both scenarios and there are no performance variations in using CTX against THS.

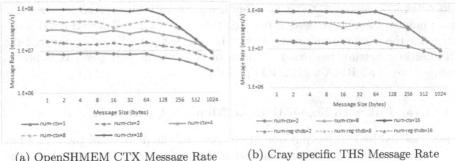

(a) OpenSHMEM CTX Message Rate   (b) Cray specific THS Message Rate

Fig. 10. Multithreaded inter-node OpenSHMEM message rate analysis on Intel BDW with 1 PPN on 2 nodes using modified OSU NBI put microbenchmark

Cray Specific THS Performance Regression in Cray SHMEM And Cray OpenSHMEMX. Cray specific THS is not a new feature, it is already implemented in Cray SHMEM and is being used in different applications as a SHMEMX prefixed routine. In this section, we report the performance regression study of the THS feature in Cray OpenSHMEMX comparing against Cray SHMEM. We use a modified OSU NBI Put message rate microbenchmark on 2 Nodes with 1 PPN. While varying the number of registered threads from 2 to 16, we can see in Fig. 11a that Cray OpenSHMEMX performs similar to Cray SHMEM for data sizes less than 1024 bytes. We can see similar performance for other data sizes and other OpenSHMEM operations as well.

OpenSHMEM Context with Different SHMEM_MAX_CTX. Fig. 11b shows the performance of NBI Put operation using OSU Microbenchmark on 2 Nodes with 1 PPN. Only the default context is used for performance evaluation. We can see the latency for 2048 bytes on SHMEM_CTX_DEFAULT varying across different

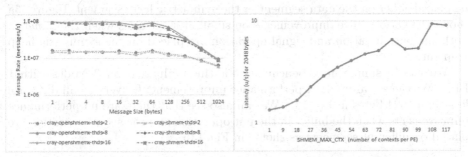

(a) Cray specific THS Message Rate in Cray SHMEM and Cray OpenSHMEMX

(b) OpenSHMEM CTX performance variation on SHMEM_MAX_CTX

Fig. 11. Multithreaded inter-node OpenSHMEM message rate and latency analysis on Intel BDW with 1 PPN on 2 nodes using modified OSU NBI put microbenchmark

SHMEM_MAX_CTX. SHMEM_MAX_CTX is an environment variable used to set the maximum number of context needed per PE. If not used Cray OpenSHMEMX can determine the maximum number of available context per PE during shmem_init initialization. Setting the exact number of contexts needed per PE improves performance of all RMA and AMO operations.

5.3 Cray Put with Signal Remote Memory Operations

A put followed by another put operation to signal the delivery of the initial put operation is an important usage model in OpenSHMEM. Figure 12 shows the implementation of put-with-signal with and without using shmem_fence. Cray-developed Aries interconnect has support for packing put operation with a signal value in the header to the same target PE as a single message. This optimization is available only for small message size. We can use this optimization to avoid explicit shmem_fence operation to signal the delivery of the put operation.

```
1    /* with shmem_fence implementation */
2    shmem_put(*dst, *src, nelems, pe);
3    shmem_fence();
4    shmem_put(*signal, value, pe);
5
6    /* cray-specific implementation without fence */
7    shmemx_put_signal(*dst, *src, nelems, *signal, value, pe);
```

Fig. 12. Implementing put-with-signal semantics with and without shmem_fence in Cray OpenSHMEMX

The above mentioned hardware optimization is available only when the buffer in both the put operation (dst, src) and the signal operation (signal) are on the same memory segment. As per OpenSHMEM, symmetric data objects can be placed either on the data segment or the symmetric heap segment. Figure 13a shows the performance improvements on small message sizes when the buffer in both the put operation and signal operation are placed on the symmetric heap segment.

We used a simple microbenchmark for this evaluation on 2 Nodes with 1 PPN. We can see around 3X performance improvements for very small data size less than 1024 bytes in Fig. 13a. We can also see that there are no performance improvements when the buffer in the put operation and the signal operation are placed on different segments as shown in Fig. 13b.

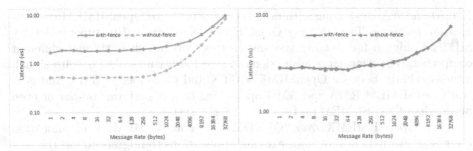

(a) Comparing put-with-signal with and without `shmem_fence`

(b) Comparing put-with-signal when target and signal in different segments

Fig. 13. Multithreaded inter-node OpenSHMEM latency analysis on Intel BDW with 1 PPN on 2 nodes using simple put-with-signal microbenchmark

6 Related Work

Software evolution is the term used to refer to the process of developing a software stack and continuously updating it for various reasons. The development of Cray OpenSHMEMX from Cray SHMEM is an adaptive approach for supporting an optimized, and scalable OpenSHMEM implementation on future Cray systems at exascale. At present many HPC software libraries and parallel programming models are undergoing a major evolution to support and exploit future exascale capable systems.

For example, the Exascale MPI project addresses in enabling applications to effectively use the latest advances in MPI [12] to scale to the largest supercomputers in the world. And, OMPI-X project prepares the MPI standard and its implementation in Open MPI for exascale through improvements in scalability, capability, and resilience. As part of both these projects, the existing MPICH [13] and Open MPI [7] software stacks are getting evolved.

Similarly, the PAGODA project helps in supporting HPC application development using the PGAS programming model. As part of the pagoda project, GASNet [1] is evolving as GASNet-EX. xGA is another similar project which enables the performance scalability of Global Arrays (GA) [6] programming model for exascale capable systems.

7 Conclusion

In this work we introduced Cray OpenSHMEMX, a new proprietary software library product from Cray Inc. It is planned to supersede the current production ready Cray SHMEM library on future Cray systems. Apart from importing existing Cray specific features from Cray SHMEM, Cray OpenSHMEMX is designed as a highly modular SHMEM implementation to support OpenSHMEM standards. Cray OpenSHMEMX supports different processor architectures like

X86_64 and AArch64 along with other new features like OpenSHMEM communication contexts. Though Cray OpenSHMEMX is planned to supersede Cray SHMEM only on future Cray systems, in this work we show through different comprehensive performance evaluations on selected features like put-with-signal, interoperability between OpenSHMEM CTX and Cray-specific THS, and general OpenSHMEM RMA and AMO operations that it performs on-par or even better than Cray SHMEM on the current Cray systems.

Cray OpenSHMEMX over SMP(DMAPP and XPMEM) communication layer is an evaluation library for existing applications to migrate to use the new library. In future, we plan to work more on the SMP(DMAPP and XPMEM) communication layer based library by adding new features, porting to other processor architectures and exporting these evaluated features to other new communication layers.

Acknowledgment and Disclaimer. The authors would like to thank all the members of Cray Message Passing Toolkit for their involvement in the design and implementation of the Cray OpenSHMEMX software stack. Any opinions, findings, and conclusions or recommendations expressed in this material are those of the authors and do not necessarily reflect the views of associated organizations.

References

1. GASNet: a portable high-performance communication layer for global address-space languages. http://gasnet.lbl.gov/pubs/258-paper.pdf
2. OpenSHMEM standard version-1.3. http://openshmem.org/site/sites/default/site_files/OpenSHMEM-1.3.pdf, a
3. OpenSHMEM standard version-1.4. http://openshmem.org/site/sites/default/site_files/OpenSHMEM-1.4.pdf, b
4. OSU Micro-benchmarks. http://mvapich.cse.ohio-state.edu/benchmarks/
5. Cavium Thunder X2 ARM Processors. https://www.cavium.com/product-thunderx2-arm-processors.html
6. Global arrays: a portable shared memory model for distributed memory computers (1994)
7. Open MPI: a flexible high performance MPI (2005)
8. Almasi, G.: In: Padua, D.A. (ed.) Encyclopedia of Parallel Computing (2011)
9. Balaji, P., et al.: PMI: a scalable parallel process-management interface for extreme-scale systems. In: Keller, R., Gabriel, E., Resch, M., Dongarra, J. (eds.) EuroMPI 2010. LNCS, vol. 6305, pp. 31–41. Springer, Heidelberg (2010). https://doi.org/10.1007/978-3-642-15646-5_4
10. Chapman, B., et al.: Introducing OpenSHMEM: SHMEM for the PGAS Community. In: Proceedings of the Fourth Conference on Partitioned Global Address Space Programming Model, PGAS 2010 (2010)
11. Doweck, J., et al.: Inside 6th-generation Intel Core: new microarchitecture code-named Skylake. IEEE Micro (2017)
12. Message Passing Forum. MPI: a message-passing interface standard. Technical report (1994)
13. Gropp, W.: MPICH2: a new start for MPI implementations. In: Kranzlmüller, D., Volkert, J., Kacsuk, P., Dongarra, J. (eds.) EuroPVM/MPI 2002. LNCS, vol. 2474, pp. 7–7. Springer, Heidelberg (2002). https://doi.org/10.1007/3-540-45825-5_5

14. Hammarlund, P., et al.: Haswell: the fourth-generation intel core processor. IEEE Micro **34**, 6–20 (2014)
15. Kandalla, K., et al.: Current state of the cray MPT software stacks on the cray XC series supercomputers. In: Cray User Group (CUG) meeting 2017 (2017)
16. Knaak, D., Namashivayam, N.: Proposing OpenSHMEM extensions towards a future for hybrid programming and heterogeneous computing. In: Gorentla Venkata, M., Shamis, P., Imam, N., Lopez, M.G. (eds.) OpenSHMEM 2014. LNCS, vol. 9397, pp. 53–68. Springer, Cham (2015). https://doi.org/10.1007/978-3-319-26428-8_4
17. Nalamalpu, A., et al.: Broadwell: a family of IA 14nm processors. In: Symposium on VLSI Circuits (VLSI Circuits) (2015)
18. Namashivayam, N., Knaak, D., Cernohous, B., Radcliffe, N., Pagel, M.: An evaluation of thread-safe and contexts-domains features in cray SHMEM. In: Gorentla Venkata, M., Imam, N., Pophale, S., Mintz, T.M. (eds.) OpenSHMEM 2016. LNCS, vol. 10007, pp. 163–180. Springer, Cham (2016). https://doi.org/10.1007/978-3-319-50995-2_11
19. OpenMP Architecture Review Board. OpenMP application program interface version 4.5, November 2015. https://www.openmp.org/wp-content/uploads/openmp-4.5.pdf
20. Sodani, S.A., et al.: Knights landing: second-generation Intel Xeon Phi product (2016)
21. ten Bruggencate, M., Roweth, D.: DMAPP: an API for one-sided programming model on baker systems. Technical report, Cray Users Group (CUG), August 2010
22. ten Bruggencate, M., Roweth, D., Oyanagi, S.: Thread-safe SHMEM extensions. In: Poole, S., Hernandez, O., Shamis, P. (eds.) OpenSHMEM 2014. LNCS, vol. 8356, pp. 178–185. Springer, Cham (2014). https://doi.org/10.1007/978-3-319-05215-1_13

An Initial Implementation of Libfabric Conduit for OpenSHMEM-X

Subhadeep Bhattacharya[1]([⊠]), Shaeke Salman[1], Manjunath Gorentla Venkata[2],
Harsh Kundnani[1], Neena Imam[2], and Weikuan Yu[1]

[1] Department of Computer Science, Florida State University, Tallahassee, USA
{bhattach,salman,kundnani,yuw}@cs.fsu.edu
[2] Oak Ridge National Laboratory, Oak Ridge, USA
{manjugv,imamn}@ornl.gov

Abstract. As a representative of Partitioned Global Address Space models, OpenSHMEM provides a variety of functionalities including one-sided communication, atomic operations, and collective routines. The communication layer of OpenSHMEM-X plays a crucial role for its functionalities. OFI Libfabric is an open-source network library that supports portable low-latency interfaces from different fabric providers while minimizing the semantic gap across API endpoints. In this paper, we present the design and implementation of OpenSHMEM-X communication conduit using Libfabric. This Libfabric conduit is designed to support a broad range of network providers while achieving excellent network performance and scalability. We have performed an extensive set of experiments to validate the performance of our implementation, and compared with the Sandia OpenSHMEM implementation. Our results show that the Libfabric conduit improves the communication bandwidth on the socket provider by up to 42% and 11%, compared to an alternative OpenSHMEM implementation for put and get operations, respectively. In addition, our implementation of atomic operations has achieved similar latency to that of the Sandia implementation.

This work was sponsored by the U.S. Department of Energy's Office of Advanced Scientific Computing Research. This manuscript has been authored by UT-Battelle, LLC under Contract No. DE-AC05-00OR22725 with the U.S. Department of Energy. The United States Government retains and the publisher, by accepting the article for publication, acknowledges that the United States Government retains a non-exclusive, paid-up, irrevocable, world-wide license to publish or reproduce the published form of this manuscript, or allow others to do so, for United States Government purposes. The Department of Energy will provide public access to these results of federally sponsored research in accordance with the DOE Public Access Plan (http://energy.gov/downloads/doe-public-access-plan). This research used resources of the Oak Ridge Leadership Computing Facility at the Oak Ridge National Laboratory, which is supported by the Office of Science of the U.S. Department of Energy under Contract No. DE-AC05-00OR22725.

© Springer Nature Switzerland AG 2019
S. Pophale et al. (Eds.): OpenSHMEM 2018, LNCS 11283, pp. 56–69, 2019.
https://doi.org/10.1007/978-3-030-04918-8_4

1   Introduction

SHMEM is known as a collection of programming libraries that provide parallel processing capabilities. Cray systems developed the first implementation. Other organizations later followed suit with their own implementations, including SGI, IBM and many others. One-sided communication, shared view of memory, atomic and collective operations are some critical aspects of SHMEM library implementation. It has been used in the context of parallel programming model to implement partitioned global address space (PGAS) systems.

The presence of various implementations of SHMEM prompted the need of a standard specification and API. In addition, performance and code portability is also critical due to diverged behaviors and API syntax from different implementations of SHMEM. The OpenSHMEM community was formed to standardize the specification, and they introduced OpenSHMEM [3], integrating different implementation efforts of SHMEM.

PGAS (Partitioned Global Address Space) languages are popular due to their capability of providing shared memory programming model over distributed memory machines. OpenSHMEM [9] realizes a PGAS model by allocating remotely accessible objects and enabling easy data sharing among the processing elements (PEs) in an application. It can be leveraged in developing parallel, scalable and portable programs, achieving low latency and high bandwidth. OpenSHMEM data distribution is carried out by one-sided communication and synchronization routines. Such one-sided operations allow a local PE to be independent of the communication at a remote PE when executing and completing a data transfer operation. It also facilitates a simplified exhibition of parallelism allowing overlap between communication and computation that hide data transfer latencies.

Libfabric [6, 8] is an open-source software library for various network fabrics. It is implemented by the OpenFabrics Interface (OFI) working group. Libfabric aims to reduce the technical complexities between applications and underlying fabric services and support many application semantics directly. It has been carefully designed by fabric hardware providers and application developers, so that HPC users can get the utmost benefit. Libfabric is agnostic to the underlying hardware implementation and networking protocols. Its goal is to utilize high-bandwidth and low-latency network interface cards (NICs) to deliver a highly scalable and portable network implementation.

In this work, we introduce an implementation of a new Libfabric conduit for OpenSHMEM to achieve high-performance communication. We take on an existing OpenSHMEM implementation, OpenSHMEM-X [10] from ORNL. Currently, OpenSHMEM-X includes a couple of existing network conduits: GASNet [5] and UCX [15], which supporting mapping between OpenSHMEM calls and network operations. UCX [13] consists of a collection of network libraries and interfaces having the capability of rendering high scalability and throughput. UCX maintains the networking paradigms of high-performance computing, allowing RMA operations, tag matching, remote atomic operations and active messages. From the OpenSHMEM perspective, Libfabric and UCX provide functionality similar to GASNet. Like UCX, Libfabric also provides similar kind of APIs for initialization, shutdown, data transfer, atomic operations.

Our objective is to design the Libfabric conduit in OpenSHMEM-X communication layer with the purpose of providing a broad range of network support while enhancing the performance and scalability. We carefully devise the initialization and shutdown of the network layer with the most suitable options provided by Libfabric. PMIx is utilized as the out-of-band channel for exchanging the necessary information among the PEs. We focus more on designing the point-to-point and atomic operations as these provide the foundation for most of the other OpenSHMEM-X functionalities. Additionally, we utilize the different data transfer operations of Libfabric depending on data size to achieve optimal network performance.

We assess our work in the Eos system of Oak Ridge Leadership Computing Facility and compare it with the Sandia OpenSHMEM implementation. Therefore, we choose Libfabric as the communication layer while configuring both the application. After accumulating the results for point-to-point and atomic data transfer operations, we observe that our implementation outperforms Sandia OpenSHMEM for blocking put, get and atomic operations.

The rest of this paper is organized as follows: In Sect. 2, we present some backgrounds on OpenSHMEM-X and Libfabric. In Sect. 3, we describe some works that are related to our implementation. We then elaborate our design of Libfabric conduit in Sect. 4. Section 5 presents the performance evaluation of our implementation and a comparison with Sandia OpenSHMEM Libfabric implementation. Finally, we discuss possible tuning and feature enhancements in Sect. 6 and conclude in Sect. 7.

2   Background

2.1   OpenSHMEM-X

SHMEM programs follow the Single Program Multiple Data (SPMD) parallel programming model where all PEs run the same program. The actual number of PEs is set during the start of the program. They are numbered from 0 to $N - 1$, where N stands for the total number of PEs. SHMEM library routines offer remote data transfer, synchronization, collective and atomic memory operations to attain high-performance communication. It creates a symmetric view of memory for the participating PEs, where they can allocate symmetric variables maintaining their copies. This feature allows remote direct memory access (RDMA) between the processing elements. One participating PE can directly put or get data from the particular memory location of another PE. RDMA capable interconnects are particularly attractive to the PGAS community as they provide high-throughput, low-latency networking. Vendors such as Intel, HPE, Cray have provided high-performance OpenSHMEM implementations. In addition to that, there are implementations by ORNL known as OpenSHMEM-X. The current OpenSHMEM-X implementation features GASNet and UCX communication conduits.

2.2 Libfabric

Libfabric is aimed to support low-latency communication on network hardware. Libfabric library is designed to support many different programming models such as MPI, and PGAS over various fabric hardware (such as sockets, InfiniBand, Cray GNI, Intel TrueScale, Intel Omni-Path, and Cisco VIC). The design of libfabric provides a set of standard interfaces to set up the communication environment. Libfabric APIs are developed by different underlying providers, each operating over specific fabric hardware or software abstraction. The standard interface functions need to be implemented by each provider. Each provider can also choose the interface functions they want to support. Moreover, the application has the option to scrutinize the capabilities of providers and accordingly, choose to use the most appropriate providers for communications support.

3 Related Work

For its popularity, there has been a large body of research and development studies on OpenSHMEM. Here we selectively provide a discussion on a few studies. Hammond et al. [7] developed an OpenSHMEM implementation using many new communication features proposed by the MPI-3 community. Particularly, this study emphasized the integration of MPI-3 network capabilities such as remote atomic functionalities and a memory model similar to the model required for an OpenSHMEM implementation. Similar to MPI-3 communication routines, Libfabric supports remote atomic functionalities and an optimized memory management scheme, which makes it a viable choice as the network conduit for OpenSHMEM. To this end, our work represents a new attempt to develop the Libfabric conduit for the OpenSHMEM-X implementation from Oak Ridge National Lab.

New network layers have also been introduced in recent times. It helps to achieve portability and scalability across various networks while providing high-performance for different HPC applications. Shamis et al. [14] introduces the implementation of OpenShmem using Universal Common Communication Substrate (UCCS) to optimize its performance by redesigning the network layer. UCCS is a low-level communication library explicitly designed to implement parallel programming models. It supports atomic and remote memory operations which are required by any PGAS programming model. UCCS implementation in OpenSHMEM shows that it outperforms state of the art SGI's SHMEM. Baker et al. [1] has developed an implementation of OpenSHMEM on UCX, validated its suitability for OpenSHMEM programming model, evaluated its performance and scalability on Cray XK systems. UCX have a close semantic match with OpenSHMEM APIs and provides portability and scalability to HPC applications. Built on top of these prior implementations for various SHMEM frameworks, our implementation extends the OpenSHMEM-X implementation with an additional conduit that supports the Libfabric library.

Seager et al. [12] have developed the Sandia OpenSHMEM implementations using Libfabric, which is the closest to our work for OpenSHMEM-X. They have demonstrated the outstanding improvement in bandwidth when OFI Libfabric is used as a transport layer. The Sandia implementation has been enabled on the Aries interconnect that uses u-GNI as the low-level software interface. Compared to the Cray SHMEM that uses DMAPP instead of u-GNI, they have achieved a significant bandwidth improvement. Moreover, Sandia OpenSHMEM uses the message injection feature of Libfabric to enable high bandwidth for small messages. Compared to Sandia OpenSHMEM, our work enables a Libfabric conduit for the OpenSHMEM-X library. Similar to Sandia OpenSHMEM, we also utilize the message injection to get higher performance characteristics for small messages and atomic operations.

Overall, we have designed the OpenSHMEM-X implementation using salient features available from Libfabric to enable efficient, scalable and portable communication.

4   Design of Libfabric Conduit

In this section, we describe the design of Libfabric conduit as an additional communication path for OpenSHMEM-X. We will focus on the description of initialization, out-of-band configuration, memory management, address translation and communication routines.

4.1   Architectural Overview of Libfabric Conduit

OpenSHMEM-X provides a dedicated layer to integrate any network conduit for communication. The communication layer is designed in a way that common functionalities can be shared across different network conduits. Thus, any implementation of an additional conduit needs to take a close architectural examination and make careful choices to design a thin yet high-performance network path.

As a communication library, Libfabric delivers its portability across many popular network providers. It hides the complexity of network management and data transfer inside its implementation, and offers a thin-layer of APIs for application performance and scalability. Figure 1 depicts the software architecture of OpenSHMEM-X with particular details on its communication functionalities. Besides the existing UCX and GASNet, we extend OpenSHMEM-X with Libfabric conduit. We plan to organize the communication architecture of the conduit into four major components including connection management, control functionalities, data transfer operations and completion events. PMIx [2,11] is used as the RTE layer that enables out-of-band communication. To avoid redundancy, we leverage useful data structures from the OpenSHMEM-X and Libfabric as much as possible.

We elaborate the details of communication functionalities on remote memory access routines, atomic operations and point-to-point synchronization operations in the rest of this section.

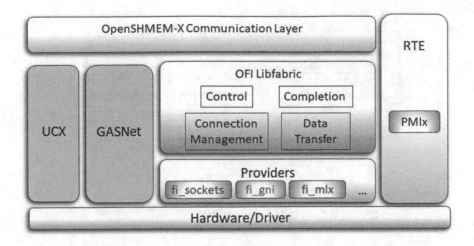

Fig. 1. Software architecture of OpenSHMEM-X with Libfabric conduit

4.2   Initialization and Out-of-Band Configuration

The primary responsibility while implementing any scalable network layer is to configure resources and initialize their parameters before any communication, and properly shut down the resources in the end. Figure 2 describes the initialization and shutdown of Libfabric conduit in an OpenSHMEM-X program. We leverage the control operations from Libfabric for handling these functionalities. The capabilities for a Libfabric provider can be obtained via an initial query to the underlying provider library shown in Step 1. The discovery API then fetches a set of fabric interfaces with their capabilities based on the requirements specified in the query.

As shown in Step 2 of Fig. 2, our conduit proceeds to query the fabric domain, determining access attributes and endpoint configurations. Libfabric can be utilized in a system containing multiple hardware and software resources for network operations. Hence, it is necessary to query the fabric domain after the provider discovery has identified available resources for communication. After the determination of a fabric domain, an access domain for communication also needs to be determined for a single logical connection to the fabric. Then active endpoints will be configured for data transfer operations. Detailed parameters for the access domain are configured. Furthermore, we will initialize the memory regions and address vectors for each PE before enabling the communication endpoints.

Note that the out-of-band communication layer plays a significant role in OpenSHMEM-X because the addresses of connection endpoints and memory regions for each PE need to be exchanged among all the PEs. Steps 4 and 5 in Fig. 2 describe the steps of address translation and exchange of memory region information. We leverage the PMIx (**P**rocess **M**anagement **I**nterface **E**xascale) component for out-of-band communication in our implementation. Step 6 repre-

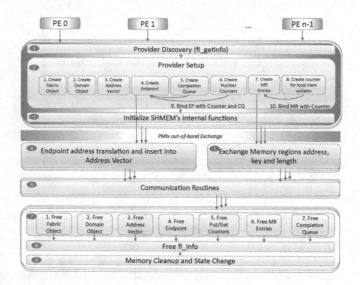

Fig. 2. Initialization and shutdown of Libfabric conduit in OpenSHMEM-X

sents the communication routines which is described in the following subsections in details. Finally, in Steps 7, 8 and 9, we free the resources before shutting down the conduit.

4.3 Memory Management and Address Translation

OpenSHMEM provides symmetric memory so that data movement can be performed directly via a memory address to any location in the Heap, BSS, and Data sections. Thus all these memory regions need to be registered via the communication conduit before the one-sided operations. The information on the Heap, Data and BSS segments shall be made available via their start addresses and range. In the current implementation of OpenSHMEM-X, basic memory registration is first performed for these sections by the PE. Then the start address, length and key of all registered memory regions are to be extracted. An array of IO vectors (fi_rma_iov) from Libfabric is used to record the memory region information for each PE. All the PEs then exchange this array through the PMIx out-of-band communication channel. For the exchange of these vectors at the beginning of an OpenSHMEM program, fabric specific addresses are used for data transfer operations. These addresses are different from the high-level logical addresses.

Figure 3 shows the exchange of these vectors through PMIx and the steps involved in address translation. Libfabric provides address vectors, which allows the mapping of addresses without expensive address resolution. The source address of each PE is fetched and exchanged among all the PEs using PMIx. After getting endpoint addresses of all the PEs, the addresses are stored in a single buffer linearly using the length of each endpoint address. The address buffer is then used as the translation table for address vectors. Any logical address

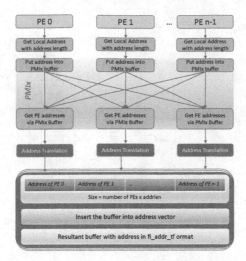

Fig. 3. Address translation using PMIx

from a remote PE can be translated to the fabric specific address. For proper indexing, the address vectors from different PEs are linearly ordered according to the ranks of all PEs.

4.4 Completion Queues and Counters

Libfabric point-to-point operations are non-blocking. Thus there must be some form of progress tracking and completion notification mechanism to ensure the completion of an operation which can be properly detected and notified to the pertinent components. Libfabric provides completion queues and counters for this purpose. A completion queue is bound to the endpoint for getting the completion event of any read, write, or atomic operations. Lightweight counters are also used to keep track of put and get operations. An extra counter is bound with the local memory region to keep track of update operations to the local memory region. This additional counter helps to achieve *wait* functionality of OpenSHMEM-X.

4.5 Remote Memory Access Routines and Atomic Operations

OpenSHMEM requires the support of remote memory accesses and atomic operations from the underlying conduit in order to achieve the functionalities of blocking and non-blocking operations (put, get and atomics). Figure 4 shows the steps involved in any data transfer operation in OpenSHMEM-X using Libfabric. For any data transfer operation, OpenSHMEM-X first determines the memory segment in the local PE based on the memory address and offset for the remote PE address segment. Once the address segment information including the key

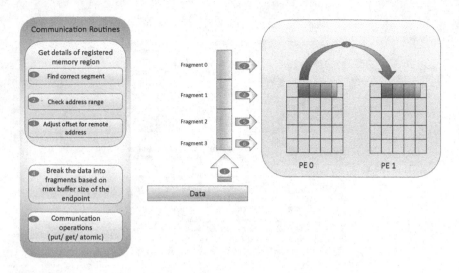

Fig. 4. Data transfer operations

and address is available, the data can be written to the remote location using Libfabric APIs.

However, data that need to be written in the remote PE can be of any length. For very large messages, we need to send the data into chunks to avoid overflowing the transmit and receive buffers at the endpoints. The maximum data size that can be sent in each iteration is determined by querying the underlying provider for the maximum supported size of the endpoint. The data is broken into fragments. We iterate the data transfer operations in a loop until the operation on entire data gets completed.

5   Performance Evaluation

In this section, we describe our experimental setup and the evaluation results. We measure the performance of point-to-point data movement and atomic operations across multiple nodes.

5.1   Experimental Setup

We conduct all our experiments on the *Eos* system [4] located at Oak Ridge National Laboratory. Eos is an XC30 computing cluster built by Cray. It is equipped with Intel Xeon E5-2670 CPUs, 16 cores per node. The whole system consists of 736 nodes with a total of 47.104 TB of memory where each node comprises of 64 GB memory. Eos uses Cray's Aries interconnect and Dragonfly network topology.

For our measurements, we use the OpenSHMEM-X code base and configure its communication path to use our implementation of Libfabric conduit. In our conduit, the Sockets provider of Libfabric is used for our initial implementation. We also configure Sandia OpenSHMEM with Libfabric on the Eos system, for which the sockets provider is also chosen for Sandia OpenSHMEM (SOS). The Sandia OpenSHMEM is configured with hard and completion polling. For a fair comparison of the Libfabric conduits in the two OpenSHMEM libraries, we also disable the scalable memory registration and multi-threading in Sandia OpenSH-MEM, because these functionalities are not implemented in the OpenSHMEM-X Libfabric conduit. We use OpenSHMEM micro-benchmarking suite (SHOMS) to measure the performance of point-to-point operations. OSU Micro-Benchmarks tool is used to measure the latency of atomic operations. Fabtest is used for measuring the Libfabric read and write performances.

5.2 Performance of Point-to-Point Data Movement Operation

We run our tests across multiple nodes in EOS. For point-to-point data movement operations in SHOMS, node 0 sends a fixed sized message to all other nodes and collects the bandwidth. We use the default configuration for SHOMS which use 1000 iterations for data size 8 bytes to 16 KB, 500 iterations for data size of 16 KB to 512 KB and 250 iterations for messages greater than 512 KB. Minimum and maximum message sizes are 8 bytes and 1 MB, respectively. We collected the aggregated bandwidth and average latency measurements for our evaluation. We also compare the bandwidth and latency with Sandia OpenSH-MEM implementation and Libfabric read/write operations.

Put Latency. Figure 5(a) shows the comparison of latency measurements between OpenSHMEM-X Libfabric conduit, Sandia OpenSHMEM Libfabric implementation and the unidirectional write operation of Libfabric. SOS performs slightly better by about 2% for the message size upto 128 bytes. However, our implementation shows a better latency measurement for message size greater than 128 bytes with almost 30% improvement for 2 KB messages.

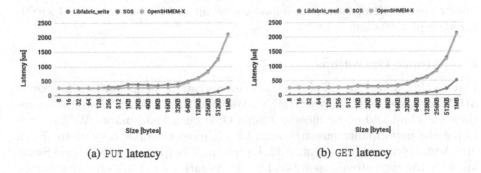

(a) PUT latency   (b) GET latency

Fig. 5. Latency comparisons

Get Latency. Figure 5(b) shows the latency measurements for OpenSHEMEM-X, Sandia OpenSHMEM and Libfabric read operation. Our implementation performs better than SOS in terms of latency. We get a latency improvement up to 10% for 16 KB message size.

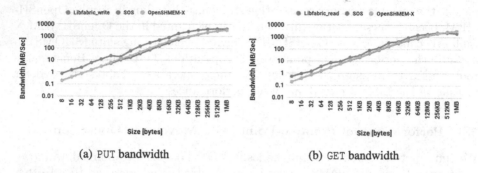

(a) PUT bandwidth   (b) GET bandwidth

Fig. 6. Bandwidth comparisons

Put Bandwidth. Figure 6(a) shows the bandwidth of PUT operation for OpenSHMEM-X Libfabric conduit, Sandia OpenSHMEM Libfabric implementation and unidirectional write bandwidth of Libfabric. The *shmem_int_put* operation is used as the test case for measuring the PUT benchmark. Our evaluation results show that the performance of PUT operations in Sandia OpenSHMEM is 2-5% better than our implementation for small data sizes up to 128 bytes. However, the performance of our implementation improves for messages greater than 256 bytes. The bandwidth improvement can be up to 42% for 2 KB messages.

Get Bandwidth. Figure 6(b) compares the bandwidth of GET operations between OpenSHEMEM-X, Sandia OpenSHMEM and Libfabric read operation. The *shmem_int_get* operation is used for measurements in this case. Our experimental results demonstrate an improvement up to 11% over Sandia OpenSHMEM implementation.

5.3   Atomic Operations

Figures 7(a) and 7(b) show the atomic operation performances for Open SHMEM-X and Sandia OpenSHMEM. We collect the latency of atomic operations for 32-bit and 64-bit messages using OSU microbenchmarks. We have collected the performance measurements for six integer atomic operations: Fetch and Add, Fetch and Increment, Add, Increment, Compare and Swap, and Swap. We have run each atomic operation for 1000 iterations and collected the average latency measurements. The performance of these atomic operations from our implementation is comparable with, or slightly better than, the Sandia OpenSHMEM implementation.

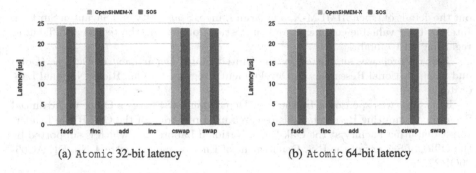

(a) Atomic 32-bit latency   (b) Atomic 64-bit latency

Fig. 7. Atomic operation performance

6   Discussion

Libfabric offers support for many provider implementations such as verbs, mlx, and gni. We have tried verbs and mlx providers using Libfabric. However, *fi_verbs* and *fi_mlx* both do not support full atomic functionalities required by the OpenSHMEM-X. One of the most common Libfabric providers for Cray systems is uGNI, which is fully supported on ORNL systems. We are still working on enabling the uGNI provider for the OpenSHMEM-X Libfabric conduit. Furthermore, we are going through additional tuning and optimization efforts. When these steps are completed, we expect to see a further performance improvement on the OpenSHMEM-X Libfabric conduit.

7   Conclusion

Libfabric offers a communication library that minimizes the semantic gap and maintains application performance while delivering scalability. Its application-centric design allows us to enable operations on different networking interface without considering the internal hardware management. In this paper, we have designed and prototyped an implementation of Libfabric conduit for the OpenSHMEM-X library from ORNL. We have evaluated the performance of our implementation and compared it with the Sandia OpenSHMEM implementation. Our assessment demonstrates that our Libfabric conduit can indeed enable OpenSHMEM portably on different network providers while achieving excellent performance and scalability. We are working on further tuning and optimizations of our Libfabric conduit. We will also work on enabling more Libfabric providers for OpenSHMEM-X.

Acknowledgment. This work is supported in part by a contract from Oak Ridge National Laboratory and the National Science Foundation awards 1561041 and 1564647.

We are thankful to Amit Kumar Nath for his valuable suggestions and feedbacks to the paper. We would like to thank Matthew B. Baker (ORNL) for his help in figuring out the details of OpenSHMEM-X, and Arun Ilango, Sean Hefty and Sayantan Sur from Intel for their valuable comments and suggestions on solving the technical difficulties regarding OFI Libfabric.

This research was supported by the United States Department of Defense (DoD) and Computational Research and Development Programs at Oak Ridge National Laboratory.

This work was sponsored by the U.S. Department of Energy's Office of Advanced Scientific Computing Research. This research used resources of the Oak Ridge Leadership Computing Facility at the Oak Ridge National Laboratory, which is supported by the Office of Science of the U.S. Department of Energy under Contract No. DE-AC05-00OR22725.

References

1. Baker, M., Aderholdt, F., Venkata, M.G., Shamis, P.: OpenSHMEM-UCX: evaluation of UCX for implementing OpenSHMEM programming model. In: Gorentla Venkata, M., Imam, N., Pophale, S., Mintz, T.M. (eds.) OpenSHMEM 2016. LNCS, vol. 10007, pp. 114–130. Springer, Cham (2016). https://doi.org/10.1007/978-3-319-50995-2_8
2. Castain, R.H., Hursey, J., Bouteiller, A., Solt, D.: PMIx: process management for exascale environments. In: Proceedings of the 24th European MPI Users' Group Meeting, EuroMPI 2017, New York, NY, USA, pp. 14:1–14:10. ACM (2017)
3. Chapman, B., et al.: Introducing OpenSHMEM: SHMEM for the PGAS community. In: Proceedings of the Fourth Conference on Partitioned Global Address Space Programming Model, PGAS 2010, New York, NY, USA, pp. 2:1–2:3. ACM (2010)
4. EOS, Cray® XC30TM. https://www.olcf.ornl.gov/for-users/system-user-guides/eos/
5. GASNet. https://gasnet.lbl.gov/
6. Grun, P., et al.: A brief introduction to the openfabrics interfaces - a new network api for maximizing high performance application efficiency. In: 2015 IEEE 23rd Annual Symposium on High-Performance Interconnects, pp. 34–39, August 2015
7. Hammond, J.R., Ghosh, S., Chapman, B.M.: Implementing OpenSHMEM using MPI-3 one-sided communication. In: Poole, S., Hernandez, O., Shamis, P. (eds.) OpenSHMEM 2014. LNCS, vol. 8356, pp. 44–58. Springer, Cham (2014). https://doi.org/10.1007/978-3-319-05215-1_4
8. Libfabric. https://ofiwg.github.io/libfabric/
9. OpenSHMEM. http://www.openshmem.org/site/
10. OpenSHMEM-X. https://github.com/ornl-languages/ornl-openshmem.git
11. PMIx. https://pmix.org/
12. Seager, K., Choi, S.-E., Dinan, J., Pritchard, H., Sur, S.: Design and implementation of OpenSHMEM using OFI on the aries interconnect. In: Gorentla Venkata, M., Imam, N., Pophale, S., Mintz, T.M. (eds.) OpenSHMEM 2016. LNCS, vol. 10007, pp. 97–113. Springer, Cham (2016). https://doi.org/10.1007/978-3-319-50995-2_7
13. Shamis, P., et al.: UCX: An open source framework for HPC network APIs and beyond. In: 2015 IEEE 23rd Annual Symposium on High-Performance Interconnects, pp. 40–43, August 2015

14. Shamis, P., Venkata, M.G., Poole, S., Welch, A., Curtis, T.: Designing a high performance OpenSHMEM implementation using universal common communication substrate as a communication middleware. In: Poole, S., Hernandez, O., Shamis, P. (eds.) OpenSHMEM 2014. LNCS, vol. 8356, pp. 1–13. Springer, Cham (2014). https://doi.org/10.1007/978-3-319-05215-1_1
15. UCX. https://www.openucx.org/

The OpenFAM API: A Programming Model for Disaggregated Persistent Memory

Kimberly Keeton[(⊠)], Sharad Singhal, and Michael Raymond

Hewlett Packard Enterprise, Palo Alto, CA 94304, USA
{kimberly.keeton, sharad.singhal, mraymond}@hpe.com

Abstract. Recent technology advances in high-density, byte-addressable non-volatile memory (NVM) and low-latency interconnects have enabled building large-scale systems with a large disaggregated fabric-attached memory (FAM) pool shared across decentralized compute nodes. The OpenFAM API is an API for programming with persistent FAM that is inspired by the Open-SHMEM partitioned global address space (PGAS) model. Unlike OpenSHMEM, where each node contributes local memory toward a logically shared global address space, FAM isn't associated with a particular node and can be addressed directly from any node without the cooperation or involvement of another node. The OpenFAM API enables programmers to manage FAM allocations, access FAM-resident data structures, and order FAM operations. Because state in FAM can survive program termination, the API also provides interfaces for naming and managing data beyond the lifetime of a single program invocation.

Keywords: Disaggregated memory · Fabric-attached memory ·
Persistent memory · Non-volatile memory · Gen-Z

1 Introduction

Recent technology advances in high-density, byte-addressable non-volatile memory (NVM) and low-latency interconnects have enabled building large-scale systems with a large disaggregated fabric-attached memory (**FAM**) pool shared across heterogeneous and decentralized compute nodes [20]. NVDIMMs and new NVM technologies (e.g., [13, 30, 34, 36, 37]) provide byte-addressable persistent storage accessible through loads and stores, rather than the block I/O path used today. In addition to persistence, these new technologies provide the potential for increased memory density and increased energy efficiency, relative to DRAM. NVM technologies are expected to have 2X to 4X higher read latency and 4X to 8X lower write bandwidth than DRAM [5]. High-performance system interconnects, such as Gen-Z [11], OmniPath [17], and RDMA over InfiniBand [31], provide low-latency access from compute nodes to fabric-attached memory, enabling rack-scale disaggregated memory. Several proposals are based on forward-looking silicon photonics [32] and high-radix optical switches, but disaggregated memory architectures are already being constructed with today's RDMA-based interconnects [2, 24]. These nascent architectures are already capable of providing low-latency remote memory access (e.g., 1 μs to send 1 KB over RDMA over InfiniBand FDR 4x [2]). Co-packaged or 3D-stacked local memory [19] continues

S. Pophale et al. (Eds.): OpenSHMEM 2018, LNCS 11283, pp. 70–89, 2019.
https://doi.org/10.1007/978-3-030-04918-8_5

to play an important role, providing a high-bandwidth memory tier to complement the high-capacity disaggregated memory tier. Research proposals for rack-scale disaggregation include FireBox [1], memory blades [22], scale-out NUMA [25] and network-attached memory [2]. Commercial proposals include The Machine prototype from HPE [6, 7], HPE's Superdome Flex product with Software-Defined Scalable Memory [14], Huawei's DC3.0 [15], Intel's Rack Scale Design [18], and Intel and Facebook's Disaggregated Rack [16]. For example, HPE's Machine prototype system [7] contains 160 TB of shared fabric-attached memory accessible via loads and stores from 40 Cavium ThunderX2 ARM processors [3], in addition to node-local DRAM. More recently, HPE's Superdome Flex product with Software-Defined Scalable Memory [14] allows the firmware to configure a subset of the system's memory as disaggregated memory.

These disaggregated memory architectures share several characteristics. First, they provide a high-capacity pool of fabric-attached memory that can be shared by heterogeneous computing resources at low latency. Because compute nodes are decoupled from FAM, processing and memory can scale and evolve independently, allowing the compute-to-fabric-memory ratio to be tailored to the specific needs of the workload. Second, they provide a *partially disaggregated* architecture, in that they treat node-local memory as private and disaggregated memory as shared. Third, most systems assume a heterogeneous memory system [5], containing both volatile DRAM and NVM. The persistence of disaggregated memory offers the potential to eliminate traditional overheads from slow storage, such as data copies and (de)serialization between memory and storage representations of data. Fourth, disaggregated memory has no explicit owner among application compute nodes. Thus, access to disaggregated memory by one compute node doesn't need to be mediated by any other compute node. This unmediated access is provided by one-sided loads/stores or gets/puts and facilitated through atomic operations (e.g., compare-and-swap as in RDMA [33] or Gen-Z [9]), which bypass processor caches to make updates directly to FAM in an all-or-nothing fashion. Fifth, disaggregation provides separate fault domains between processing and memory, meaning that failure of a compute node doesn't render disaggregated memory unavailable. Any updates propagated to FAM by the failed compute node remain visible to other compute nodes. Persistence further enables data durability and survival of power cycles and power failures. Finally, the hardware-enforced cache coherence domain is usually limited to a single compute node, although recent industry efforts such as Gen-Z [10], CCIX [8] and OpenCAPI [26], propose instruction set architecture (ISA) agnostic methods to extend processor cache coherency beyond a single node (e.g., to a small number of processors, accelerators and I/O (network and storage) adapters).

Disaggregated FAM architectures provide new opportunities to applications, as compared to traditional shared nothing system architectures. Shared nothing architectures partition data between compute nodes, where each compute node "owns" its local data and relies on heavyweight two-sided message passing and data copying to coordinate with other nodes. Data owners mediate access to their data, performing work on behalf of the requester. This model suffers mediation overheads and doesn't sufficiently leverage the data sharing potential of FAM systems.

In contrast, the large capacity of the FAM pool means that large working sets can be maintained as in-memory data structures. The fact that all compute nodes share a common view of memory means that data sharing and communication may be done efficiently through shared memory, without requiring explicit messages to be sent over heavyweight network protocol stacks. Additionally, data sets no longer need to be partitioned between compute nodes, and data access can avoid message-based coordination overheads. Any compute node can operate on any data item, which enables more dynamic and flexible load balancing. More generally, sharing permits new approaches to cooperation.

In this paper, we describe an application programming interface (API) for use in systems that contain FAM. Because the API is patterned after one-sided partitioned global address space (PGAS) libraries such as OpenSHMEM [27], we refer to it as the OpenFAM API. The primary distinctions between OpenFAM and OpenSHMEM are:

1. OpenFAM APIs provide access to fabric-attached disaggregated memory, rather than remote node memory. Since FAM is no longer associated with a specific PE, it can be addressed directly from any PE without the cooperation and/or involvement of any other PE.
2. Because state in FAM can outlive a single program invocation, OpenFAM provides interfaces that let programmers associate user-friendly names to data in FAM, to simplify management for long-lived data.
3. Disaggregated memory can provide non-functional attributes (such as hardware-level redundancy) that are not normally present in DRAM. OpenFAM introduces a two-level allocation scheme to take advantage of such characteristics.
4. OpenFAM includes an API for mapping portions of fabric-attached disaggregated memory into a PE's virtual address space, thus permitting direct load/store access to FAM over fabrics that support memory semantics.

In the following sections, we describe the system model assumed by the OpenFAM API (Sect. 2), and then provide the details of the API organized in functional categories patterned after the OpenSHMEM specification: initialization and finalization (Sect. 3), querying state and names (Sect. 4), allocating and deallocating FAM (Sect. 5), reading and writing FAM data (Sect. 6), atomics (Sect. 7), and memory ordering (Sect. 8). Subsequent sections describe failure semantics, open issues and related work. For each functional category, we provide give an overview of the anticipated functionality behind the API. For the detailed API specification in C11, we refer readers to [28]. Our goal is to keep the API minimal in this initial specification. We expect that implementations will optimize this API for different hardware environments. As we gain experience with implementing and using the library and gather feedback from users, we expect the API will evolve.

2   System Model

Figure 1 shows the system model assumed in OpenFAM. The system consists of a multi-OS environment where each compute node runs a separate operating system instance, with locally attached memory that is "private" to the OS instance. In addition, the system provides fabric attached memory that is also directly addressable (as memory) in a Global Address Space (GAS). Programmable data movers, e.g., direct memory access (DMA) engines, support efficient high-speed movement of data between local memory and fabric attached memory, and within different parts of fabric attached memory at a hardware level. To distinguish references to the two types of memory, we will use the term **FAM** to refer to fabric attached memory and **local memory** to refer to the DRAM (or persistent memory) attached locally to a processing node in the discussion below. We also assume in the API that parts of FAM may be persistent to enable data to be shared not only within a running program, but also across program instances in larger computational workflows.

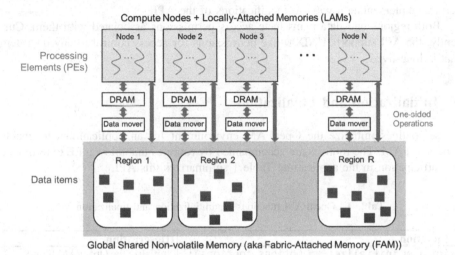

Fig. 1. System view in OpenFAM

The application spans compute nodes, and is composed of a group of processing elements (**PEs**) that cooperate with one another. Each PE represents a (potentially multi-threaded) process that uses both local memory and FAM to perform its tasks. FAM acts as a shared (and potentially persistent) space where PEs may place and access data. As in other PGAS programming models, the application is responsible for coordination of accesses between PEs to any shared data and for managing data consistency in FAM.

We assume that the system manages FAM in a two level hierarchy. At the coarser level programs can create FAM **regions**, which are large blocks of memory. Regions may have non-functional properties (e.g., persistence or resilience properties) associated with them. At the more granular level, memory managers can allocate **data items** that correspond to program data structures within the regions. Data items inherit the non-functional characteristics of the regions within which they are allocated.

FAM is addressed by **descriptors**, which are opaque read-only data structures within applications that contain sufficient information to uniquely locate the corresponding region or data item in FAM. Because regions and data items may persist beyond the lifetime of the application that created them, OpenFAM provides APIs for associating user-friendly names with regions and data items. These names can be used by other processes (concurrent or time shifted) to find the corresponding region or data item. A **metadata service** is used primarily to maintain mappings from names to descriptors that locate data in FAM, and also to maintain limited metadata (e.g., region and data item permissions and sizes, region redundancy levels). Currently, the API leaves the structure of names open. Each region is required to have a unique name associated with it. Data items may optionally have associated names. In line with the two-level memory hierarchy represented by regions and data items, data items within a given region must be named uniquely, relative to other data items in that region. If a hierarchical name space is desirable, it can be accommodated within the metadata service implementation with no modifications of the API.

Both regions and data items have access permissions associated with them. Currently, the API supports UNIX®-like permissions for access control to any data item that is long-lived.

3 Initialization and Finalization

These routines initialize the OpenFAM environment for an application and enable access to FAM. The routines are accompanied by routines that allow a PE to terminate its participation in the application. Table 1 summarizes this API.

Table 1. OpenFAM functions for initialization and finalization

Function	Description
`int fam_initialize(Fam_Options *options);`	Initialize the OpenFAM library
`void fam_finalize(void);`	Finalize the OpenFAM library
`void fam_abort(int status);`	Forcibly terminate the program

At the start of the program each PE calls fam_initialize() and provides options that are application (or PE) specific. Options represent an extensible data structure determined by the implementation that contains library-specific variables, including state that might otherwise be captured as environment variables. Specifying options through environment variables can lead to non-deterministic execution, so we prefer to explicitly set such parameters as library options using this mechanism. The library creates FAM-resident data structures for internal use by the OpenFAM library. If the library finds that the required data structures already exist, it simply adds information about the current PE to the data structures. The library returns success or failure to allow graceful termination in case of errors.

When the program finishes, each PE calls the fam_finalize() method. This disconnects the PE from the overall FAM environment, although the PE may continue to run without further involvement of the OpenFAM library.

Finally, a PE may invoke fam_abort() with a status flag. This causes a signal to be propagated asynchronously to all PEs indicating that termination of the application is desired. The OpenFAM library will forcibly terminate a PE as the signal is received at that PE. Since data consistency in FAM cannot be assured under this scenario, the programmer should not use this mechanism as a normal termination mechanism—each PE should invoke fam_finalize() to gracefully disconnect from the FAM environment when it is finished, and terminate using normal process exit mechanisms.

4 Querying State and Names

These routines provide any PE the ability to query the pre-defined state variables maintained by the OpenFAM library environment. The maintained state may include library and system information (e.g., library version, number of nodes, size of memory) or additional information specific to the executing program available via the OpenFAM library (e.g., number of PEs, maximum region size possible). We assume that implementations may extend the base list of pre-defined variables as needed. Rather than embedding specific information within function names, for flexibility and extensibility, the API provides an interface for querying such state as {name, value} pairs. Note that the interface accesses a set of pre-defined state variables, and does *not* represent a generic key/value store for use by the application. Table 2 outlines this API.

Table 2. OpenFAM functions for querying state and names

Function	Description
`const char **fam_list_options(void);`	Get the list of pre-defined OpenFAM library option names
`const void *fam_get_option(const char *optionName);`	Get the value for a pre-defined OpenFAM library option
`Fam_Region_Descriptor *fam_lookup_region(const char *regionName);`	Look up a descriptor to a FAM region in the metadata service
`Fam_Descriptor *fam_lookup(const char *itemName, const char *regionName);`	Look up a descriptor to a FAM data item in the metadata service

fam_list_options() allows the application to query the library for currently defined state variables. Any PE can query for the value of the corresponding variable using fam_get_option().

In addition, the query group provides an interface to the metadata service, which permits PEs to request the descriptor associated with a region or data item name via fam_lookup(). Regions are automatically registered with the metadata service during creation and unregistered when they are destroyed. Data items can optionally be associated with a name for later retrieval (either within the executing program or within a different program). Corresponding to the two-level memory hierarchy (regions and data items), data item names are scoped within the region within which they are created. *Note that if a descriptor is not registered with the metadata service during allocation, then the program itself is responsible for saving and tracking the descriptor if required later, since the data in FAM will be unreachable without the descriptor.* Implementations may optionally choose to automatically register unnamed data items during creation using special names, and/or allow background services to eventually garbage collect data items if their descriptors are not named. Such services and mechanisms for garbage collection are outside the scope of the OpenFAM API.

5   Allocating and Deallocating Fabric-Attached Memory

These routines provide mechanisms for allocating/deallocating FAM regions and data items within those regions. The API provides a two-level hierarchy:

* **Regions** represent (large) containers within FAM that have associated properties, such as desired resilience levels, which may be specified by the user when the region is created. All data items within a region have the same resilience as the region. Management services use regions as the allocation units to reserve large address ranges in FAM, and may enforce quotas to limit the total size of FAM allocated to a given user or application.
* **Data items** represent (smaller) areas of FAM that are allocated within the regions. Each region provides a heap allocator abstraction, which can be used to allocate individual data items. Management services may delegate per-region heap allocator functionality to distributed brokers within operating systems or other middleware.

As mentioned earlier, FAM is referenced through a descriptor (much like a file descriptor), not a standard pointer that can be de-referenced to access the content directly. The allocation API returns opaque (to the application) read-only descriptors that are portable in the sense that they can be used by any PE to access the data. Descriptors enable applications to specify global/virtual references that will work for any PE regardless of where the region may be mapped into the PE's virtual address space.

Because FAM regions and data items can be long-lived, access permissions are associated with both allocated data items and regions. Currently, the API assumes that standard Unix® permissions can be used, although implementations may choose additional mechanisms for managing access. Permissions can be changed if desired (assuming that the requestor has the appropriate access rights). Assuming appropriate access rights, any PE has the ability to allocate data items in FAM and/or use data items allocated by other PEs, enabling much more efficient mechanisms for passing data between PEs and even within larger computational workflows consisting of multiple stages.

Table 3 provides an overview of these APIs. fam_create_region() creates a new region in FAM for use by the application, and returns a descriptor that can be used portably across PEs (or programs in a larger workflow) to reference that region. Regions are named and registered with the metadata service when they are created to enable PEs to retrieve the descriptor associated with the region using user-friendly names. Regions may be resized using fam_resize_region(). If the region size is reduced, data items that reside within the truncated part of the region will be lost. Region size can be safely increased without affecting existing data items within it.

Finally regions can be destroyed using fam_destroy_region(), which deallocates the region (and all data items within it) and frees the corresponding FAM. Deallocation occurs asynchronously after the fam_destroy_region() call to allow other PEs using the region to finish. The behavior of the library if a PE accesses a region (data item) after it has been destroyed (deallocated) by a different PE is implementation dependent.

Table 3. OpenFAM functions for allocating and deallocating fabric-attached memory

Function	Description
Fam_Region_Descriptor ***fam_create_region(const char** *name, uint64_t size, mode_t permissions, Fam_Redundancy_Level redundancyLevel, ...);**	Create a new region in FAM
void fam_destroy_region(Fam_Region_Descriptor *descriptor);	Destroy an existing region in FAM
int fam_resize_region(Fam_Region_Descriptor *descriptor, uint64_t nbytes);	Resize an existing region in FAM
Fam_Descriptor ***fam_allocate(const char** *name, uint64_t nbytes, mode_t accessPermissions, Fam_Region_Descriptor *region);	Allocate a named data item in a region of FAM
Fam_Descriptor ***fam_allocate(**uint64_t nbytes, mode_t accessPermissions, Fam_Region_Descriptor *region);	Allocate an unnamed data item in a region of FAM
void fam_deallocate(Fam_Descriptor *descriptor);	Deallocate space being used by a data item in a region of FAM
int fam_change_permissions(Fam_Region_Descriptor *descriptor, mode_t accessPermissions);	Change permissions associated with a region in FAM
int fam_change_permissions(Fam_Descriptor *descriptor, mode_t accessPermissions);	Change permissions associated with a data item in FAM

Space for data items within a region can be allocated using fam_allocate(), which returns a descriptor to that data item, and de-allocated by calling fam_deallocate(). Optionally, data items may be named to simplify access to them by other PEs or programs after allocation. The application is responsible for de-allocating unnamed data items or ensuring that the corresponding descriptors are persisted.

Finally, assuming that the caller has the correct access rights, permissions on either a region or a data item can be changed using fam_change_permissions(). As mentioned earlier, the actual semantics of permissions and how they are implemented or enforced is system dependent.

6 Reading and Writing FAM Data

This group of APIs provide routines to read/write FAM data. Table 4 outlines the API, which is broken into four groups:

1. A **get/put** API supports movement of data between FAM and local memory.
2. A **map/unmap** API provides the ability to directly map data items in FAM into the local process virtual address space, enabling direct load-store access from the CPU to data in FAM.
3. The third group provides the ability to **gather (scatter)** data from (to) disjoint parts of FAM to (from) a contiguous array in local memory.
4. Finally, a **copy** API provides a hardware-assisted mechanism to replicate data from one part of FAM to another part of FAM.

Table 4. OpenFAM functions for reading and writing FAM data

Function	Description
`int fam_get_blocking(const void *local, Fam_Descriptor *descriptor, uint64_t offset, uint64_t nbytes);`	Blocking call to copy data from FAM to local memory
`void fam_get_nonblocking(const void *local, Fam_Descriptor *descriptor, uint64_t offset, uint64_t nbytes);`	Non-blocking call to copy data from FAM to local memory
`int fam_put_blocking(const void *local, Fam_Descriptor *descriptor, uint64_t offset, uint64_t nbytes);`	Blocking call to copy data from local memory to FAM
`void fam_put_nonblocking(const void *local, Fam_Descriptor *descriptor, uint64_t offset, uint64_t nbytes);`	Non-blocking call to copy data from local memory to FAM
`void *fam_map(Fam_Descriptor *descriptor);`	Map a FAM data item into the process virtual address space
`void fam_unmap(const void *local, Fam_Descriptor *descriptor, uint64_t nbytes);`	Unmap a FAM data item from the process virtual address space
`void fam_invalidate(const void *local, uint64_t nbytes);`	Invalidate mapped FAM data cached in processor cache
`void fam_flush(const void *local, uint64_t nbytes);`	Flush mapped FAM data cached in processor cache to FAM
`int fam_gather_blocking(const void *local, Fam_Descriptor *descriptor, uint64_t nElements, uint64_t firstElement, uint64_t stride, uint64_t elementSize);`	Blocking call to copy disjoint elements of a data item from FAM to local memory, with constant stride
`int fam_gather_blocking(const void *local, Fam_Descriptor *descriptor, uint64_t nElements, uint64_t *elementIndex, uint64_t elementSize);`	Blocking call to copy disjoint elements of a data item from FAM to local memory, with non-constant (indexed) stride
`void fam_gather_nonblocking(const void *local, Fam_Descriptor *descriptor, uint64_t nElements, uint64_t firstElement, uint64_t stride, uint64_t elementSize);`	Non-blocking call to copy disjoint elements of a data item from FAM to local memory, with constant stride

`void fam_gather_nonblocking(const void *local, Fam_Descriptor *descriptor, uint64_t nElements, uint64_t *elementIndex, uint64_t elementSize);`	Non-blocking call to copy disjoint elements of a data item from FAM to local memory, with non-constant (indexed) stride
`int fam_scatter_blocking(const void *local, Fam_Descriptor *descriptor, uint64_t nElements, uint64_t firstElement, uint64_t stride, uint64_t elementSize);`	Blocking call to copy elements of a data item from local memory to disjoint parts of FAM, with constant stride
`int fam_scatter_blocking(const void *local, Fam_Descriptor *descriptor, uint64_t nElements, uint64_t *elementIndex, uint64_t elementSize);`	Blocking call to copy elements of a data item from local memory to disjoint parts of FAM, with non-constant (indexed) stride
`void fam_scatter_nonblocking(const void *local, Fam_Descriptor *descriptor, uint64_t nElements, uint64_t firstElement, uint64_t stride, uint64_t elementSize);`	Non-blocking call to copy elements of a data item from local memory to disjoint parts of FAM, with constant stride
`void fam_scatter_nonblocking(const void *local, Fam_Descriptor *descriptor, uint64_t nElements, uint64_t *elementIndex, uint64_t elementSize);`	Non-blocking call to copy elements of a data item from local memory to disjoint parts of FAM, with non-constant (indexed) stride
`void fam_copy(Fam_Descriptor *src, uint64_t srcOffset, Fam_Descriptor *dest, uint64_t destOffset, uint64_t nbytes);`	Create a second copy of a data item in FAM

fam_put() creates a copy of an object from local memory in FAM. Similarly fam_get() creates a copy of an object from FAM in local memory. Note that subsequent modifications to the two copies are made independently, and no synchronization should be assumed between the two copies. Both APIs specify data movement in bytes, enabling movement of smaller chunks of data within larger data items (such as parts of a large array resident in FAM). Both fam_put() and fam_get() have blocking and non-blocking variants. The non-blocking calls return once the transfer has been initiated, and don't wait for completion. For example, fam_put_nonblocking() returns once data has been dispatched to FAM, and does not wait until the object has reached fabric-attached memory. If multiple calls to fam_get_nonblocking() or fam_put_nonblocking() are made in succession, the order of data delivery is not guaranteed. To ensure ordering and completion, either blocking versions of the API or memory ordering operations (see Sect. 8) should be used. Non-blocking calls permit overlap of the round-trip latencies to FAM for multiple related operations, thereby improving efficiency over a set of blocking operations. The blocking call variants wait until the data transfer has been completed. For example, fam_get_blocking() waits until data is delivered to local memory.

fam_map() and fam_unmap() directly map and unmap FAM addresses into the local process virtual address space—no copy exists in local memory in this case. These APIs enable the processor to use load/store instructions to directly access FAM: the application can treat FAM the same way it treats local memory. However, there may be performance differences associated with the use of map/unmap versus get/put depending on the access patterns and characteristics of the underlying hardware, so the programmer should use the API that makes sense for the application's computation and memory accesses. fam_map() and fam_unmap() require support from the underlying memory fabric components (e.g., Gen-Z's Memory Management Unit (ZMMU) [12]) to maintain node physical address-to-fabric address mappings. Traditional address translation mechanisms then perform virtual-to-physical address translations.

Similar to data in local memory, mapped FAM data is eligible for caching by the processor caches. At large scale, the underlying architecture won't provide hardware support for cache coherence between nodes; thus accesses to FAM from PEs on different nodes will not be cache-coherent. Thus, if multiple nodes map the same descriptors into memory, the application will need to explicitly manage synchronization, including cache invalidation and flushes. The API provides fam_invalidate() and fam_flush() for this purpose.

Just as there is no coherence between multiple PEs on different nodes that have mapped a FAM data item, there is also no coherence or coordination between PEs that map a FAM data item and PEs that use fam_get() and fam_put() to access that data item. The application must provide coordination between PEs using multiple modes of interacting with FAM.

Both get/put and map/unmap APIs deal with contiguous bytes in FAM. To support commonly used data access patterns, the API also provides the ability to gather elements from an array data item in FAM into a contiguous part of local memory, and scatter them back from a contiguous part of local memory to disjoint parts of the array in FAM. A fam_gather() operation allows the programmer to specify a starting element, a stride, the number of elements, and the size of each element. The library then makes multiple parallel copies from FAM to adjacent regions of local memory. Conversely, a fam_scatter() operation copies array elements placed sequentially in local memory, and scatters them in parallel to disjoint parts of the corresponding array in FAM. As with fam_get() and fam_put(), the OpenFAM API provides both blocking and non-blocking variants of fam_gather() and fam_scatter(). The API also provides an indexed gather/scatter variant, where the stride between consecutive array elements is not assumed to be constant, but can be specified as an array of indexes into the data item.

Finally, fam_copy() supports direct movement of data between two parts of FAM, possibly from one region of FAM to another region of FAM. fam_copy() is non-blocking. No synchronization is assumed between the copies, and they can be modified independently after the copy is complete.

7 Atomics

The atomics APIs provide mechanisms to ensure that operations in FAM are done in an atomic (all-or-nothing) fashion, i.e., do not result in torn reads or writes when the same location in FAM is accessed at the same time from different processing elements. Atomic operations are broken into two categories: non-fetching (which update data in FAM without returning a result) and fetching (which update data in FAM and return a result). Atomic operations that return values block until the operation completes, while those that do not return data values simply dispatch the operation to FAM, but do not wait for acknowledgements before returning (i.e., are non-blocking). Table 5 shows these categories.

Table 5. OpenFAM functions for atomically accessing FAM data. Unless otherwise specified, arithmetic types <AT> include (u)int32_t, (u)int64_t, float and double. Logical types <LT> include uint32_t and uint64_t.

Function	Description
`void fam_set(Fam_Descriptor *descriptor, uint64_t offset, <AT> value);`	Atomically set a value of type <AT> in FAM.
`void fam_add(Fam_Descriptor *descriptor, uint64_t offset, <AT> value);`	Atomically add a value of type <AT> to a data item in FAM.
`void fam_subtract(Fam_Descriptor *descriptor, uint64_t offset, <AT> value);`	Atomically subtract a value of type <AT> from a data item in FAM.
`void fam_min(Fam_Descriptor *descriptor, uint64_t offset, <AT> value);`	Atomically replace a value in FAM with the minimum of it and a given value of type <AT>.
`void fam_max(Fam_Descriptor *descriptor, uint64_t offset, <AT> value);`	Atomically replace a value in FAM with the maximum of it and a given value of type <AT>.
`void fam_and(Fam_Descriptor *descriptor, uint64_t offset, <LT> value);`	Atomically replace a value in FAM with the logical AND of that value and a given value of type <LT>.
`void fam_or(Fam_Descriptor *descriptor, uint64_t offset, <LT> value);`	Atomically replace a value in FAM with the logical OR of that value and a given value of type <LT>.
`void fam_xor(Fam_Descriptor *descriptor, uint64_t offset, <LT> value);`	Atomically replace a value in FAM with the logical XOR of that value and a given value of type <LT>.
`<AT> fam_fetch_<AT>(Fam_Descriptor *descriptor, uint64_t offset);`	Atomically fetches a value of type <AT> from FAM.
`<AT> fam_swap(Fam_Descriptor *descriptor, uint64_t offset, <AT> value);`	Atomically replace a value of type <AT> in FAM with the given value and return the old value.
`<AT> fam_compare_swap(Fam_Descriptor *descriptor, uint64_t offset, <AT> oldValue, <AT> newValue);`	Atomically conditionally replace a value of type <AT> in FAM with the given value and return the old value. Type <AT> includes `(u)int32_t`, `(u)int64_t`, and `int128_t`.
`<AT> fam_fetch_add(Fam_Descriptor *descriptor, uint64_t offset, <AT> value);`	Atomically adds a value of type <AT> to a value in FAM, and returns the old value.
`<AT> fam_fetch_subtract(Fam_Descriptor *descriptor, uint64_t offset, <AT> value);`	Atomically subtracts a value of type <AT> from a value in FAM, and returns the old value.
`<AT> fam_fetch_min(Fam_Descriptor *descriptor, uint64_t offset, <AT> value);`	Atomically replaces a value of type <AT> in FAM with the smaller of the value in FAM and a given value, and returns the old value.
`<AT> fam_fetch_max(Fam_Descriptor *descriptor, uint64_t offset, <AT> value);`	Atomically replaces a value of type <AT> in FAM with the larger of the value in FAM and a given value, and returns the old value.

`<LT> fam_fetch_and(Fam_Descriptor *descriptor, uint64_t offset, <LT> value);`	Atomically replaces a value of type <LT> in FAM with the logical AND of that value and some given value, and returns the old value.
`<LT> fam_fetch_or(Fam_Descriptor *descriptor, uint64_t offset, <LT> value);`	Atomically replaces a value of type <LT> in FAM with the logical OR of that value and some given value, and returns the old value.
`<LT> fam_fetch_xor(Fam_Descriptor *descriptor, uint64_t offset, <LT> value);`	Atomically replaces a value of type <LT> in FAM with the logical XOR of that value and some given value, and returns the old value.

In the initial version of the API, non-fetching operations include fam_set(), fam_add(), fam_subtract(), fam_min(), fam_max(), fam_and(), fam_or(), and fam_xor(). Fetching operations include fam_fetch(), fam_swap(), fam_compare_ *swap*(), fam_fetch_add(), fam_fetch_subtract(), fam_fetch_min(), fam_fetch_ *max*(), fam_fetch_and(), fam_fetch_or(), and fam_fetch_xor().

fam_set(), fam_fetch(), fam_swap(), and arithmetic operators ((non-)fetching add, subtract, min, and max) are specified for 32-bit and 64-bit signed and unsigned integer and floating point operands. Logical operators ((non-)fetching and, or and xor) are specified for 32-bit and 64-bit unsigned integer operands. Compare and swap (CAS) operations (compare for equality and swap if equal) are specified for 32-bit and 64-bit signed and unsigned integer operands. In addition, the API defines a 128-bit integer compare and swap.

We note that atomic operations bypass the processor cache on the node that issues the request. Thus, if a PE that has mapped a FAM data item subsequently issues an atomic operation for part of the mapped data item, any cached versions of the atomically updated operand will no longer be valid.

8   Memory Ordering

These operations, outlined in Table 6, provide ordering to FAM operations.

Table 6. OpenFAM functions for memory ordering

Function	Description
`void fam_fence(void);`	Ensures that FAM operations issued by the calling thread before the fence are completed before FAM operations issued after the fence are dispatched.
`void fam_quiet(void);`	Ensures that all pending operations to FAM issued by the calling thread have completed before proceeding

fam_fence() is a non-blocking call that enables ordering of FAM operations from a PE: any FAM operations (put, scatter, atomics, copy) issued by the calling thread before the fence operation will be delivered before any FAM operations by the same thread after the fence are dispatched. fam_quiet() blocks the calling thread until pending FAM operations from that thread are complete. To provide ordering operations *to a single memory location* requires memory-side hardware support, and we are currently not aware of systems that provide such support for FAM. Hence we do not include those operations in the API at this time.

Note that unlike other PGAS implementations, since all PEs have equal access to all data items in FAM, the need for collectives, reductions, and all-to-all messaging when addressing FAM is unclear. For simplicity, we omit these operations from the API at this time. PEs that wish to synchronize with one another can poll on a location in FAM (e.g., using fam_compare_swap()) or use external-to-OpenFAM collectives (e.g., OpenSHMEM). If necessary, such operations can be added in a later version.

9 Failure Semantics

OpenFAM calls may be unsuccessful due to failures in fabric components, fabric-attached memory controllers or the fabric-attached memory media itself. We expect that lower-layer hardware and software will implement failure mitigation strategies (e.g., request retry, memory bad block remapping, inter-controller replication or erasure coding) that will mask (and in some cases, recover from) these failures. As a result, we interpret any failures reported to the OpenFAM layer to be unrecoverable.

The OpenFAM API provides two alternative approaches for dealing with failures: *failure-reporting* operation and *fail-fast* operation. With failure-reporting operation, failures are detected and associated with the call that triggered or experienced them. As a result, this mode can only be used with blocking OpenFAM calls. The type of error is reported to the OpenFAM layer, which can pass the error code to the application, allowing for application-specific error handling based on the severity of the error. For example, an application that implements its own application-level replication may choose to recover from a failed fam_get_blocking() request to an inoperable replica by retrying the operation with a different replica. A disadvantage of the failure-reporting approach is that performance is lower, due to the need to use only blocking calls for attributable error reporting.

FAM failures may affect the operation of a non-blocking call well after the call has returned, so it isn't always possible to attribute the failure to the call that first experienced it. Rather than support out-of-band error reporting (e.g., through exceptions), OpenFAM provides a fail-fast mode of operation. In this approach, which mimics commonly supported OpenSHMEM failure behavior, unrecoverable FAM errors cause the application (including all its PEs) to be terminated. Because fail-fast operation supports non-blocking calls, it provides the potential for higher performance.

Neither failure-reporting operation nor fail-fast operation guarantees all-or-nothing execution of failed OpenFAM calls; partial completion is a possible outcome under failure scenarios. For fail-fast operation, any partially completed update calls to data persistently stored in FAM may result in corrupted application state that the application does not get the opportunity to recover before the termination of the current program invocation. (In failure-reporting operation, the application can choose whether and how to recover any potential corruptions at the time of the failed call.) As a result, applications using fail-fast operation (and potentially those using failure-reporting operation) should be structured to explicitly check at initialization whether persistent data needs to be recovered, and to perform the appropriate application-specific recovery. As an extreme approach, applications may even choose to treat FAM data as ephemeral, deleting any residual regions or data items and starting with a clean slate.

10 Discussion

This section covers open issues for future consideration in OpenFAM.

Access Control. Accesses to FAM-resident data are permitted only if the requesting user has sufficient permissions for the request. Verification of these rights must be performed by a trusted entity (e.g., the operating system); however, due to the potential cost of these operations, per-request verification is to be avoided. Future versions of the API will consider adding fam_open() and fam_close() calls, to perform a mandatory name-to-descriptor translation including a permission check before data item or region access. Under these assumptions, a Fam_Descriptor(Fam_Region_Descriptor) would be considered a capability, which both identifies the corresponding data item (region) and associates access rights granted to the requester. This approach could also simplify delayed reclamation of data items (regions), because the system could check whether there are any currently active descriptors before removing the associated item (region).

Memory Ordering. The current API provides ordering of FAM operations from the calling PE thread to all of fabric-attached memory. This approach will limit the application's ability to pipeline and overlap FAM requests with computation. Open-SHMEM introduced contexts to address this issue. If hardware support is provided, future OpenFAM API versions may also include methods to order outstanding FAM operations using a context-like abstraction. Such an approach would give the application the flexibility to order requests on a per-region basis (i.e., operations to a particular region would be ordered independently of FAM operations to other regions).

Scratch Regions. Applications may wish to create regions that are automatically garbage collected at the end of the application's execution (either through successful completion or through fail-fast termination in the event of a FAM error). This abstraction could be provided by the application deallocating any scratch regions during its finalization phase (for successful completion) or during its initialization phase (to handle any residual scratch regions from fail-fast termination). If open/close calls are introduced, it may be possible to include system-level support for scratch regions (e.g., through region allocation-time scratch specification and automatic garbage collection at the end of the program).

PE Synchronization. Because data in FAM can be accessed from PEs running on multiple nodes at the same time, data conflicts are possible (either using fam_get()/fam_put() or if the same descriptor is accessed using fam_map() from multiple PEs). Given the large scale envisioned (up to thousands of nodes and petabytes of FAM), it will be difficult to maintain cache coherence between the nodes and to efficiently ensure that large regions of FAM are updated atomically. We currently leave such synchronization to the PEs accessing FAM as part of the application. PEs may poll on locations in FAM using atomics (e.g., fam_compare_swap()) or rely on external-to-OpenFAM collective communication (e.g., OpenSHMEM).

Error Reporting and Handling. For simplicity, the current OpenFAM API proposes a fail-fast approach for errors resulting from implicit non-blocking calls. Richer error notification may be possible, for example, by delaying asynchronous error notification until a subsequent fam_quiet() call; this approach may require introducing a requirement for such a blocking call after a group of non-blocking calls. If open/close calls are introduced into the API, asynchronous error notifications could be raised during the fam_close() call. Alternately, all non-blocking API calls could be extended to return a handle, which the application could use to check the call's progress and completion status (success vs. failure). Using this explicit non-blocking approach, the API could also include calls for coalescing handles, to simplify status checking of multiple outstanding requests. In the future, we will evaluate the merits of these approaches.

Data Item Resizing. Currently the OpenFAM API does not support resizing (or automated re-packing) of data items within a region. This constraint may be relaxed in the future, as implementations become available.

Multi-item Gather/Scatter. The current fam_gather() and fam_scatter() operate on the elements of a single data item in FAM. In the future, we will consider whether it is useful to gather (scatter) from (to) multiple FAM-resident data items.

Data Item Snapshots. The current fam_copy() performs an inconsistent copy, in that the copied data may reflect updates that are performed concurrently with the copy operation. To ensure a consistent copy without the need to quiesce application accesses to the copied region, future versions of the API will consider including functions to snapshot the source data item.

Metadata Service. The current version of the API primarily uses the metadata service to map user-friendly names to FAM descriptors and to store minimal metadata. Based on past experience from adjacent fields like file systems, providing a metadata service that scales to a large number of items and a large number of users is challenging [23]. By re-envisioning persistent data management in the context of FAM regions and data items accessed through the OpenFAM API, rather than files accessed via the POSIX file API, we believe that an OpenFAM metadata service can overcome the scalability challenges of traditional file metadata services. In a FAM environment the shared state represented by region and data item metadata can be implemented as data structures stored in FAM, and directly accessible by any node. As a result, trusted code running on any node can use one-sided accesses and atomics to access and update metadata in a scalable fashion.

11 Related Work

The OpenFAM API is designed to enable HPC and distributed data analytics applications to manage and access disaggregated persistent memory. It borrows ideas from PGAS programming models that use one-sided operations, such as OpenSHMEM [27] and Cray DMAPP [4], with several important distinctions. PGAS programs use a single-program multiple data (SPMD) model, where a group of processes (PEs) executes the same executable in parallel. The model exposes the global address space as a symmetric heap, with the assumption that all PEs in a job make the same calls to the symmetric heap management functions in the same sequence. The SPMD and symmetric heap model is a natural match for many traditional HPC applications, but is generally too restrictive for distributed data analytic applications, which typically use a multiple program multiple data (MPMD) model and independent data management operations across processes. Because the OpenFAM API is intended to support both HPC application and distributed data analytic applications, it cannot adopt traditional PGAS models wholesale.

PGAS models form their global address space from node-local DRAM contributed by each PE, meaning that the global address space lives only as long as the application lifetime; as a result, data structures are ephemeral. In contrast, OpenFAM's global address space comes from disaggregated memory, which isn't associated with any single PE. Since the disaggregated memory is likely to be non-volatile, OpenFAM is designed to support persistent data structures that outlive a single program invocation. The independence of state maintained in disaggregated FAM provides additional opportunities for managing application availability in the presence of component failure. OpenFAM also includes an API for mapping portions of fabric-attached disaggregated memory into a PE's virtual address space, thus permitting direct load/store access to FAM over fabrics that support memory semantics.

OpenFAM enables applications to manage and access named persistent data, a role traditionally filled by POSIX file systems. Although OpenFAM borrows several key concepts from file systems, including namespace management and memory mapping content into the process virtual address space, POSIX I/O semantics include some unnecessary features [23] and are missing some desired features. POSIX semantics dictate that writes must be strongly consistent (i.e., a write() is required to block application execution until the system can guarantee that any other read() call will see the data that was just written). Although this is tractable on a single node that is writing to locally attached storage, ensuring such strong consistency across multiple nodes, each with its own page cache, is very challenging. Approaches include eliminating the page cache (which increases request latency), relaxing POSIX consistency semantics (e.g., providing no consistency guarantees if two nodes try to modify the same part of the same file), or implementing complex locking mechanisms to avoid concurrent activity by multiple nodes. Additionally, POSIX requires that metadata such as mtime and atime be updated in concert with fully consistent reads and writes. Such strong consistency semantics are overkill for programs that coordinate their access to shared data through application-specific means, and their implementation will severely limit performance for a layer designed primarily for accessing disaggregated memory.

POSIX shared memory APIs [21] provide a memory-oriented alternative to the POSIX I/O APIs. Like the POSIX I/O APIs, they enable naming of objects and enforce access permissions using an explicit (shm_)open() call. Unlike the POSIX I/O semantics, the shared memory interface does not require strict consistency; synchronization of accesses to shared memory objects is handled by the application outside the scope of the shared memory API (e.g., using POSIX semaphores). POSIX mmap APIs, which can be used with both files and shared memory, provide user-level memory semantic accesses to file or shared memory data. However, they do not permit explicit management of near (e.g., node local) vs. far (e.g., FAM) memories in non-uniform memory access (NUMA) systems, nor do they permit explicit management of persistent memory (e.g., flushing cache contents to persistent memory in an order controlled by program rather than the cache replacement policy). Additionally, mmap APIs don't provide support for easy sharing of data in non-cache coherent environments; application programmers still need to explicitly manage cache line invalidations and flushes to make updates visible to processes on other nodes. Finally, POSIX I/O and shared memory APIs don't include support for scatter/gather functions or atomic memory operations. Thus, to provide the desired functionality, the OpenFAM API must go beyond existing POSIX APIs, borrowing useful concepts where appropriate.

HPC burst buffers provide persistent storage close to the compute nodes (i.e., separate from the campaign storage in the parallel file system) for storing intermediate and final results from a computation for the lifetime of a job or potentially a small number of related jobs in a workflow. During the job execution, the burst buffer is treated as an ephemeral file system, which can be accessed through normal file API calls. At the end of a job/workflow run, any data that is to be preserved longer than the resource allocation needs to be copied back to the parallel file system. In contrast, OpenFAM is intended to permit long-term storage of persistent data without the need to explicitly move data to a separate system.

The emergence of persistent memory technologies has led to standardized efforts such as the Storage Networking Industry Association (SNIA) NVM Programming Model [35] and implementations such as Intel's Persistent Memory Development Kit (PMDK) [29]. PMDK, for example, is a collection of libraries that builds upon the direct access (DAX) features of Linux and Windows file systems, to allow applications direct load/store access to persistent memory by memory-mapping files on a persistent memory aware file system. With the exception of librpmem, which replicates content of local persistent memory regions to persistent memory on a remote node over RDMA, these libraries focus on accessing local persistent memory. In contrast, the OpenFAM API is intended to support applications in managing and accessing data stored in disaggregated persistent memory in non-cache coherent multi-node environments.

12 Summary

The OpenFAM API provides an API for programming with persistent fabric-attached memory (FAM). FAM is disaggregated and hence independent of compute nodes, and can be addressed directly from any node without the involvement of another node. The

OpenFAM API includes functions for managing FAM allocations, accessing FAM-resident data structures, and ordering FAM operations. We have released an initial version of the detailed spec [28], and welcome feedback from the community. A reference implementation is under way. We hope to work with the OpenSHMEM community to introduce OpenFAM concepts into future OpenSHMEM versions.

References

1. Asanovic, K.: FireBox: a hardware building block for 2020 warehouse-scale computers. Keynote at USENIX Conference on File and Storage Technologies (FAST) 2014
2. Binnig, C., Crotty, A., Galakatos, A., Kraska, T., Zamanian, E.: The end of slow networks: it's time for a redesign. Proc. VLDB Endow. **9**(7), 528–539 (2016)
3. Cavium, ThunderX2 ARM Processors. https://www.cavium.com/product-thunderx2-arm-processors.html. Accessed 22 July 2018
4. Cray: Cray XC Series GNI and DMAPP API User Guide (CLE 6.0.UP05) S-2446. https://pubs.cray.com/pdf-attachments/attachment?pubId=00478935-DA&attachmentId=pub_00478935-DA.pdf. Accessed 28 July 2018
5. Dulloor, S.R., et al.: Data tiering in heterogeneous memory systems. In: Proceedings of 11th ACM European Conference on Computer Systems (EuroSys) (2016)
6. Faraboschi, P., Keeton, K., Marsland, T., Milojicic, D.: Beyond processor-centric operating systems. In: Proceedings of Workshop on Hot Topics in Operating Systems (HotOS) (2015)
7. Funk, M.: Drilling down into the machine from HPE. The Next Platform, 4 January 2016. https://www.nextplatform.com/2016/01/04/drilling-down-into-the-machine-from-hpe/. Accessed 22 July 2018
8. Funk, M.: Drilling into the CCIX coherence standard. The Next Platform, 13 July 2016. https://www.nextplatform.com/2016/01/04/drilling-down-into-the-machine-from-hpe/. Accessed 22 July 2018
9. Gen-Z Consortium: Gen-Z Atomics, October 2017. https://genzconsortium.org/wp-content/uploads/2018/05/1711_Gen-Z-Atomics.pdf. Accessed 25 July 2018
10. Gen-Z Consortium: Gen-Z Coherency, October 2017. http://genzconsortium.org/wp-content/uploads/2017/08/Gen-Z-Coherency.pdf. Accessed 25 July 2018
11. Gen-Z Consortium: Gen-Z Core Specification. https://genzconsortium.org/specification/core-specification-1-0/. Accessed 22 July 2018
12. Gen-Z Consortium: Gen-Z ZMMU and Memory Interleave, June 2018. https://genzconsortium.org/wp-content/uploads/2018/06/Gen-Z-MMU-and-Memory-Interleave-1.pdf. Accessed 25 July 2018
13. Hewlett Packard Enterprise: HPE Persistent Memory: The Performance of Memory with the Persistence of Storage. https://www.hpe.com/us/en/servers/persistent-memory.html. Accessed 25 July 2018
14. Hewlett Packard Enterprise: New HPE Pointnext Capabilities Accelerate Transition to Memory-Driven Computing. https://news.hpe.com/new-hpe-pointnext-capabilities-accelerate-transition-to-memory-driven-computing/. Accessed 22 July 2018
15. Huawei: High Throughput Computing Data Center Architecture: Thinking of Data Center 3.0. http://www.huawei.com/ilink/en/download/HW_349607. Accessed 25 July 2018
16. Intel: Facebook Collaborate on Future Data Center Rack Technologies, Intel Newsroom, 16 January 2013. http://goo.gl/6h2Ut. Accessed 25 July 2018

17. Intel: Intel Omni-Path Architecture (Intel OPA) Driving Exascale Computing and HPC. http://www.intel.com/content/www/us/en/high-performance-computing-fabrics/omni-path-architecture-fabric-overview.html. Accessed 25 July 2018
18. Intel Rack Scale Design: Data Center Agility at Scale. http://www.intel.com/content/www/us/en/architecture-and-technology/rack-scale-design-overview.html. Accessed 25 July 2018
19. High Bandwidth Memory (HBM) DRAM, JEDEC Standard JESD235A, November 2015. http://www.jedec.org/standards-documents/results/jesd235. Accessed 25 July 2018
20. Keeton, K.: Memory-driven computing. Keynote at 33rd International Conference on Massive Storage Systems and Technology (MSST), May 2017. http://storageconference.us/2017/Presentations/Keeton.pdf
21. Kerrisk, M.: Linux/UNIX System Programming: POSIX Shared Memory, February 2015. http://man7.org/training/download/posix_shm_slides.pdf. Accessed 30 July 2018
22. Lim, K., et al.: System-level implications of disaggregated memory. In: Proceedings of International Symposium on High Performance Computer Architecture (HPCA) (2012)
23. Lockwood, G.: What's so bad about POSIX I/O?. The Next Platform, 11 September 2017. https://www.nextplatform.com/2017/09/11/whats-bad-posix-io/. Accessed 29 July 2018
24. Loesing, S., Pilman, M., Etter, T., Kossmann, D.: On the design and scalability of distributed shared-data databases. In: Proceedings of 15th ACM SIGMOD International Conference on Management of Data (SIGMOD), pp. 663–676 (2015)
25. Novakovic, S., Daglis, A., Bugnion, E., Falsafi, B., Grot, B.: Scale-out NUMA. In: Proceedings of Symposium on Architectural Support for Programming Languages and Operating Systems (ASPLOS) (2014)
26. OpenCAPI Overview, 14 October 2016. http://opencapi.org/wp-content/uploads/2016/09/OpenCAPI-Overview.10.14.16.pdf. Accessed 25 July 2018
27. OpenSHMEM API Version 1.4. http://openshmem.org/site/sites/default/site_files/OpenSHMEM-1.4.pdf. Accessed 25 July 2018
28. The OpenFAM API. https://github.com/OpenFAM/API. Accessed 27 June 2018
29. pmem.io: Persistent Memory Programming. http://pmem.io. Accessed 29 July 2018
30. Qureshi, M.K., Srinivasan, V., Rivers, J.A.: Scalable high performance main memory system using phase-change memory technology. In: Proceedings of 36th International Symposium on Computer Architecture (ISCA), pp. 24–33 (2009)
31. RDMA Consortium: http://www.rdmaconsortium.org. Accessed 25 July 2018
32. Seyedi, M.A., Fiorentino, M.: Silicon photonics; ring modulator transmitters. In: Guenther, R., Steel, D. (eds.) Encyclopedia of Modern Optics, 2nd edn, vol. 4, pp. 216–223 (2018)
33. Shah, H., Marti, F., Noureddine, W., Eiriksson, A., Sharp, R.: Remote Direct Memory Access (RDMA) Protocol Extensions, IETF RFC 7306, June 2014. https://tools.ietf.org/html/rfc7306. Accessed 25 July 2018
34. Spelman, L.: Reimagining the Data Center Memory and Storage Hierarchy, Intel Newsroom, 30 May 2018. https://newsroom.intel.com/editorials/re-architecting-data-center-memory-storage-hierarchy/. Accessed 25 July 2018
35. Storage Networking Industry Association (SNIA): NVM Programming Model (NPM), Version 1.2. https://www.snia.org/sites/default/files/technical_work/final/NVMProgrammingModel_v1.2.pdf. Accessed 29 July 2018
36. Strukov, D.B., Snider, G.S., Steward, D.R., Williams, R.S.: The missing memristor found. Nature **453**, 80–83 (2008)
37. Xie, Y.: Modeling, architecture and applications for emerging memory technologies. IEEE Design and Test of Computers **28**(1), 44–51 (2011)

SHCOLL - A Standalone Implementation of OpenSHMEM-Style Collectives API

Srđan Milaković[1]([⊠]), Zoran Budimlić[1], Howard Pritchard[2], Anthony Curtis[3], Barbara Chapman[3], and Vivek Sarkar[4]

[1] Rice University, Houston, USA
srdjan@rice.edu
[2] Los Alamos National Laboratory, Los Alamos, USA
[3] Stony Brook University, Stony Brook, USA
[4] Georgia Institute of Technology, Atlanta, Georgia

Abstract. The performance of collective operations has a large impact on overall performance in many HPC applications. Implementing multiple algorithms and selecting optimal one depending on message size and the number of processes involved in the operation is essential to achieve good performance. In this paper, we will present SHCOLL, a collective routines library that was developed on top of OpenSHMEM API point to point operations: puts, gets, atomic memory update, and memory synchronization routines. The library is designed to serve as a plug-in to OpenSHMEM implementations and will be used by the OSSS OpenSHMEM reference implementation to support OpenSHMEM collective operations. In this paper, we describe the algorithms that have been incorporated in the implementation of each OpenSHMEM API collective routine and evaluate them on a Cray XC30 system. For long messages, SHCOLL shows an improvement by up to a factor of 12 compared to the vendor's implementation. We also discuss future development of the library, as well as how it will be incorporated into the OSSS OpenSHMEM reference implementation.

1 Introduction

OpenSHMEM includes both point-to-point communication and collective operations in its specification. These collectives involve synchronization (barriers), data movement (e.g. broadcast, alltoall) and computation (reductions).

A number of platforms provide hardware support for collective operations and vendor solutions will take advantage of this. For portable solutions where such hardware support is not available, it is desirable to provide software implementations of collectives. SHCOLL is such a library for community use, providing a number of algorithms for OpenSHMEM collectives. OpenSHMEM developers, or other developers working on similar problems, can then incorporate SHCOLL into their implementations to avoid reinventing the wheel.

The rest of the paper is organized as follows: in Sect. 2 we compare SHCOLL with related work; in Sect. 3 we introduce the OpenSHMEM specification; in

© Springer Nature Switzerland AG 2019
S. Pophale et al. (Eds.): OpenSHMEM 2018, LNCS 11283, pp. 90–106, 2019.
https://doi.org/10.1007/978-3-030-04918-8_6

Sect. 4 we discuss the implementation of OpenSHMEM that this work is based on; in Sect. 5 we elaborate the different algorithms provided by the SHCOLL library; in Sect. 6 we include and discuss the experimental results; and in Sect. 7 we discuss future work and ideas.

2   Related Work

Most of the previous work focuses on collective communication for the Message Passing Interface (MPI) such as work by Thakur et al. that investigates the performance of different algorithms in MPICH [2,26]. Also, some researchers designed algorithms for specific message sizes such as Rabenseifner's algorithm for large reductions [22] or Van de Gejin's algorithm for large broadcast [6]. Awan et al. investigated design and performance of non-blocking collectives in Open-SHMEM using MVAPICH2-X [3,5]. Jose et al. optimized performance of Open-SHMEM collective operations by developing a light-weight mapping between collective operations in OpenSHMEM and MPI [17]. In this paper, we focus on optimizing OpenSHMEM collective operations using only OpenSHMEM API operations.

3   OpenSHMEM

OpenSHMEM is a specification [20] in the Partitioned Global Address Space (PGAS) family for a distributed parallel programming library that focuses on fast, low-latency, communication using Remote Direct Memory Access (RDMA) to address remote variables directly.

'SHMEM" is a family of PGAS libraries that was developed by various vendors since the early 1990s, but unfortunately drifted from each other over time with subtly different behaviors and APIs that caused portability problems. This led, at least in the C language, to unwieldy preprocessor conditional macro definitions that attempted to iron out the differences [21].

OpenSHMEM is the process that unifies these "SHMEM" libraries under a common, agreed upon and ratified, specification.

4   The OSSS-UCX OpenSHMEM Implementation

4.1   Initial Implementation with GASNet

After the OpenSHMEM specification was first drafted around 2010, the reference implementation library was developed by the University of Houston [12]. This library used GASNet [8] as its communications substrate. GASNet is a portable communications library that was initially developed for use in UPC [23] but has found use in other projects, for example Chapel [13], Legion [7], and in a runtime for Fortran CoArrays [19].

Although GASNet supports a wide range of underlying networks (e.g. Infiniband, Cray Aries, Intel OmniPath, portable MPI), some functionality required by OpenSHMEM is not exposed to the programmer. In particular, GASNet does not, as yet, expose remote atomics, nor does it allow arbitrary memory registration, which would be required to support multiple symmetric heaps with different memory kinds in the future.

4.2 New Implementation with UCX

The current reference implementation, named "OSSS-UCX" after Open Source Software Solutions, for OpenSHMEM specification 1.4 (and beyond) is based on UCX [24]. UCX is a multi-party open-source project to produce a best-of-breed communications substrate that can be used by different HPC paradigms, but predominantly MPI and PGAS libraries and languages.

OSSS-UCX uses UCX for its communications. The OpenSHMEM API maps quite naturally to UCX's upper layer, called UCP ("P" for Protocol). UCP then drops to UCT ("T" for Transport) to target individual network layers. UCX also contains UCS for Operating System services, and UCM for memory management. By targeting UCP, OSSS-UCX does not have to concern itself with network details and thus will work on any network supported by UCX.

4.3 Process Management Interface

OSSS-UCX uses PMIx [11], the Process Management Interface for Exascale, as its launch mechanism. Open-MPI and the PMIx Reference Runtime Environment (PRRTE) [4] provide a launcher with a PMIx server that coordinates the initial bootstrap of information required by UCX for RDMA and atomics. The OpenSHMEM Processing Elements (PEs) contain PMIx clients that exchange information through the server. PMIx will also be used for fault-tolerance.

OSSS-UCX also incorporates some third-party software to, for example, manage symmetric memory allocations.

5 Collective Operations Algorithms

As mentioned earlier in Sect. 2, most of the previous work focuses on collective operations for Message Passing Interface (MPI). For the purpose of this paper, we have implemented all collective operations in OpenSHMEM. In MPI when a process is supposed to receive data, it must call a receive method. However, in OpenSHMEM that is not required because OpenSHMEM supports one-sided remote memory access. When a receive method returns in MPI, there is a guarantee that the data is delivered. Since OpenSHMEM does not have an analogous method, it is necessary to notify the remote node that the data transfer has completed. To ensure the transfer order between the data and the notification, it is required to call shmem_fence in between. Also, Cray SHMEM supports extensions to OpenSHMEM API that combine data transfer with data delivery notification (shmemx_putmem_signal) so in addition to an approach that uses `shmem_fence`, we also used the Cray SHMEM extensions to improve the performance. Additionally, for remote memory accesses in OpenSHMEM, there is no need to calculate the addresses for remote writes in the user code because remotely accessible memory locations have symmetric addresses.

5.1 Barrier

The barrier is a synchronization collective routine that registers the arrival of a PE at the barrier and blocks the execution until all other PEs arrive at the barrier [20]. The library we implemented supports three types of barrier algorithms: linear, tree and dissemination barrier.

In linear barrier, when a PE reaches the barrier, it will increment a counter at PE 0. When the counter reaches the number of PEs, PE 0 will notify all other PEs that they can continue with execution.

For tree barrier, all PEs are organized in a tree. When a non-root PE reaches the barrier, it will wait until the value of its local counter becomes equal to the number of children. Then the PE will increment a counter at the parent. When the counter at root PE becomes equal to the number of children, the root PE will notify its children, and the children will start propagating the notification to the leaf PEs. The library supports two types of trees, k-ary and k-nomial trees (Fig. 1).

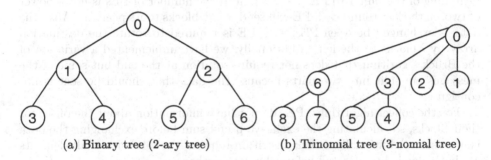

(a) Binary tree (2-ary tree)   (b) Trinomial tree (3-nomial tree)

Fig. 1. Examples of k-ary and k-nomial trees

Dissemination barrier belongs to the category of butterly barrier algorithms, and it has $\lceil \log p \rceil$ rounds [1]. In each round r $(0 \leq r < \lceil \log p \rceil)$, PE i will signal PE $(i + 2^k) \% p$ and wait for a signal from PE $(i - 2^k) \% p$. After getting a signal in $\lceil \log p \rceil$ round, the PE can continue with execution.

5.2 Collect, Fcollect

Collect and fcollect are collective routines that concatenate blocks of data from multiple PEs to an array in every PE. Fcollect requires that the size of each block must be the same whereas block size for collect may vary [20]. For collect, we support linear, recursive doubling, ring and Bruck algorithm. In addition to the algorithms we support for collect, we support neighbor exchange algorithm for fcollect.

In the linear algorithm, each PE issues a put operation to all other PEs in a loop. After the data from a single PE is transferred, the PE increments a counter on all other PEs or calls a barrier depending on the number of PEs.

The ring algorithm (Fig. 2) requires $p-1$ rounds. In round r $(0 \leq r < p-1)$, PE i sends block $(i-r)$ % p to PE $(i+1)$ % p and receives block $(i-r-1)$ % p from PE $(i-1)$ % p.

The neighbor exchange algorithm (Fig. 3) works only if p is even and it requires $\frac{p}{2}$ rounds. In the first round, PE i sends its block to i XOR 1. In odd rounds, even PEs send 2 blocks that were received in the previous round to PE $(i-1)$ % p and odd PEs send the blocks to PE $(i+1)$ % p. In even rounds, even PEs send 2 blocks that were received in the previous round to PE $(i+1)$ % p and odd PEs send the blocks to PE $(i-1)$ % p.

The recursive doubling algorithm (Fig. 4) works if p is a power of two and it requires $\log p$ rounds. In round r $(0 \leq r < \log p)$, PE i sends the data that was received in the previous rounds to PE i XOR 2^r.

Like the recursive doubling algorithm, the Bruck algorithm [9] (Fig. 5) also requires $\lceil \log p \rceil$ rounds but, unlike the recursive doubling algorithm, it works even if p is not a power of two. First, each PEs copies its block to the beginning of its buffer. Then, in round r $(0 \leq r < \lceil \log p \rceil)$, PE i sends 2^r blocks from the beginning of the buffer to PE $(i-2^r)$ % p. If the number of PEs is not a power of two, in the last round each PE will send $p-2^r$ blocks to its peer PE. After the data is exchanged between PEs, each PE is required to rotate the destination array by i blocks to the left. Additionally, we have implemented a variation of the Bruck algorithm that does not require rotation at the end but some of the messages are split into two parts because the data that should be sent is not contiguous.

For the collect algorithms, PEs do not have information about the offset for their blocks, so calculating the exclusive prefix sum before exchanging the data is necessary. Additionally, Bruck algorithm requires the total size of all elements so that value is broadcasted before the data exchange.

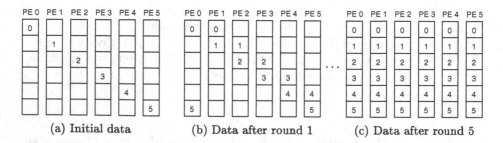

(a) Initial data   (b) Data after round 1   (c) Data after round 5

Fig. 2. Ring collect

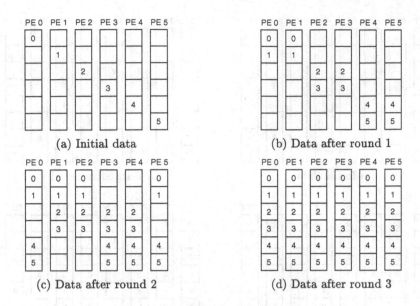

(a) Initial data

(b) Data after round 1

(c) Data after round 2

(d) Data after round 3

Fig. 3. Neighbor exchange collect

5.3 Broadcast

The broadcast is a collective routine that sends data from the root PE to all other PEs in the active set. The library supports three types of the broadcast algorithms: linear, tree, and Van de Geijn's algorithm.

In the linear algorithm, all PEs (except root PE) will call the get method to retrieve the data from the root. To ensure that the root has the data, a barrier is called before and after calling the get method.

For tree broadcast, all PEs are organized in a tree with the PE that has the data as a root. When the root PE invokes broadcast it will send the data to its children, and the children will start propagating the data down the tree. The library supports two types of trees: k-ary and binomial trees (Fig. 1).

Van de Geijn's algorithm [6] is good for large messages. First, the data is scattered across all PEs and then it is concatenated using a method analogous to collect. For scattering, we use binomial scatter, and for collect, we use the ring algorithm (Fig. 2).

5.4 Alltoall, Alltoalls

Alltoall and alltoalls are collective routines in which each PE exchanges a fixed amount of data with all other PEs in the active set. The data that is exchanged in alltoall has to be contiguous whereas the data in alltoalls can be strided [20].

For both collectives, we support three algorithms: shift exchange, XOR pairwise exchange, and generalized pairwise exchange [25]. All three algorithms have

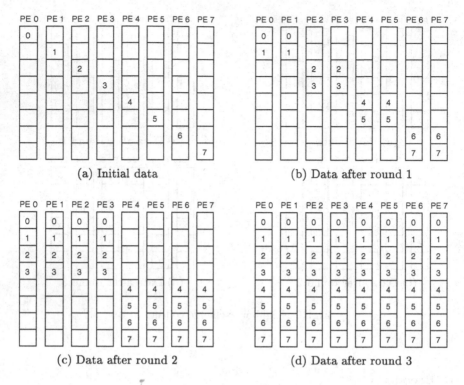

(a) Initial data   (b) Data after round 1

(c) Data after round 2   (d) Data after round 3

Fig. 4. Recursive doubling collect

p rounds and in each round, a put is issued to a different PE (put to self is done using memcpy). However, each algorithm issues put in a different order.

Shift exchange is the simplest algorithm among the algorithms we implemented. In round r ($1 \leq r \leq p$), PE i will send its data to PE $(i + r)$ % p. This algorithm tries to avoid the bottleneck that would happen if all PEs were writing to PE r in round r.

XOR pairwise exchange works only when the number of PEs is a power of 2. In each round of this algorithm, each PE has a partner PE and communicates exclusively with its partner PE. (it sends the data to the partner and it receives the data from the partner). In round r ($1 \leq r \leq p$), the id of the partner PE for PE i is calculated as i XOR r.

Like XOR pairwise exchange, each PE has a partner in each round of generalized pairwise exchange. However, generalized pairwise exchange does not require the number of processes to be a power of 2. The problem of finding a partner can be solved by solving the edge-coloring problem in a complete graph. The complete algorithm can be found in [25].

After the data from a single PE is transferred, the PE increments a counter on all other PEs, or call a barrier depending on the number of PEs.

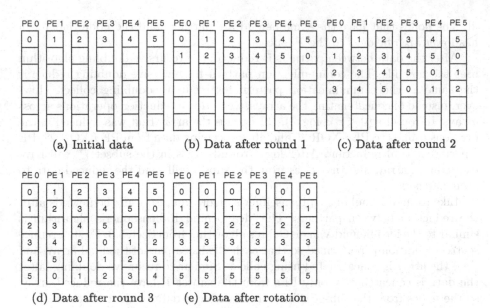

(a) Initial data   (b) Data after round 1   (c) Data after round 2

(d) Data after round 3   (e) Data after rotation

Fig. 5. Bruck collect

In alltoall implementations, we used non-blocking put. However, the Open-SHMEM API [20] does not support non-blocking strided put so we implemented a naive version of non-blocking strided put which we use it in the alltoalls implementations.

5.5 Reductions

Reductions are a set of collective routines that perform associative arithmetic and logical operations across arrays on PEs from the active set [20]. The library we implemented supports a recursive doubling algorithm and Rabenseifner's algorithm.

For both algorithms, we have to first choose the greatest subset of PEs $\mathcal{P}'$ such that the number of nodes p' in the subset is a power of two. After choosing the subset, we assign a unique node from the subset a partner node, which is not in the subset, and then we perform reduction between the partner nodes.

Rabenseifner suggests that the new subset should be a union of even PEs less than $2 * (p - p')$ and PEs greater or equal to $2 * (p - p')$. If we have multiple PEs per node and use Rabenseifner's approach for choosing the subset $\mathcal{P}'$, the PEs from the subset will not be balanced across nodes. Consequently, the nodes that have more PEs than others will have to perform more reduce operations and they will have to exchange more data. To solve this problem, we use a different approach. First we assign a new id to each PE, which is calculated as $\mathrm{id}_{new} = \lfloor \mathrm{id}_{old} \times \frac{p'}{p} \rfloor$. Since $\frac{p}{2} < p' \leq p$, at most two PEs can have the same new id. The nodes that have the same new id are partners and the node that has a has lower id_{old} belongs to the $\mathcal{P}'$ subset.

After the data between partners is reduced, the recursive doubling algorithm uses the new ids. The communication pattern for recursive doubling reduce is the same as the communication pattern for recursive doubling collect. However, instead of concatenating the arrays, we perform reduction operations across arrays. In round r $(0 \leq r < \log p')$, PE i sends the array that was reduced in the previous rounds to PE i XOR 2^r and after receiving data from PE i XOR 2^r, PE i performs local reduction. After $\log p'$ rounds, PEs in the subset $\mathcal{P}'$ will have the reduced array, and the nodes from the subset will send the reduced data to their partners.

Like recursive doubling, Rabenseifner's algorithm also uses the new ids after the reduction between partners. The idea behind Rabenseifner's algorithm is similar to the idea behind Van de Geijn's algorithm from Sect. 5.3. First, a reduce scatter operation is performed so that each PE has a part of the final array, and then the array is concatenated using collect. Similar to recursive doubling, after the data is concatenated, only PEs from the subset $\mathcal{P}$ have the reduced array, so the nodes from the subset will send the reduced data to their partners.

6   Results

In this section, we present a performance evaluation of SHCOLL's collective functions and compare their performance against the equivalent OpenSHMEM functions provided by Cray SHMEM. Note, SHCOLL uses Cray's OpenSHMEM put and memory sychronization methods for data transfers Sect. 5.

6.1   Evaluation Platform and Software

All experimental results presented were collected on the NERSC Edison machine. Edison is a Cray* XC30 with 2×12-core Intel® Xeon® Processors E5-2695 v2 and 64 GB DDR3 in each node. The system was running Cray's CLE 6.0.UP05 operating system. Cray's Intel Programming Environment 6.0.4 was used to compile SHCOLL and its performance tests. Cray's OpenSHMEM 7.6.2 was used for linking against SHCOLL and to obtain Cray OpenSHMEM performance results. Jobs were submitted to Edison using SLURM's *contiguous* option to try and get closely packed sets of nodes. The SLURM nodelists for the jobs indicated that the allocations obtained were generally closely packed, taking into account locations of service and I/O nodes within cabinets.

The OSU OpenSHMEM benchmark tests [3] were initially used for comparing the performance of SHCOLL against the vendor's OpenSHMEM implementation. However, there were limitations in the OSU tests which reduced their usefulness for this evaluation: they don't include all OpenSHMEM collectives, iteration count and transfers are not easily configurable, and they don't check for correctness, even during the warm-up phase. For thes reason, we decided to write tests specifically for this evaluation.

6.2   Barrier

In Fig. 6, timings for SHCOLL's shcoll_barrier are compared to Cray's shmem_barrier for 1 to 512 nodes using 1 and 24 PEs/node. The plot reports time per iteration in milliseconds. The vendor's shmem_barrier performs significantly better at all node counts both for the 1 PE and 24 PEs per node runs. This is expected as Cray OpenSHMEM makes use DMAPP API collective calls [10,14] to access the Aries collective engine (CE) [16] for the inter-node stage of the barrier operation. The significant jump from 256 to 512 nodes can be attributed to the fact that at 512 nodes, the job spans more than a single electrical group of the Cray XC30.

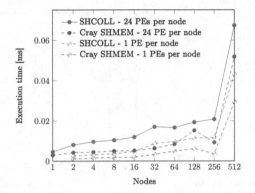

Fig. 6. Barrier

6.3   Broadcast

Figure 7 compares time for broadcast operations for 4, 1KB, 1MB, and 256MB byte transfer sizes for SHCOLL's shcoll_bcast32 and the vendor's shmem_broadcast32 functions for 1 to 512 nodes, and 1 and 24 PEs per node. The plot gives times for a broadcast operation plus a subsequent shmem_barrier_all, to ensure we are timing the full transfer to all participating PEs, and not just the time spent in the broadcast operation by the root PE. For the 4-byte broadcast, SHCOLL uses the *k-nomial* algorithm. The Cray OpenSHMEM broadcast significantly outperforms the SHCOLL implementation, particularly for the 1 PE per node case. This indicates the Cray implementation may be employing the Aries CE to do the broadcast by using its reduction engine with only the root PE supplying a non-zero value. For the 1 KB broadcast, the *k-nomial* algorithm gives optimal performance as well. Using Cray's put-with-signal operation gives best performance for the *k-nomial* algorithm. This helps particularly for 256 and 512 nodes, where SHCOLL performs significantly better than the Cray implementation. The 24 PEs per node timings

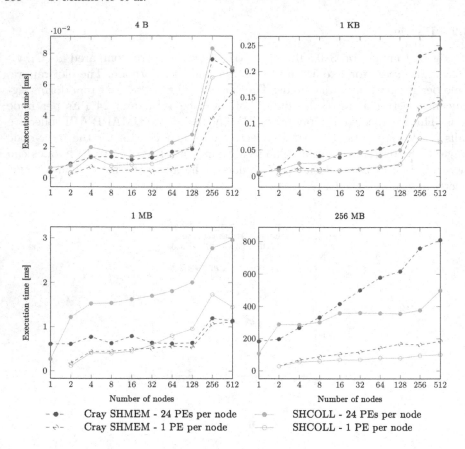

Fig. 7. Broadcast

show a similar performance difference between the Cray and SHCOLL broadcast implementations. For the 1 MB transfer size, the *binomial tree* algorithm gave the best results for SHCOLL, although the Cray implementation shows better performance. For the 256 MB broadcast, SHCOLL uses the *Van de Geijn's't* algorithm. The results for the Cray implementation are similar to those obtained using the *binomial tree* method. The *Van de Geijn's* gives better performance for both the 1 and 24 PE cases compared to the vendor's implementation.

The SHMEM_USE_OPT_MASSIVE_BCAST environment variable was used to check for the best timings using Cray OpenSHMEM. At some PE counts and transfer sizes setting the environment variable helped, in which case timings were taken with it set.

6.4   Reduce

Figure 8 shows times for OpenSHMEM shmem_double_sum_to_all and the SHCOLL equivalent for 8 and 2 KB reductions. Timings include a preceding

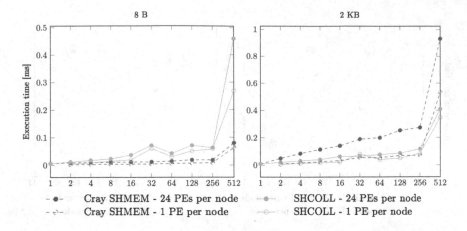

Fig. 8. Reduction

shmem_barrier_all to ensure the pSync array is properly armed. The results for the 8 byte reduction show that Cray's implementation is making use of the Aries CE, consequently performing significantly better than SHCOLL's *recursive doubling* approach. For 2 KB reductions SHCOLL uses *recursive doubling* for 1 PE per node (power of two), and the *Rabenseifner* algorithm for 24 PEs per node. This algorithm gives better results for all node counts, leading to superior performance for SHCOLL in this case. Note the Aries CE can't be efficiently used for these size reductions. Performance is similar to Cray when using recursive doubling.

The Cray OpenSHMEM SHMEM_USE_LARGE_OPT_REDUCE variable was set when it gave better performance.

6.5   Fcollect

Figure 9 presents timing results for shmem_fcollect32 and its SHCOLL equivalent for 4 and 16 KB per PE operations. As with the reduction tests, a shmem_barrier_all is included in the *fcollect* timing loop. For the 4 bytes per PE operation, SHCOLL employees the *Bruck* algorithm and makes use of Cray's put-with-signal extension to OpenSHMEM [18]. The SHCOLL implementation at this transfer size gives comparable performance to the Cray implementation for 1 PE per node up to 128 nodes, and better performance beyond. For 24 PEs per node, the SHCOLL approach yields much better performance. The significant difference at 24 PEs per node verses 1 PE per node hints that the Cray algorithm may be doing something suboptimal - perhaps leading to network congestion - particularly as the performance deteriorates significantly at higher node counts.

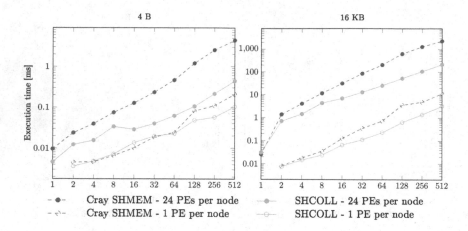

Fig. 9. Fcollect

For 16 KB size transfers and 24 PEs per node, the *ring* algorithm gives the best results for SHCOLL, likely due to the pipelining effect offered by this algorithm. Using this algorithm, SHCOLL performs much better than the vendor implementation, especially at 16 and higher node counts. For 16 KB per PE operations and 1 PE per node, we use the `linear` method up to 256 nodes and the `Bruck` algorithm for 512 nodes.

6.6   Collect

Results for timing of `shmem_collect32` and `shcoll_collect32` are presented in Fig. 10. The *collect* method involves more inter-PE data exchange as each PE supplies its contribution to the transfer, and the implementation must assemble this information in order to do the actual data exchange correctly. For 4 byte per PE (in these tests each PE contributes the same amount of data), SHCOLL uses the *recursive doubling* algorithm and Cray's put-with-signal feature for 1 PE per node, and *linear* for low node counts and *Bruck* for higher node counts. The *Bruck* algorithm yields significantly better results than the method used by the vendor, as shown by the 24 PE/node results at nodes counts of 16 and higher.

For the 16 KB, the *linear* method was optimal up to 32 nodes, with the *Bruck* algorithm performing better for higher node counts. Both algorithms give superior performance to the approach used in the vendor implementation.

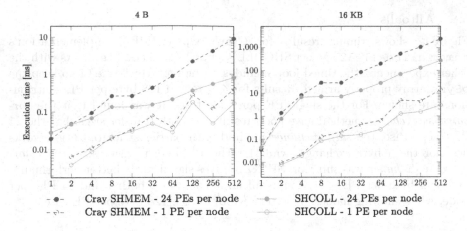

Fig. 10. Collect

6.7 Alltoall

Figure 11 compares performance of Cray OpenSHMEM shmem_alltoall32 against that of SHCOLL's equivalent shcoll_alltoall32 function. The *color-pairwise* exchange method generally performed best for all transfer sizes. At low node or PE counts, the Cray put-with-signal approach works well, but a barrier based synchronization is employed for higher numbers of processes. The algorithm could be more efficient if the underlying network (and the OpenSHMEM API), supported a put-with-counter mechanism [15]. The vendor implementation [18] modestly outperforms the SHCOLL implementation suggesting that the Cray implementation is similar to that used by SHCOLL.

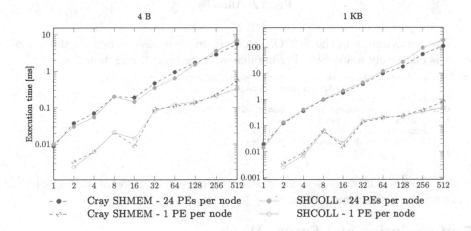

Fig. 11. Alltoall

6.8   Alltoalls

Figure 12 shows timing results for Cray's OpenSHMEM implementation's `shmem_alltoalls32` against SHCOLL's `shcoll_alltoalls32`. As with the other experiments, the timed loop includes a `shmem_barrier_all` to keep the `pSync` array properly armed. Results for 4 byte and 128 byte per PE contributions are shown. For the single PE per node tests, it was found that the *xor-pairwise exchange* method gave good results for both transfer sizes. For the 24 PEs/node case, the *shift_exchange* method with barrier synchronization works best for the 4 byte exchange, while for the 128 byte transfer size, the *color-pairwise exchange* was superior. SHCOLL gives significantly better performance for the 4 byte per PE operation at all node counts for both 1 and 24 PEs per node, while showing modestly better results for the 128 byte per PE case.

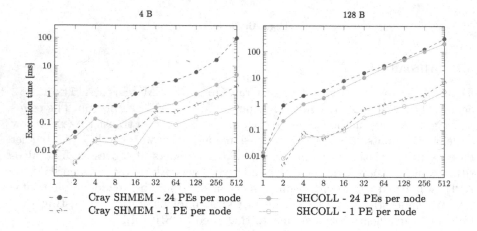

Fig. 12. Alltoalls

The performance of the SHCOLL algorithms was also helped by the use of what is effectively a non-blocking implicit `shmem_iputX_nbi` function:

```
void shmem_iput32_nbi(void* dest, const void* source, ptrdiff_t dst,
                      ptrdiff_t sst, size_t nelems, int pe) {
    uint32_t* dest_ptr = (uint32_t*)dest;
    const uint32_t* source_ptr = (const uint32_t*)source;
    for (int i = 0; i < nelems; i++) {
        shmem_put32_nbi(dest_ptr, source_ptr, 1, pe);
        dest_ptr += dst; source_ptr += sst;
    }
}
```

This approach was used for the data movement part of the `shcoll_alltoalls32` implementation.

7   Conclusion and Future Work

In this paper we have shown that implementing multiple algorithms and selecting the optimal one depending on message size and the number of processes involved in the operation is essential to achieving good performance. Currently, the optimal algorithm for both transfer size and the number of PEs involved in the collective is chosen manually. In future we plan to develop methods to better automate the selection of the optimal algorithm for a particular message size and number of processes. Also, to improve the performance for flat Open-SHMEM applications that use collective operations, we plan add topology aware collectives using PMIx [11]. We further plan to integrate SHCOLL into a future OSSS OpenSHMEM collective plugin framework.

Acknowledgments. This research was funded in part by the United States Department of Defense, and was supported by resources at Los Alamos National Laboratory. This publication has been approved for public, unlimited distribution by Los Alamos National Laboratory, with document number LA-UR-18-27273.

This research used resources of the National Energy Research Scientific Computing Center (NERSC), a U.S. Department of Energy Office of Science User Facility operated under Contract No. DE-AC02-05CH11231.

References

1. Introduction to barrier algorithms. https://6xq.net/barrier-intro/
2. MPICH. https://www.mpich.org
3. MVAPICH2-X. http://mvapich.cse.ohio-state.edu/
4. PMIx Reference RunTime Environment. https://github.com/pmix/prrte
5. Awan, A.A., Hamidouche, K., Chu, C.H., Panda, D.: A case for non-blocking collectives in OpenSHMEM: design, implementation, and performance evaluation using MVAPICH2-X. In: Gorentla Venkata, M., Shamis, P., Imam, N., Lopez, M.G. (eds.) OpenSHMEM 2014. LNCS, vol. 9397, pp. 69–86. Springer, Cham (2015). https://doi.org/10.1007/978-3-319-26428-8_5
6. Barnett, M., Shuler, L., van De Geijn, R., Gupta, S., Payne, D.G., Watts, J.: Interprocessor collective communication library (intercom). In: Proceedings of the Scalable High-Performance Computing Conference, pp. 357–364. IEEE (1994)
7. Bauer, M.E.: Legion: programming distributed heterogeneous architectures with logical regions (2014)
8. Bonachea, D.: GASNet specification, v1.1. Technical report, Computer Science Department, University of California, Berkeley (2002)
9. Bruck, J., Ho, C.T., Kipnis, S., Upfal, E., Weathersby, D.: Efficient algorithms for all-to-all communications in multiport message-passing systems. IEEE Trans. Parallel Distrib. Syst. **8**(11), 1143–1156 (1997)
10. ten Buggencate, M., Roweth, D.: DMAPP: an API for one-sided programming models on baker systems. In: Proceedings of Cray User Group (2010)
11. Castain, R.H., Solt, D., Hursey, J., Bouteiller, A.: Pmix: process management for exascale environments. In: Proceedings of the 24th European MPI Users' Group Meeting, EuroMPI 2017, pp. 14:1–14:10. ACM, New York (2017). http://doi.acm.org/10.1145/3127024.3127027
12. Chapman, B., et al.: Introducing OpenSHMEM: SHMEM for the PGAS community. In: Proceedings of the Fourth Conference on Partitioned Global Address Space Programming Model, PGAS 2010, pp. 2:1–2:3. ACM, New York (2010). http://doi.acm.org/10.1145/2020373.2020375

13. Cray, Inc.: Chapel Language Specification. Technical report, Cray, Inc. (2010)
14. Cray Inc.: Using the GNI and DMAPP APIs (2011)
15. Dinan, J., Cole, C., Jost, G., Smith, S., Underwood, K., Wisniewski, R.W.: Reducing synchronization overhead through bundled communication. In: Poole, S., Hernandez, O., Shamis, P. (eds.) OpenSHMEM 2014. LNCS, vol. 8356, pp. 163–177. Springer, Cham (2014). https://doi.org/10.1007/978-3-319-05215-1_12
16. Faanes, G., et al.: Cray cascade: a scalable HPC system based on a dragonfly network. In: Proceedings of the International Conference on High Performance Computing, Networking, Storage and Analysis (SC 2012), November 2012
17. Jose, J., Kandalla, K., Zhang, J., Potluri, S., Panda, D.: Optimizing collective communication in openshmem. In: 7th International Conference on PGAS Programming Models, p. 185 (2013)
18. Knaak, D., Namashivayam, N.: Proposing OpenSHMEM extensions towards a future for hybrid programming and heterogeneous computing. In: Gorentla Venkata, M., Shamis, P., Imam, N., Lopez, M.G. (eds.) OpenSHMEM 2014. LNCS, vol. 9397, pp. 53–68. Springer, Cham (2015). https://doi.org/10.1007/978-3-319-26428-8_4
19. Namashivayam, N., Eachempati, D., Khaldi, D., Chapman, B.M.: OpenSHMEM as a portable communication layer for PGAS models: a case study with coarray fortran. In: 2015 IEEE International Conference on Cluster Computing, CLUSTER 2015, Chicago, IL, USA, 8–11 September 2015, pp. 438–447 (2015). http://dx.doi.org/10.1109/CLUSTER.2015.66
20. OpenSHMEM Specification Committee: OpenSHMEM Specification. http://www.openshmem.org/site/Specification
21. Poole, S.W., Hernandez, O., Kuehn, J.A., Shipman, G.M., Curtis, A., Feind, K.: OpenSHMEM - toward a unified RMA model. In: Padua, D. (ed.) Encyclopedia of Parallel Computing. Springer, Boston (2011). https://doi.org/10.1007/978-0-387-09766-4_490
22. Rolf Rabenseifner: A new optimized MPI reduce algorithm. https://fs.hlrs.de/projects/par/mpi//myreduce.html
23. Chauvin, S., Saha, P., Cantonnet, F., Annareddy, S., El-Ghazawi, T.: UPC Manual (2003)
24. Shamis, P., et al.: UCX: an open source framework for HPC network APIS and beyond. In: 2015 IEEE 23rd Annual Symposium on High-Performance Interconnects, pp. 40–43, August 2015
25. Tam, A., Wang, C.L.: Efficient scheduling of complete exchange on clusters. In: 13th International Conference on Parallel and Distributed Computing Systems (PDCS 2000), Las Vegas, vol. 4 (2000)
26. Thakur, R., Rabenseifner, R., Gropp, W.: Optimization of collective communication operations in MPICH. Int. J. High Perform. Comput. Appl. **19**(1), 49–66 (2005)

OpenSHMEM Use and Applications

HOOVER: Distributed, Flexible, and Scalable Streaming Graph Processing on OpenSHMEM

Max Grossman[1(✉)], Howard Pritchard[2], Tony Curtis[3], and Vivek Sarkar[1]

[1] Rice University, Houston, USA
jmg3@rice.edu
[2] Los Alamos National Laboratory, Los Alamos, USA
[3] Stony Brook University, Stony Brook, USA

Abstract. Many problems can benefit from being phrased as a graph processing or graph analytics problem: infectious disease modeling, insider threat detection, fraud prevention, social network analyis, and more. These problems all share a common property: the relationships between entitites in these systems are crucial to understanding the overall behavior of the systems themselves. However, relations are rarely if ever static. As our ability to collect information on those relations improve (e.g. on financial transactions in fraud prevention), the value added by large-scale, high-performance, dynamic/streaming (rather than static) graph analysis becomes significant.

This paper introduces HOOVER, a distributed software framework for large-scale, dynamic graph modeling and analyis. HOOVER sits on top of OpenSHMEM, a PGAS programming system, and enables users to plug in application-specific logic while handling all runtime coordination of computation and communication. HOOVER has demonstrated scaling out to 24,576 cores, and is flexible enough to support a wide range of graph-based applications, including infectious disease modeling and anomaly detection.

1 Motivation

The value of graph analytics has grown over the past decade, as new applications arise in the areas of intrusion detection, infectious disease modeling, social networks, fraud prevention, and more. The value of graph analytics lies in the emphasis on analyzing relationships between elements of a system, rather than simply attributes of the elements themselves.

In many high-value applications of graph analytics, timeliness is key; while detecting a network intrusion one month after it occurs is still useful, detecting it as it occurs is much more so. As a result, focus is shifting from static graphs towards dynamic or streaming graph analyses.

However, with the growth in the use of streaming graph analysis has come a growth in the size and diversity of the graph datasets that graph analytics

© Springer Nature Switzerland AG 2019
S. Pophale et al. (Eds.): OpenSHMEM 2018, LNCS 11283, pp. 109–124, 2019.
https://doi.org/10.1007/978-3-030-04918-8_7

frameworks are applied to. Graphs have grown in scale, with increased numbers of vertices and edges. Graphs have also grown in complexity and imbalance, with widely varying densities and connectivity within a single graph. To support the continuation of these trends into the future, graph analysis frameworks will need to:

1. Support bringing to bear larger amounts of memory and compute.
2. Use sufficiently high level abstractions such that the framework's runtime can make automatic performance tuning decisions transparently, and so that user workloads can be mapped to new and exotic hardware.
3. Use sufficiently low level and flexible abstractions such that the framework does not overly restrict the problems that a user can express on top of it.
4. Demonstrate good scalability, such that adding memory and compute leads to an increase in the problem sizes that can be solved.

Without these properties, future graph datasets will be un-analyzable because of their size, or because of how long processing them requires.

In this paper, we introduce the HOOVER graph analysis and simulation framework. HOOVER is a general purpose, distributed, scalable, and flexible framework for (1) modeling systems that are naturally expressed as a graph, and (2) running analyses on the graph representation of that system. HOOVER is a framework for modeling dynamic graphs and supports addition and removal of vertices and edges in the graph, as well as updates to attributes on graph elements. This paper offers an overview of the problem scope of HOOVER, HOOVER's runtime, HOOVER's API, and uses two mini-apps to evaluate its scalability. HOOVER is available open source at https://github.com/agrippa/hoover.

2   Design

HOOVER is a C/C++ distributed framework for modeling and analyzing systems represented as streaming/dynamic graph problems. HOOVER emphasizes flexibility without sacrificing scalability, allowing users to plug in application-specific logic while:

1. Using OpenSHMEM [2] as a scalable backend for inter-PE communication.
2. Using communication-avoiding techniques to reduce inter-PE communication.
3. Being PGAS-by-design from the beginning, leveraging one-sided communication and de-coupled execution to reduce blocking and increase asynchrony.

HOOVER is, to some extent, specialized for a particular class of dynamic graph problems. The archetypical HOOVER problem follows this high level execution flow:

1. The application defines a large number of vertices partitioned across PEs, as well as callbacks to update the state of the graph. This information is passed to HOOVER.

2. The HOOVER framework begins iterative modeling of vertex behavior through repeated callbacks to user-level functions, evolving vertex and graph state over time. All PEs execute entirely de-coupled from each other. While each PE is asynchronously made aware of summaries of the state change in other PEs, no PE ever blocks on or performs two-sided communication with any other PE.

3. After some time, two or more PEs discover their state is related. This "relationship" is entirely user-directed and in the control of user callbacks. After this connectivity is discovered, those PEs enter lockstep execution with each other and share data on each iterative update to their local graph state. Multiple clusters of "coupled" PEs may evolve over time, with separate groups of PEs becoming interconnected or all PEs evolving into a single, massive cluster depending on application behavior.

4. Individual PEs may decide to leave the simulation at any time. A PE exiting a simulation does not imply a barrier; hence, all other PEs may continue in the simulation. PEs may also be configured with a maximum number of iterations to perform. Of course, this says nothing about process termination: all PEs would be expected to call `shmem_finalize` eventually.

An illustrative example may be useful: malware spread over Bluetooth. Malware propagation can be expressed as a graph problem, where vertices in the graph represent Bluetooth devices and edges represent direct connectivity between two devices. Malware propagation and analysis could be modeled on the HOOVER framework:

1. The application developer would define the actors in the simulation as vertices. Each actor would represent a device, and may include attributes such as the range of its Bluetooth hardware, the model of its Bluetooth hardware/-software, the speed at which it can move, or its initial infected/uninfected status.

2. HOOVER would then begin execution, updating device infection status, position, and connectivity with other devices based on user callbacks and other information passed in by the application developer. As iterations progress, more and more devices might become infected from a small initial seed of infected devices.

3. Eventually, two or more PEs may become coupled at the application developer's direction. For example, the developer might instruct two PEs to become coupled if a device resident on one PE infects a device resident on another. By entering coupled, lockstep execution those two PEs can now compute several joint metrics about the infectious cluster they collectively store, such as number of infected devices or rate of infection progression. Note that even when PEs create a tightly coupled cluster, they still interact as usual with any other PEs in the simulation which they are not coupled with.

2.1 OpenSHMEM

HOOVER is built on top of the PGAS OpenSHMEM programming model, and derives much of its scalability from being designed for the PGAS/OpenSHMEM execution model.

The SHMEM programming model was first created by Cray Research for the Cray* T3D machine and has subsequently been supported by a number of vendors across many platforms. The OpenSHMEM specification was created in an effort to improve the consistency of the library across implementations and, more importantly, to provide a forum for the user and vendor communities to discuss and adopt extensions to the SHMEM API.

The OpenSHMEM library provides a single program, multiple data (SPMD) execution model in which N instances of the program are executed in parallel. Each instance is referred to as a processing element (PE) and is identified by its integer ID in the range from 0 to $N - 1$. PEs exchange information through one-sided *get* (read) and *put* (write) operations that access remotely accessible *symmetric objects*. Symmetric objects are objects that are present at all PEs and they are referenced using the local address to the given object. By default, all objects within the data segment of the application are exposed as symmetric; additional symmetric objects are allocated through OpenSHMEM API routines. OpenSHMEM's communication model is unordered by default. Point-to-point ordering is established through *fence* operations, remote completion is established through *quiet* operations, and global ordering is established through *barrier* operations.

3 HOOVER's API

This section describes the user-facing HOOVER data structures, concepts, and APIs to illustrate how an application developer interacts with HOOVER.

3.1 Vertex APIs

The core data structure of HOOVER is the graph vertex, represented by objects of type hvr_vertex_t. A graph vertex is represented as a sparse vector-like data structure.

Creating new vertices is accomplished with hvr_vertex_create_n (before or during the simulation). This will return initialized but empty vertices to the user, to be populated with initial state. Vertices are deleted using hvr_vertex_delete_n.

Given a vertex in the graph, a new attribute can be set or an old attribute updated to a new value using hvr_vertex_set. Similarly, hvr_vertex_get can be used to fetch the current value of an attribute.

```
hvr_vertex_t *hvr_vertex_create_n(size_t nvecs,
        hvr_graph_id_t graph, hvr_ctx_t ctx);
void hvr_vertex_set(unsigned feature, double val,
```

```
        hvr_vertex_t *vec, hvr_ctx_t in_ctx);
double hvr_vertex_get(unsigned feature, hvr_vertex_t *vec,
        hvr_ctx_t in_ctx);
void hvr_vertex_delete_n(hvr_vertex_t *vecs, size_t nvecs,
        hvr_ctx_t ctx);
```

3.2   Core APIS

The core of HOOVER is encapsulated in four APIS.

hvr_ctx_create initializes the state of a user-allocated HOOVER context object. The HOOVER context is used to store global state for a given HOOVER simulation. HOOVER assumes that the user has already called shmem_init to initialize the OpenSHMEM runtime before calling hvr_ctx_create.

```
extern void hvr_ctx_create(hvr_ctx_t *out_ctx);
```

hvr_init completes initialization of the HOOVER context object by populating it with several pieces of user-provided information (e.g. application callbacks) and allocating internal data structures. hvr_init does not launch the simulation itself, but is the last step before doing so.

```
void hvr_init(const uint16_t n_partitions,
        hvr_start_iteration start_iteration,
        hvr_update_metadata_func update_metadata,
        hvr_check_abort_func check_abort,
        hvr_might_interact_func might_interact,
        hvr_actor_to_partition actor_to_partition,
        const double connectivity_threshold,
        const unsigned min_spatial_feature_inclusive,
        const unsigned max_spatial_feature_inclusive,
        const hvr_iter_t max_iteration, hvr_ctx_t ctx);
```

The arguments passed are described below:

1. n_partitions - During execution, HOOVER divides the simulation space up into partitions. These partitions are used to detect possible interactions between vertices in different PEs by first checking for vertex-to-partition interaction. This argument specifies the number of partitions the application developer would like used.
2. start_iteration - A user callback that is called at the beginning of each iteration and passed an iterator over the vertices in the local PE.
3. update_metadata - On each iteration, update_metadata is called on each local vertex one-by-one along with the vertices that vertex has edges with (including remote vertices). update_metadata is responsible for making any changes to the state of the vertex, and deciding if based on those updates any remote PEs should become coupled with the current PE's execution.

4. `check_abort` - A callback used by the application developer to determine if the current PE should exit the simulation based on the state of all local vertices following a full iteration. `check_abort` also computes local metrics, which are then shared with coupled PEs.
5. `might_interact` - A callback used by the runtime to determine if a vertex in the provided partition may interact with any vertex in another partition.
6. `actor_to_partition` - A callback that computes the partition for a given vertex.
7. `connectivity_threshold`,   `min_spatial_feature_inclusive`, `max_spatial_feature_inclusive` - These arguments are all used to update graph edges. HOOVER automatically updates edges based on their "nearness" to other vertices in the simulation, by some distance measure. Today, that is simply a Euclidean distance measure on the features in the range [`min_spatial_feature_inclusive`, `max_spatial_feature_inclusive`]. If the computed distance is less than `connectivity_threshold` those vertices have an edge created between them.
8. `max_iteration` - A limit on the number of iterations for HOOVER to run.
9. `ctx` - The HOOVER context to initialize.

`hvr_body` is then used to launch the simulation problem, as specified by the provided `ctx`, and `hvr_finalize` is used to clean up HOOVER's state. `hvr_body` only returns when the local PE has completed execution, either by exceeding the maximum number of iterations or through a non-zero return code from the `check_abort` callback. HOOVER assumes that `shmem_finalize` is called after `hvr_finalize`.

```
extern void hvr_body(hvr_ctx_t ctx);
extern void hvr_finalize(hvr_ctx_t ctx);
```

3.3 HOOVER Application Skeleton

Given the above APIs, a standard HOOVER application has the following skeleton:

```
hvr_ctx_t ctx;
hvr_ctx_create(&ctx);
hvr_graph_id_t graph = hvr_graph_create(hvr_ctx);

// Create and initialize the vertices in the simulation
hvr_sparse_vec_t *vertices = hvr_sparse_vec_create_n(...);
...

hvr_init(...);

// Launch the simulation
hvr_body(ctx);
```

```
// Analyze and display final results of the simulation
...

hvr_finalize(ctx);
```

Internally, the kernel of hvr_body follows the following workflow:

```
while not abort and iter < max_iter:
  start_time_step(local_vertices)

  foreach vert in local_vertices:
    neighbors = gather_neighbors_along_edges(vert)
    update_metadata(vert, neighbors)

  iter += 1

  update_my_partitions()

  foreach vert in local_vertices:
    update_edges(vert)

  abort = check_abort()

  block_on_coupled_pes()
```

4   HOOVER's Runtime

The core of HOOVER's coordination logic is included under the hvr_body API. hvr_body is responsible for coordinating the execution of the simulation from start to end.

The core of hvr_body is a loop. On each iteration, the following high level actions are taken:

1. **Start Iteration**: The user-provided start_iteration is called, which is passed an iterator over the vertices in the local part of the graph. This gives the user the opportunity to (optionally) perform any application-specific, per-iteration logic.
2. **Update Local Vertices**: All local vertices have their attributes updated using the update_metadata user callback.
3. **Update Local Partitions**: Information on the problem space partitions that contain local vertices is updated on the local PE and made visible to remote PEs.
4. **Find Nearby PEs**: Based on the partition information of other PEs, construct a list of all PEs which have vertices that local vertices may have edges with.

5. **Update Graph Edges**: Communicating only with the PEs that may have nearby vertices, update all inter-vertex edges.
6. **Check Abort**: Check if any updates to local vertices lead to this PE aborting using the check_abort user callback, and compute the local PE's contribution to any coupled metric.
7. **Compute Coupled Metric**: If coupled with other PEs, jointly compute a coupled metric with them.
8. Continue to the next iteration if no abort was indicated and we have not reached the maximum number of iterations.

The following sections provide additional details on subtleties in HOOVER's execution and data structures.

4.1   Versioned Vertices

While HOOVER vertices expose simple get and set APIs to the user, they are subtly complex.

The root of this complexity is the decoupled nature of HOOVER's execution. For scalability reasons, HOOVER was designed to avoid all two-sided, blocking, or collective operations between any two de-coupled PEs. As such, any PE may fetch vertex data from any other PE at any time during the simulation without any involvement from the remote PE. As such, the sparse vector data structure used to represent vertices must be designed to be remotely consistent.

Additionally, because HOOVER is iterative it has some measure of ordering of operations. De-coupled PEs may have reached very different iterations in the simulation before their first interaction. It may be undesirable (in some applications) for the slower PE to be able to read data from future iterations on the faster PE - we would like any information accessed to be mostly consistent for a given iteration. As a result, it is necessary to have some history or versioning built in to HOOVER's sparse vector data structure such that de-coupled PEs on different iterations can still fetch consistent data from each other.

Hence, internally the vertex data structure stores its state going back many iterations. Additionally, when updating a vertex with new values, those values are tagged with the current iteration. A simplified version of the actual sparse vector data structure used to represent graph vertices is shown below:

```
typedef struct _hvr_vertex_t {
    // Features, all entries in each bucket guaranteed unique
    unsigned features[HVR_BUCKETS][HVR_BUCKET_SIZE];

    // Values for each feature in each bucket
    double values[HVR_BUCKETS][HVR_BUCKET_SIZE];

    // Number of features present in each bucket
    unsigned bucket_size[HVR_BUCKETS];

    // Creation iteration for each bucket
```

```
    hvr_iter_t iterations[HVR_BUCKETS];
} hvr_vertex_t;
```

The sparse vector above has the ability to store history for this sparse vector's state going back HVR_BUCKETS iterations, with up to HVR_BUCKET_SIZE features in the sparse vector.

Each time the first attribute is set on a new iteration, a bucket is allocated to it by finding the oldest bucket (i.e. least recently used eviction policy). The most recent state of the sparse vector from the most recent iteration is copied to the new bucket. Then, additional changes for the current iteration are made on top of those copied values.

Anytime a feature needs to be read from a sparse vector, an iteration to read the value for is also passed in (either explicitly from the HOOVER runtime or implicitly using the calling PE's context). The bucket that is closest to that iteration but not past it is then used to return the requested feature. Finding the correct bucket is O(HVR_BUCKETS) in the worst case, but HOOVER maintains two indices into each vertex's buckets to accelerate lookups: (1) the index of the last bucket requested and the iteration that was requested, and (2) the index of the most recently created bucket.

While this design is flexible and solves the problem of de-coupled data accesses in a massively distributed system, it naturally comes with drawbacks. It is memory inefficient, consuming many times the number of bytes than what would be needed to simply store the current state of the sparse vector. Of course, this also has implications for bytes transferred over the network.

Edge Updates. Updating the edges on a given vertex is an expensive operation. Each check to see if an edge should exist between two vertices may include both a remote vector fetch as well as a distance measure. Hence, edge updating is a multi-step process during which we try to eliminate as many remote vertices from consideration as possible without fetching the vertex itself. Key to this is the concept of partitions.

Partitions were introduced earlier, but will be described in more detail here. A partition is simply some subset of the current simulation's problem space, where the problem space is defined as all possible values that may be taken on by the positional attributes of any vertex. One of the simplest forms of partition would be a regular two-dimensional partitioning/gridding of a flat, two-dimensional problem space. However, the concept of a partition in HOOVER is more flexible than that as the user is never asked to explicitly specify the shape or bounds of any partition. They simply must define:

1. A total number of partitions (passed to hvr_init).
2. A callback for returning the partition for a given vertice's state.
3. A callback that tests for the possibility of partition-to-partition interaction (i.e. the possibility of any vertex in partition A interacting with any vertex in partition B)..

Partitions are key to reducing the number of pairwise distance checks needed during edge updating.

During an update to the edges of local actors, we iterate over all other PEs. For each PE we fetch the current actor-to-partition map of that PE. The actor-to-partition map is simply an array storing the partition of each actor on a PE, which is updated on each iteration. Then, for each actor on the remote PE in a partition which one of our locally active partitions may interact with we take a Euclidean distance with each of our local actors to determine which should have edges added.

To further reduce the number of remote memory accesses required we also use a fixed-size, LRU cache for remotely fetched vertices.

OpenSHMEM Read-Write Locks. One common pattern repeated throughout HOOVER was the desire to atomically fetch a large, contiguous region of memory from a remote PE (similar to shmem_atomic_fetch but on larger numbers of bytes). In general, these regions of memory are remotely read and only locally written.

Currently, HOOVER supports this requirement by implementing read-write locks on top of OpenSHMEM APIs. Like the standard OpenSHMEM lock APIs, a read-write lock is a symmetrically allocated long, though in our case we add a custom allocator to allow for custom initialization:

```
long *hvr_rwlock_create_n(const int n);
```

These read-write locks have some semantic differences with standard Open-SHMEM locks (beyond the differences between read-write locks and standard locks). When locking an OpenSHMEM lock, mutual exclusion is guaranteed globally across all PEs for that lock. If a user has a distributed data structure and would like to lock only the chunk of it sitting in a particular PE, this leads to an (undesirable) pattern of allocating npes locks, each for mutual exclusion on a different PE's chunk.

Instead, allocating a single read-write lock in HOOVER is semantically allocating a lock per PE. When acquiring or releasing a read-write lock, a target PE must be specified along with the symmetrically allocated lock object. Mutual exclusion is only guaranteed for a given lock targeting a given PE. The APIs for read-write locks are listed below:

```
void hvr_rwlock_rlock(long *lock, const int target_pe);
void hvr_rwlock_runlock(long *lock, const int target_pe);
void hvr_rwlock_wlock(long *lock, const int target_pe);
void hvr_rwlock_wunlock(long *lock, const int target_pe);
```

Under the covers, the highest order bit in the symmetrically allocated long on each PE is set to acquire a write lock for that PE, while the remaining bits are used to count readers. If a reader attempts to lock and finds the highest order bit set, it will spin until the write lock clears. If a writer attempts to lock and finds one or more readers in the critical section, it will spin until they have all unlocked their read locks.

Dynamic Vertex Allocation and Deallocation. To support adding and removing vertices, we must support dynamic allocation and de-allocation of HOOVER vertices from OpenSHMEM's symmetric heap. Today, that is accomplished with a memory pool that tracks free and used vertices in a pre-allocated chunk of the symmetric heap.

One subtlety of vertex deletion in the presence of de-coupled execution is that remote PEs may still request information on a deleted vertex after it is locally deleted, depending on how the problem is configured and which iteration they are on. As a result, deleted vertices are retained until all PEs have progressed past the point where any would request information on the deleted vertices. PEs share information on their current iteration with neighboring PEs, which in term share this information with their neighbors, leading to all PEs asynchronously receiving slightly out-of-date information on the current iteration of all other PEs. Once all PEs have passed the iteration on which a given vertex was deleted, it is safe to delete that vertex.

5   Performance Results

5.1   Mini-apps

We focus our evaluation on two mini-apps developed as part of this work: a simplified infectious disease model and an intrusion detection model.

Infectious Disease Model. In our infectious disease model each node in the graph represents an actor, i.e. a person or device that could be infected by a bacterial or electronic bug. Actors are assigned a home location, and then repeatedly given random destinations to travel to that are within some radius of their home. Edges between actors indicate some physical proximity to each other, allowing infection to spread between nearby actors. One or more actors in the simulation are initialized to be infected, with the remainder initialized to uninfected. On each HOOVER iteration, an actor's location is updated based on the current destination it is traveling towards, and it becomes infected if any of the vertices it shares edges with are also infected. PEs couple when an actor from one PE infects an actor on another PE.

Intrusion Detection Model. Our intrusion detection model is based on the GBAD graph-based anomaly detection algorithm [4]. In GBAD, the goal is to find anomalies (i.e. rarities) in the structure of a graph which look similar to common patterns, but which are not the same. Nodes in this graph might represent system events, network packets, or other user activities. In our implementation, each PE computes a local set of normative/common subgraph patterns. These patterns are then shared globally and asynchronously among PEs, and used to compute a global set of normative patterns. Each PE then locally looks for patterns which are similar to the normative patterns, but not the same. Note that these patterns may contain edges that cross PEs and include remote vertices. PEs couple when an anomalous pattern is discovered with cross-PE edges.

5.2   Evaluation Platform

HOOVER has been tested on the OSSS, SoS, Cray, HPE, and OpenMPI Open-SHMEM implementations. It has also been tested on ARM- and Intel-based platforms.

The experiments presented here were run on the NERSC Edison machine. Edison is a Cray* XC30 with 2 × 12-core Intel® Xeon® Processors E5-2695 v2 and 64 GB DDR3 in each node. Edison nodes are connected by the Aries interconnect. All experiments are run on Cray SHMEM 7.7.0. All tests are run with one PE per core (24 PEs per node).

5.3   Scaling Results

For strong scaling experiments of the infectious disease model, we use a problem consisting of a 16,000 × 24,000 two-dimensional grid with 9,830,400 actors moving on it. Strong scaling results out to 256 nodes are shown in Table 1. Thanks to its decoupled-by-default design, HOOVER is able to continue to show strong scaling performance improvements out to over 6,000 PEs.

Table 1. Strong scaling tests with 9,830,400 actors in the infectious disease model on the Edison supercomputer.

# PEs	Execution time (ms)	Speedup relative to previous
384	56,296	
1,536	13,229	4.26×
6,144	6,642	1.99×
24,576	4,472	1.49×

Table 2 shows the results of weak scaling experiments of our intrusion detection model out to 3,072 PEs. In these tests, each PE inserts a random number of random nodes in the graph on each iteration as part of the start_iteration callback. This emulates the ingestion of new events in a real world auditing system. Tests are run for a fixed walltime. Table 2 reports the number of nodes that were handled by the end of the simulation, demonstrating that with more hardware the system is able to process events at a consistently higher rate.

Decoupled execution is a foundational component of HOOVER's performance, but also leads to overheads that other systems lack. In particular, decoupled execution eliminates synchronization but requires that the history of a vertex's attributes be kept and communicated between PEs. It is important to test that the overheads removed by decoupled execution are greater than the overheads introduced. To that end, experiments were run using the intrusion

Table 2. Weak scaling tests of the intrusion detection model on the Edison supercomputer.

# PEs	Nodes processed	Improvement relative to previous
384	2,228,526	
768	3,788,324	1.70×
1,536	6,143,523	1.62×
3,072	9,087,829	1.48×
6,144	12,787,045	1.41×

detection model at 3,072 PEs with vertex history tracking disabled and a global barrier per iteration to ensure PEs remain in-sync. While decoupled execution was able to process 9,087,829 nodes, the synchronized version only processed 3,672,764 (~40%).

6   Related Work

6.1   Distributed Graph Analytics

While most of today's graph analytics frameworks are single node and shared memory, we summarize the distributed frameworks here.

GraphX [5] is a popular graph processing framework built on top of the Apache Spark framework. As a result, it supports scaling out to large distributed systems (though the original paper only measures scalability out to 16 nodes) and composability with other frameworks built on Spark. GraphX represents graphs as distributed arrays of vertex and edge attributes stored in Spark RDDs, which are often presented as arrays of "triplets" where each triplet contains an edge and references to the vertices it connects. GraphX adds graph-specific operators on top of Spark to make processing GraphX graphs easier (e.g. a mapE operation that maps a function across edges).

LFGraph [6] is a distributed graph processing framework that focuses on value propagation problems (rather than computing on the graph itself) on static graphs. The dataflow API focuses on fetching the updated values of neighboring vertices, and updating the current value of the current vertex. Hence, LFGraph is focused on computing classical graph statistics (e.g. PageRank, Undirected Triangle Count, etc) rather than modeling more complex systems. While LFGraph is fault tolerant and is designed to run on commodity hardware, its experimental evaluation only measures its scalability out to 64 nodes.

Distributed GraphLab [8] is a distributed graph processing framework for static graphs. GraphLab's programming abstractions consist of a "data graph" which allows user's to attach metadata to each vertex and edge in the static graph, "update functions" which updates the state of a vertex and may schedule processing of other vertices, and "sync operations" which update global data structures based on read-only access to the data graph. GraphLab uses a pre-processing step to initially over-partition the target graph into many files on the storage system, and then loads these partitions (similar to HOOVER's partitions) in a distributed fashion across nodes. GraphLab uses its own custom execution engine to manage computation and communication across nodes (i.e., does not sit on top of Spark or some other framework).

Pregel [9] offers a message-based programming model for dynamic, distributed graph processing: "Programs are expressed as a sequence of iterations, in each of which a vertex can receive messages sent in the previous iteration, send messages to other vertices, and modify its own state and that of its outgoing edges or mutate graph topology". Pregel has its own execution engine that coordinates the communication of messages and their processing at each vertex.

Apache Flink [1] is an open source system for distributed stream and batch processing, which exposes a graph API called Gelly [7]. Gelly offers common graph operations, supports dynamic graph mutation, and supports both vertex-centric and edge-centric APIs.

Many of the frameworks above and in other literature have several properties in common that contrast them with HOOVER:

1. Bulk synchronous execution: Most frameworks make frequent use of global barriers to coordinate execution, limiting scalability.
2. Focus on static rather than dynamic graphs: Most frameworks focus on static rather than dynamic graphs (with some exceptions, such as Pregel and Gelly).
3. Custom execution/coordination engines: Many frameworks implement their own custom execution, coordination, and communication engines for scheduling work. HOOVER, on the other hand, leverages years of work tuning OpenSHMEM runtimes for performance and stability.
4. Support for fault tolerance: HOOVER does not currently support fault tolerance, though active work is exploring this avenue of research.

6.2   Graph-Based Intrusion Detection

While not the primary contribution of this work, the intrusion detection mini-app described in Sect. 5.1 is inspired by earlier work.

GBAD [4] is the seminal graph-based anomaly detection algorithm on which our intrusion detection mini-app is based. The GBAD paper introduced the idea of thinking about anomalies as patterns in a graph which look similar to a common, normative pattern but which is not exactly identical.

Eberle et al. [3] introduced a distributed version of the GBAD algorithm. While this distributed extension is bulk synchronous, it shares similarities to our intrusion detection mini-app by computing local normative patterns, using them to find global normative patterns, and then reporting local anomalies based on those global normative patterns.

7   Future Work

While HOOVER's decoupled approach to graph processing offers promise for scaling to larger graph problems than are solveable with existing frameworks, HOOVER is still an active and evolving project with several avenues of future and ongoing investigation:

1. Explicit edge creation: HOOVER's current approach to edge creation is implicit – edges are created when two vertices become close by some distance measure. We plan to explore alternative, explicit ways to prescribing edge creation and study their impact on performance.
2. Automatic load balancing of vertices between PEs.
3. Experiment with hybrid and heterogeneous parallelism.
4. Improved infectious disease model: Work is actively exploring making the simple infectious disease model into a more realistic application.
5. Improved vertex memory efficiency: Versioned vertices consume large amounts of space to store their state over many iterations. This costs memory and bytes over the wire. Exploring ways to compress these large data structures without a loss of information would be beneficial for performance.
6. Cross OpenSHMEM implementation performance comparison: While HOOVER has been tested across several OpenSHMEM implementations for correctness, we are interested in using it as a point-of-comparison for performance.

8   Conclusion

When it comes to distributed streaming graph processing, the choice of frameworks is extremely limited today. Most graph processing frameworks do one or the other (distributed or streaming), but not both. The underlying reason for this is the challenge of efficiently scaling graph applications on rapidly mutating graphs with highly irregular computation and memory access, all using a bulk synchronous model.

HOOVER avoids this problem by using OpenSHMEM to enable fully decoupled parallel execution, minimizing communication and synchronization by keeping it local to only those PEs that must interact. HOOVER offers a sufficiently flexible API to support a wide range of graph processing applications, while enabling scaling out to thousands of PEs and terabytes of memory.

Acknowledgments. The authors would like to thank Steve Poole (LANL) for his valuable feedback on the HOOVER project and this manuscript.

Work on HOOVER was funded in part by the United States Department of Defense, and was supported by resources at Los Alamos National Laboratory. This research used resources of the National Energy Research Scientific Computing Center, a DOE Office of Science User Facility supported by the Office of Science of the U.S. Department of Energy under Contract No. DE-AC02-05CH11231. Los Alamos National Laboratory publication number LA-UR-18-27825.

References

1. Carbone, P., Katsifodimos, A., Ewen, S., Markl, V., Haridi, S., Tzoumas, K.: Apache flink: stream and batch processing in a single engine. Bull. IEEE Comput. Soc. Tech. Committee Data Eng. **36**(4) (2015)
2. Chapman, B., et al.: Introducing OpenSHMEM: SHMEM for the PGAS community. In: Proceedings of the Fourth Conference on Partitioned Global Address Space Programming Model, p. 2. ACM (2010)
3. Eberle, W., Holder, L.: Scalable anomaly detection in graphs. Intell. Data Anal. **19**(1), 57–74 (2015)
4. Eberle, W., Holder, L.B.: Mining for structural anomalies in graph-based data. In: DMIN, pp. 376–389 (2007)
5. Gonzalez, J.E., Xin, R.S., Dave, A., Crankshaw, D., Franklin, M.J., Stoica, I.: Graphx: graph processing in a distributed dataflow framework. In: OSDI, vol. 14, pp. 599–613 (2014)
6. Hoque, I., Gupta, I.: LFGraph: simple and fast distributed graph analytics. In: Proceedings of the First ACM SIGOPS Conference on Timely Results in Operating Systems, p. 9. ACM (2013)
7. Kalavri, V.: Gelly: Large-Scale Graph Processing with Apache Flink (2015). https://www.slideshare.net/vkalavri/gelly-in-apache-flink-bay-area-meetup
8. Low, Y., Bickson, D., Gonzalez, J., Guestrin, C., Kyrola, A., Hellerstein, J.M.: Distributed graphlab: a framework for machine learning and data mining in the cloud. Proc. VLDB Endow. **5**(8), 716–727 (2012)
9. Malewicz, G., et al.: Pregel: a system for large-scale graph processing. In: Proceedings of the 2010 ACM SIGMOD International Conference on Management of Data, pp. 135–146. ACM (2010)

Tumbling Down the GraphBLAS Rabbit Hole with SHMEM

Curtis Hughey[✉]

US Department of Defense, 9800 Savage Road,
Ft. George G. Meade, MD 20755, USA
curtis.r.hughey.civ@mail.mil

Abstract. In this paper we present shgraph, a SHMEM implementation of the GraphBLAS standard, which enables the user to redefine complex graph algorithms in terms of simple linear algebra primitives. Graph-BLAS offers many nice features such as type abstractions, the ability to perform generalized matrix/vector operations over a semiring, and executing graph operations out-of-order (non-blocking mode).

shgraph seeks to efficiently manage and process billion-edge or greater sparse graphs on an HPC system. We walk through sample GraphBLAS code and discuss the shgraph development process. In particular, we explain how SHMEM was used and where it was necessary to tweak the GraphBLAS specification to be compatible with a distributed system. Additionally, we analyze some preliminary performance results, map out next steps, and suggest potential applications.

Keywords: shgraph · GraphBLAS · OpenSHMEM · Sparse matrix

1 Definitions and Notation

We define a graph to be the ordered pair $G = (V, E)$, where V is a set of vertices and E a set of edges, each of which connects two vertices in V together. Throughout this paper we assume that the graphs we use are undirected, meaning that for any $u, v \in V$, u is connected to v if and only if v is connected to u. Directed graphs need only satisfy one side of the previous statement, but that is also easily handled in GraphBLAS and our implementation.

Graphs are represented broadly in one of two ways: adjacency lists and matrices. An adjacency list is a collection of vertex and list pairs, where for each vertex v in the adjacency list, and its corresponding list W, W is the collection of vertices that v is connected to. An adjacency matrix A for a given graph $G = (V, E)$ with $n = |V|$ is an n-by-n matrix of 0's and 1's. Given a mapping between V and the integers $0..n-1$, if vertex i is connected to vertex j, then $A_{ij} = 1$, otherwise, $A_{ij} = 0$. For undirected graphs, this matrix will be symmetric. Weighted graphs are also trivial to represent by expanding the domain of the values in the matrix.

Supported by the US Department of Defense.

S. Pophale et al. (Eds.): OpenSHMEM 2018, LNCS 11283, pp. 125–136, 2019.
https://doi.org/10.1007/978-3-030-04918-8_8

2   GraphBLAS

GraphBLAS [1–3] is a collection of linear algebra primitives used to express a rich variety of graph algorithms, where graphs are represented as adjacency matrices. Generally, the graphs modeled in GraphBLAS are assumed to be *sparse*, which by convention means that for a graph $G = (V, E)$, we have $|E| = O(|V|)$. This means that if the graph were represented in memory as an adjacency matrix, the vast majority of entries would be 0. This suggests compression schemes where entries not explicitly listed are implied to be 0. The simplest technique is storing the matrix as an array of triples of rows, columns, and values, although there are many more exotic schemes, such as Compressed Sparse Rows (CSR), Compressed Sparse Columns (CSC), etc. [4].

BLAS (Basic Linear Algebra Subroutines) [6] is a collection of low-level linear algebra functions codified in the late 1970's. To handle sparse matrices, Sparse BLAS [7] was defined in the early 2000's. The GraphBLAS model was first proposed in 2011 as a method for solving graph computations using matrix operations. Version 1.0 of the specification was formalized in 2017 [1–3]. See Fig. 1 below for a complete listing of the GraphBLAS primitives; while there are additional support functions for e.g. matrix/vector building, these consistute the core GraphBLAS operations.

Operation	Description
mxm	Matrix-matrix multiply
mxv	Matrix-vector multiply
vxm	Vector-matrix multiply
eWiseAdd	Matrix/vector addition
eWiseMult	Matrix/vector Hadamard product
reduce (row)	Row-wise matrix reduction
reduce (scalar)	Scalar matrix/vector reduction
apply	Matrix/vector function application
transpose	Matrix transpose
extract	Matrix/vector tuple extraction
assign	Matrix/vector assignment

Fig. 1. GraphBLAS primitives

The primary distinguishing feature between GraphBLAS and Sparse BLAS is that GraphBLAS offers a wide range of *semiring* operators rather than just normal addition and multiplication. Semirings provide a generalization of the underlying mathematical operations on vectors and matrices. It is composed of an identity element, a commutative and associative addition operator, and a multiplication operator. See Fig. 2 for an example of a Boolean semiring. Additionally, typical adjacency matrices for graphs may have exploitable patterns that cannot be assumed for generic sparse matrices. Finally, GraphBLAS offers a much wider range of flexibility to control how results are written to output vectors/matrices through the use of masks, descriptors, user-defined types (UDTs), and index ordering.

Figure 2 on the following page is an implementation of a simple top-down breadth-first search algorithm (BFS) using GraphBLAS, taken from the GraphBLAS specification [1].

3   shgraph Overview

shgraph is our mostly completed implementation of the GraphBLAS specification [1], using a proprietary light wrapper of OpenSHMEM [8]. The main functionality for building, assignment, matrix-matrix and matrix-vector multiplication and addition, etc., have been fully implemented. Development time took less than 6 months in total and a month was spent on optimizing code. The majority of GraphBLAS functions do not need any calls to OpenSHMEM, but the performance results we go over rely heavily on it.

While GraphBLAS certainly anticipates implementations with parallel code, it is not completely compatible with an SPMD application. Probably the simplest distinguishing feature is that for many of the GraphBLAS calls such as GrB_Matrix_build, GrB_Vector_build, etc., each PE is responsible for passing in only a subset of the row-column-value triples. One area of the specification that we chose not to implement was GraphBLAS indexing, which essentially amounts to computing a distributed permutation. This turns out to be computationally somewhat intensive, and it seems to not provide much functionality benefit.

Another feature that proves difficult to implement on a distributed system is the GraphBLAS error model. Without imposing severe synchronization constraints, it is hard to cleanly manage errors that only occur on a subset of PEs. Strictly speaking, although the GraphBLAS specification does not deal with SPMD applications, the "right" way would be to have all PEs return with an error message, rather than just the ones that encountered the error. Probably the greatest issue in managing this, however, is where one PE encounters an error and has to alert the other PEs so they can collectively report back to the user, but some of the PEs have already entered a barrier. Without an interrupt mechanism built into SHMEM, this is awkward to handle. On the other hand, only requiring that the PEs that encounter problems report error codes increases the burden on the end user to manage an SPMD program. Therefore, for full compatibility for an SPMD application, the GraphBLAS error system requirements would have to be relaxed.

Nevertheless, on the whole GraphBLAS provides a clean, expressive interface to perform many interesting graph algorithms. Since shgraph will entirely manage the distributed aspect, the end user can easily write SPMD code with minimal knowledge of OpenSHMEM or other underlying technologies.

```
1
2    #include <stdlib.h>
3    #include <stdio.h>
4    #include <stdint.h>
5    #include <stdbool.h>
6    #include "GraphBLAS.h"
7
8    /*
9     * Given a boolean n x n adjacency matrix A and a source vertex s,
10    * performs a BFS traversal of the graph and sets v[i] to the level
11    * in which vertex i is visited (v[s] == 1). If i is not reachable
12    * from s, then v[i] = 0.  (Vector v should be empty on input).
13    */
14
15   GrB_Info BFS(GrB_Vector *v, GrB_Matrix A, GrB_Index s)
16   {
17      GrB_Index n;
18      GrB_Matrix_nrows(&n,A);                        // n = # of rows of A
19
20      GrB_Vector_new(v,GrB_INT32,n);                 // Vector<int32_t> v(n)
21
22      GrB_Vector q;                                  // vertices visited in
23                                                     // each level
24      GrB_Vector_new(&q,GrB_BOOL,n);                 // Vector<bool> q(n)
25      GrB_Vector_setElement(q,(bool)true,s);         // q[s] = true, false
26                                                     // everywhere else
27
28      GrB_Monoid Lor;                                // Logical-or monoid
29      GrB_Monoid_new(&Lor,GrB_LOR,(bool)false);
30
31      GrB_Semiring Boolean;                          // Boolean semiring
32      GrB_Semiring_new(&Boolean,Lor,GrB_LAND);
33
34      GrB_Descriptor desc;                           // Descriptor for vxm
35      GrB_Descriptor_new(&desc);
36      GrB_Descriptor_set(desc,GrB_MASK,GrB_SCMP);    // invert the mask
37      GrB_Descriptor_set(desc,GrB_OUTP,GrB_REPLACE); // clear output before
38                                                     // assignment
39
40      // BFS traversal and label the vertices.
41      int32_t d = 0;                                 // d = level in BFS traversal
42      bool succ = false;                             // succ == true when some
43                                                     // child found
44      do {
45         ++d;                                        // next level (start with 1)
46         GrB_assign(*v,q,GrB_NULL,d,GrB_ALL,n,GrB_NULL);  // v[q] = d
47         GrB_vxm(q,*v,GrB_NULL,Boolean,q,A,desc);    // q[!v] = q||.&& A; finds all
48                                                     // unvisited successors from
49                                                     // the current q
50         GrB_reduce(&succ,GrB_NULL,Lor,q,GrB_NULL);  // succ = ||(q)
51      } while (succ);                                // if there is no successor
52                                                     // in q, we are done
53
54      GrB_free(&q);                                  // q vector no longer needed
55      GrB_free(&Lor);                                // Logical-or monoid no longer
56                                                     // needed
57      GrB_free(&Boolean);                            // Boolean semiring no longer
58                                                     // needed
59      GrB_free(&desc);                               // descriptor no longer needed
60
61      return GrB_SUCCESS;
62   }
```

Fig. 2. Simple GraphBLAS BFS traversal

4   Managing Large, Sparse Graphs with shgraph

Sparse graphs are prevalent in many computational areas, such as machine learning, physical systems, etc., although for this paper we focus on social networks. Famously, Dunbar's Number [5] provides a constant upper bound for the number of relationships a person can have, satisfying our requirements for a sparse matrix. Such graphs can easily exceed the billion-edge range, meaning that distributed implementations are needed to handle networks on this scale. Representing these graphs as matrices provides a host of options for partioning the data. While the simplest implementations partition the matrix by row or column (see for example STAR-P [9]), they suffer if there are highly connected vertices. It also complicates matrix-matrix multiplication. Therefore, we chose a 2D decomposition, where our PEs are arranged in a logical grid and each PE contains a certain range of matrix values by both dimensions. For example, given 4 PEs, the first PE will represent the upper left-hand quadrant of the matrix, the second will represent the upper right-hand quadrant, etc. For a more thorough treatment dealing with the scalability of 1D matrix decompositions, refer to Buluç and Gilbert's paper [10].

When a matrix is created in GraphBLAS, `GrB_Matrix_new` must first be called, and each PE will calculate the range of row and column indices that it will be locally responsible for. This information is stored in the `GrB_Matrix` struct. Note that this is independent of the matrix's non-zero distribution; it is just based off of a close-as-possible even division of the dimensions. Then `GrB_Matrix_build` is called, and each PE will be passed in a collection of triples, representing edges (row, column, value) in the graph. These must be distributed to the correct PEs as detailed below:

1. Given N PEs, each PE will locally allocate N buckets
2. Each PE calculates which remote PE each of these triples belong to, and puts them into the corresponding local bucket
3. Using OpenSHMEM value reductions, the PEs calculate the highest quantity of triples that a PE will be receiving from all other PEs
4. Using the value calculated in the previous step, all PEs make a call to `shmem_malloc`, creating a symmetric buffer
5. A static variable `index` is defined for each PE, used to record how many triples have been put into the PE's symmetric buffer
6. PEs begin independently (i.e. with no synchronization) iterating through their local buckets
7. For each bucket, given n triples, the PE uses `shmem_atomic_fetch_add` to atomically add n to the remote PE's `index`. It then performs a `shmem_put` on the remote PE's symmetric buffer at the offset corresponding to the value fetched in the atomic add operation
8. Once each PE has received all of its triples, it converts it into a sparse local storage format called DCSR (see below for details)

Note that in step 7, `shmem_atomic_fetch_add` fetches the old value of `index`. This method allows for potentially many PEs to simultaneously write to the same remote PE's symmetric buffer, since the atomic operation guarantees that they will be writing to unique areas of the buffer. This is far superior than e.g. allowing only one PE to write to a given remote PE at a time with locking routines (in fact, shgraph never locks). Efficient one-sided communication is crucial in making this build process as fast as possible. For example, each PE in step 7 has a lot of data to remotely put, but it only needs to process this data once all the buckets are processed on all the PEs. Since the data does not need to be processed right away, a two-sided communication pattern would be wasteful.

This implementation of `GrB_Matrix_build` runs fastest when the matrix represented by the triples is uniformly distributed. The less uniform it is, the larger the symmetric allocation will be in step 4. Additionally, PEs receiving more triples will have more work to do in the last step. However, generating a random isomorphism of the matrix (see below), effectively mitigates this.

Given that the triples are distributed to their correct PEs, they still must be stored in a compressed format to take advantage of its sparsity. We can consider a PE's collection of edges as a submatrix, so the traditional sparse storage formats are still applicable. One very popular format, as mentioned above, is Compressed Sparse Row (CSR); however, as Buluç and Gilbert showed [11], as the graph's dimension increases these submatrices increasingly become *hypersparse*, meaning that entire rows or columns of the submatrix will be 0. As proposed in the referenced paper above, we use the Doubly Compressed Sparse Row format (DCSR), the row analogue to DCSC, to address this. While this leads to excellent compression of the sparse data, it makes operating on them much more complex. The most obvious drawback is that for the typical 2D array implementation of a matrix, data can be accessed in constant time, whereas for DCSR to access a single point in the matrix we must first traverse the non-zero rows and then along the correct row. Fortunately, many graph algorithms require the data to be accessed in order, and not randomly. As long as the algorithm allows us to access the data by row and then column we remain largely unaffected, but DCSR makes it difficult to access data by column and then by row. This makes operations like matrix-matrix multiplication very difficult.

Inside the `GrB_Matrix` struct, there are four buffers used to represent this sparse format:

1. `nonZeroRows`: Ordered array of the rows in the matrix with non-zero elements
2. `rowPointers`: Represents where in the `nonZeroCols` the subarray of the columns corresponding to a non-zero row
3. `nonZeroCols`: An array of all column indices for the non-zero elements, first sorted by row, then by column
4. `values`: The values corresponding to the columns indices

As an example, take this 5-by-7 matrix:

$$\begin{pmatrix} & & 1 & & \\ 5 & & 3 & & \\ 4 & 7 & & & \\ & & & & \\ 1 & 0 & & 5 & \end{pmatrix}$$

Any value not explicitly listed in this matrix is an *implied zero*. Note it is entirely possible that when performing operations over a GraphBLAS monoid, the implied zero matches values in the matrix. The DCSR representation of this matrix will be:

1. `nonZeroRows = [0,1,2,4]`
2. `rowPointers = [0,1,3,5,8]`
3. `nonZeroCols = [4,0,3,0,1,0,2,6]`
4. `values = [1,5,3,4,7,1,0,5]`

The first array gives in order the rows with non-zero elements. Since there are no elements on the third row (note we're zero-indexing), 3 is not present in that array. The second array shows how to access the corresponding column indices and values for a given non-zero row. For example, the columns for row 1 will be stored between `rowPointers[1]` inclusive and `rowPointers[2]` exclusive, i.e. in the interval $[1,3)$. The corresponding values will also be stored sequentially in the same range in the `values` array. Note that the last element of `rowPointers` gives the total number of non-zero values in the matrix. shgraph must also store the number of non-zero rows in `GrB_Matrix`, as well as the dimensions of the matrix it's storing.

Many real-life and synthetic graphs will not have their non-zero elements uniformly distributed. Typical graphs will have clustered subcommunities which are relatively much more dense than the rest of the matrix. Therefore, we use a permutation polynomial to generate a random isomorphism of the input matrix. See Lidl and Mullen's paper [12] for an overview on these types of polynomials. Even a simple affine transform will generally equalize the runtimes of our Graph-BLAS algorithms over matrices whether the non-zero elements are uniformly or non-uniformly distributed. Note that this method still fails for rows or columns that are relatively dense, but the 2D decomposition partially addresses that.

Vectors are also very useful for graph operations. Since even a sparse matrix will typically represent more elements than a vector of the same dimension, we typically treat them as dense without much memory impact. This enables us to access elements of the vector in constant time, which is especially useful since vectors will often get updated in random places for graph algorithms. Vectors are first distributed by PE row and then by column, in such a way that the total length of a vector along a row of PEs matches the column-dimension of the corresponding submatrices represented along that row.

5   Vector-Matrix Products

We focused our optimization efforts on vector-matrix products (GrB_vxm) for the below performance benchmark. Given a vector and matrix with compatible dimension, distributed as described above, our overall strategy is:

1. For each row of PEs, cycle their vector chunks among themselves
2. Apply a local vector-matrix multiplication with the newly received vector chunk and the relevant portion of the PEs submatrix
3. Calculate the target PE(s) where the data yielded in the previous step belong, and send
4. Merge all the data received from the previous step, and locally store
5. Repeat until the vector chunks have been fully cycled among their row

OpenSHMEM is critical in performing steps 1 and 3. For Step 1, on every cycle iteration each PE along a row calculates the target PE for its vector chunk, and then uses shmem_put to put that data into a symmetric buffer. Step 3 is much the same, although multiple calls to shmem_put may be necessary. Both of these steps heavily take advantage of one-sided communication, because all PEs can simultaneously remotely send data with relatively low latency and overhead. Refer to Buluç and Gilbert's paper arguing for one-sided communication for graph algorithms [13] for more details. Between all of these steps, shmem_barrier_all is needed to ensure synchronization. As long as the vector and matrix are roughly distributed evenly across the PEs, each PE will do approximately the same amount of work, so the wait time in these barriers should be low.

We implemented Step 2 to specifically optimize for BFS. Although there are three GraphBLAS instructions executed on each iteration of the BFS algorithm described, GrB_vxm takes up well over 99% of the time in the algorithm. Additionally, for a typical BFS run, the majority of time is spent in one iteration. This means that on that iteration the frontier of newly-visited vertices is high, whereas on other iterations, like the beginning and end of the run, it is low. Converting the vector to a sparse format in these cases allows us to efficiently traverse it during this step. Further performance gains were achieved by optimizing matrix operations with a sparse accumulator (SPA), as described by Gilbert et al. [14], with a switch vector, first defined by Gustavson [15]. Much of our vector-matrix and matrix-matrix product implementations were based off of Buluç and Gilbert's overview on sparse matrix methods [4].

6   Performance

We compare some preliminary benchmark results against CombBLAS v1.4 [16], a C++ MPI-based sparse graph library that influenced the GraphBLAS standard. A similar test to what was described by Satish et al. [17] was used. We performed Kernels 1 and 2 of the Graph500 benchmark [18,19]. Kernel 1 builds R-MAT matrices, first introduced by Chakrabarti et al. [20]. These provide a synthetic approximation for large-scale social relationship graphs. As in the Graph500 standard, we used graph parameters [0.57, 0.19, 0.19, 0.05] and an edge factor of 16. Kernel 2 runs breadth-first search, which is a popular graph benchmark, over these graphs, using a randomly-selected source vertex. We used a Cray XC30 system with 128 GB per node, 2 Intel Haswell CPUs (2.3 GHz sockets) per node, and 16 cores per socket. We ran a weak-scaling benchmark on these two kernels, meaning that as we scale up the number of cores available for computation, we proportionally scale up the problem size. Each core on average contained approximately 2^{24} graph edges, working out to 2^{29} edges per node. BFS is roughly a linear problem for these R-MAT graphs, so ideally we would expect the total time to stay constant. In practice over a distributed system this is not the case, but keeping the line as flat as possible is a good goal.

CombBLAS can only work over a square number of cores, which is why its results are more sparse. shgraph has no such restriction. We allow only 1 core per PE because shgraph is not yet multithreaded, whereas in practice we would assign more. Finally, we used the tdbfs (top-down BFS) CombBLAS program, which approximates the BFS algorithm we implemented for shgraph, and is the simplest BFS algorithm offered by CombBLAS.

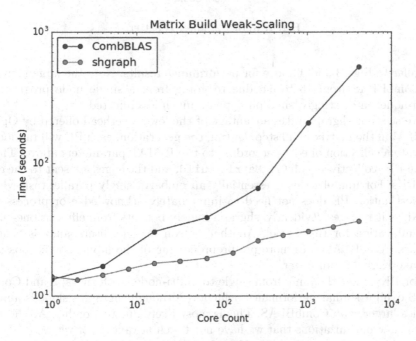

Fig. 3. Kernel 1. lower is better.

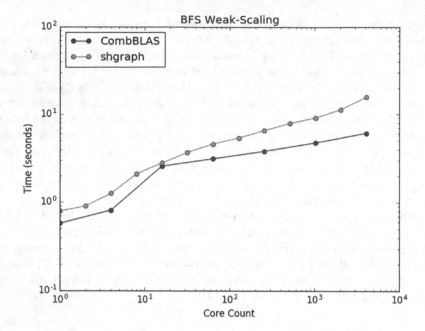

Fig. 4. Kernel 2. lower is better.

Refer to Figs. 3 and 4 above for performance results. Note the large increase for CombBLAS from 16 to 64, due to going from a single node program to multi-node. Interestingly, shgraph appears much less affected.

We see that shgraph takes advantage of the lower overhead offered by Open-SHMEM in the matrix build step. During the generation, each PE will randomly generate a collection of edges according to the R-MAT parameters above. Then, all the PEs collectively call `GrB_Matrix_build`, and the edges are sent to the correct PEs. Fortunately, this is essentially an embarrassingly parallel task where the destination PE does not need to immediately acknowledge or process the the edges it receives. Evidently, shgraph hugely benefits from efficient one-sided communication for this kernel. Another reason for the discrepancy is that it appears CombBLAS does more pre-preprocessing of the input matrix, possibly to make Kernel 2 run faster.

For BFS, after the jump from single to multi-node, both shgraph and CombBLAS exhibit similar performance behavior, although shgraph's slope is almost 3 times larger than CombBLAS. This is most likely due to CombBLAS' host of algorithmic optimizations that we have not taken advantage of yet.

Combining the runtimes for Kernels 1 and 2, shgraph runs significantly faster. While CombBLAS gets increasingly dominated by the matrix build time, shgraph is much less affected.

7   Future Work

As noted in Sect. 3, some work needs to be done to fully address error-handling for this type of SPMD application. There are numerous additional optimizations we can also exploit. We experimentally saw that 20–30% of our benchmarking runtime is spent in barrier functions, and ensuring that work is divided up evenly among the PEs can mitigate this. Providing additional overlapping for the computation and communication steps e.g. described in Sect. 5 could yield efficiency gains, although we have not explored this yet. Better permutation polynomials to distribute non-uniformly distributed matrices more evenly could also minimize the time spent in barriers.

As in Sect. 5, for most GraphBLAS operations shgraph will locally allocate N buckets on an N PE system. It is likely that there are some hierarchical decompositions of certain problems that would require fewer buckets. For example, if a vector-matrix product is relatively dense, this likely means that a lot of merging took place in Step 4 of Sect. 5. We could do repeated applications of Steps 3 and 4 where data is sent to subsets of PEs, and results are merged together (e.g. as a binary tree). This could potentially reduce the communication complexity, at the cost of some increased overhead.

8   Conclusion

shgraph demonstrates the viability of using OpenSHMEM for large-scale graph analytics. While shgraph has not been heavily engineered with space/time efficiency concerns in mind, and our focus was only for BFS, our results against CombBLAS suggest that it would be worth the effort to fully optimize the full package. By carefully structuring our algorithms, we are able to take advantage of the low overhead of OpenSHMEM's one-sided communication patterns.

To address the discrepancies between the GraphBLAS standard and SPMD implementations, an alternate standard would have to be created. Fortunately, since GraphBLAS was designed with parallelism in mind, this would be relatively reasonable to do so.

It should also be noted that while shgraph was engineered with graphs in mind, it can certainly be used for other general sparse matrix problems, such as machine learning applications.

Acknowledgments. We thank the three anonymous reviewers from the OpenSH-MEM Workshop, whose helpful and incisive advice produced a much better paper.

References

1. Buluç, A., Mattson, T., McMillan, S., Moreira, J., Yang, C.: The GraphBLAS C API specification. https://people.eecs.berkeley.edu/~aydin/GraphBLAS_API_C.pdf. Accessed 6 July 2018
2. Buluç, A., Mattson, T., McMillan, S., Moreira, J., Yang, C.: Design of the Graph-BLAS API for C. In: 2017 IEEE International Parallel and Distributed Processing Symposium Workshops, pp. 643–652. IEEE, Orlando (2017)
3. Kepner, J.: GraphBLAS Mathematics - Provisional Release 1.0 -. https://www.mit.edu/~kepner/GraphBLAS/GraphBLAS-Math-release.pdf. Accessed 6 July 2018
4. Buluç, A., Gilbert, J.R., Shah, V.B.: Implementing sparse matrices for graph algorithms. SIAM J. Sci. Comput. **22**, 287–314 (2011)
5. Dunbar, R.I.M.: Neocortex size as a constraint on group size in primates. J. Hum. Evol. **22**(6), 469–493 (1992)
6. Lawson, C.L., Hanson, R.J., Kincaid, D.R., Krough, F.T.: Basic linear algebra subprograms for FORTRAN usage. ACM Trans. Math. Softw. **5**(2), 308–323 (1979)
7. Duff, I., Heroux, M., Pozo, R.: An overview of the sparse basic linear algebra subprograms: the new standard from the BLAS technical forum. ACM Trans. Math. Softw. **28**(2), 239–267 (2002)
8. OpenSHMEM application programming interface. http://www.openshmem.org/site/sites/default/site_files/OpenSHMEM-1.3.pdf. Accessed 6 July 2018
9. Gilbert, J.R., Reinhardt, S., Shah, V.B.: Distributed sparse matrices for very high level languages. Adv. Comput. **72**, 225–252 (2008)
10. Buluç, A., Gilbert, J.R.: Challenges and advances in parallel sparse matrix-matrix multiplication. In: 2008 37th International Conference on Parallel Processing, pp. 503–510. IEEE, Portland (2008)
11. Buluç, A., Gilbert, J.R.: On the representation and multiplication of hyperspace matrices. In: 2008 IEEE International Symposium on Parallel and Distributed Processing, IEEE, Miami (2008)
12. Lidl, R., Mullen, G.L.: When does a polynomial over a finite field permute the elements of that field? Am. Math. Mon. **25**(3), 243–246 (1998)
13. Buluç, A., Gilbert, J.R.: Parallel sparse matrix-matrix multiplication and indexing: implementation and experiments. SIAM J. Sci. Comput. **32**(4), 170–191 (2011)
14. Gilbert, J.R., Moler, C., Schreiber, R.: Sparse matrices in MATLAB: design and implementation. SIAM J. Matrix Anal. Appl. **13**(1), 333–356 (1992)
15. Gustavson, F.G.: Finding the block lower triangular form of a matrix. In: Bunch, J.R., Rose, D.J. (eds.) Sparse Matrix Computations, pp. 275–289. Academic Press (1976)
16. Buluç, A., Gilbert, J.R.: The combinatorial BLAS: design, implementation, and applications. Int. J. High Perform. Comput. Appl. **25**(4), 496–509 (2011)
17. Satish, N., et al.: Navigating the maze of graph analytics frameworks using massive graph datasets. In: Proceedings of the 2014 ACM SIGMOD International Conference on Management of Data, pp. 1–12. Snowbird (2014)
18. Murphy, R., Bader, D., Snir, M.: Unveiling the first graph 500 list. In: International Conference for High Performance Computing, Networking, Storage and Analysis, New Orleans (2010)
19. Graph500. https://graph500.org/. Accessed 6 July 2018
20. Chakrabarti, D., Zhan, Y., Faloutsos, C.: R-MAT: a recursive model for graph mining. In: Proceedings of the SIAM Conference on Data Mining, Lake Buena Vista (2014)

Scaling OpenSHMEM for Massively Parallel Processor Arrays

James A. Ross[1(✉)] and David A. Richie[2]

[1] U.S. Army Research Laboratory, Aberdeen Proving Ground, MD, USA
james.a.ross176.civ@mail.mil
[2] Brown Deer Technology, Forest Hill, MD, USA
drichie@browndeertechnology.com

Abstract. The use of OpenSHMEM has traditionally focused on supporting a one-sided communication mechanism between networked processors. The US Army Research Laboratory (ARL) OpenSHMEM implementation for the Epiphany architecture has highlighted the utility of OpenSHMEM for the precise control of on-die data movement within arrays of RISC cores connected by a 2D mesh Network on Chip (NoC), and was demonstrated using a 16-core Epiphany-III coprocessor. More recently, DARPA has fabricated a much larger 64-bit 1,024-core Epiphany-V device, which ARL is presently evaluating. In support of this effort, we have developed an Epiphany-based RISC SoC device emulator that can be installed as a virtual device on an ordinary x86 platform and utilized with the existing software stack used to support physical devices, thus creating a seamless software development environment capable of targeting new processor designs just as they would be interfaced on a real platform. As massively parallel processor arrays (MPPAs) emerge as a strong contender for future exascale architectures, we investigate the application of OpenSHMEM as a programming model for processors with hundreds to thousands of cores. In this work we report on the initial results from scaling up the ARL OpenSHMEM implementation using virtual RISC processors with much larger core counts than previous physical devices.

Keywords: RISC · Network-on-Chip · Emulation · Simulation · Epiphany

1 Introduction

Recent developments in high-performance computing (HPC) provide evidence and motivation for increasing research and development efforts in low-power scalable massively parallel RISC array processor architectures. Massively parallel processors based on two-dimensional (2D) RISC arrays placed in first and fourth positions on the November 2017 list of Top500 supercomputers in the world [1] and the top three energy-efficient machines in the corresponding Green500 list [2]. Further, this was accomplished without the use of commodity processors and with instruction set architectures (ISAs) evolved from a limited ecosystem, driven primarily by research laboratories. Increasing research into new and innovative architectures has emerged as

© Springer Nature Switzerland AG 2019
S. Pophale et al. (Eds.): OpenSHMEM 2018, LNCS 11283, pp. 137–147, 2019.
https://doi.org/10.1007/978-3-030-04918-8_9

a significant recommendation as we transition into a post-Moore era [3] where old trends and conventional wisdom may no longer hold.

More rapid and open advances in hardware architectures will require unique capabilities in software development to resolve the traditional time lag between hardware availability and the software necessary to support it. This problem is long standing and one that is more pragmatic than theoretical. Significant software development for new hardware architectures will typically only begin once the hardware itself is available. Although some speculative work can be done, the effectiveness is limited. Very often the hardware initially available will be in the form of a development kit that brings unique challenges, and will not entirely replicate the target production systems. Based on our experience with Epiphany and other novel architectures, the pattern generally follows this scenario.

The focus of this research has been on the Epiphany architecture, which shares many characteristics with other RISC array processors but with emphasis on energy-efficient general purpose computation for floating point intensive applications. To the best of our knowledge, Epiphany is the only general purpose processor architecture capable of achieving the energy-efficiency projected to be necessary for exascale (50+ GFLOPS/Watt). The Adapteva Epiphany RISC array architecture [4] is a scalable 2D array of low-power RISC cores with minimal un-core functionality supported by an on-chip 2D mesh network for fast inter-core communication. The Epiphany-III architecture is scalable to 4,096 cores and represents an example of an architecture designed for power-efficiency at extreme on-chip core counts. Processors based on this architecture exhibit good performance/power metrics [5] and scalability via a 2D mesh network [6, 7], but require a suitable programming model to fully exploit the architecture. The 1024-core, 64-bit Epiphany-V was fabricated by DARPA and designed to have much higher performance and energy efficiency and scalability [8].

The overall motivation for this work stems from ongoing efforts to investigate future massively parallel processors based on the Epiphany architecture. At present we are investigating the design of a hybrid processor based on a 2D array of Epiphany-V compute cores with several RISC-V supervisor cores acting as an on-die CPU host. In support of such efforts, we developed a large-scale emulation and simulation capability to enable rapid design and specialization by allowing testing and software development using simulated virtual architectures. This work placed special emphasis on achieving a seamless transition between emulated architectures and physical systems. The overall design and implementation of the proposed emulation and simulation environment will be generally applicable to supporting more general research and development of other massively parallel RISC array processors.

As part of the exploration of massively parallel RISC array processors, an efficient on-chip programming model was required. The OpenSHMEM interface was uniquely positioned for this as it focuses on lightweight communication primitives for partitioned global address space (PGAS) platforms and was not encumbered by the complexity found in the Message Passing Interface (MPI). Here we present our approach and initial results from testing the ARL OpenSHMEM implementation on an emulated Epiphany device with up to 1,024 cores.

2 Background

The Adapteva Epiphany architecture is a scalable 2D array of RISC cores with minimal uncore functionality connected with a fast 2D mesh Network-on-Chip (NoC). Although it is capable of multiple program, multiple data (MPMD) execution, it is most easily programmed using single program, multiple data (SPMD) programming methods. The Epiphany-III (16-core) and Epiphany-IV (64-core) processors have a RISC CPU core that support a 32-bit RISC ISA with 32 KB of shared local memory per core (used for both program instructions and data), a mesh network interface, and a dual-channel DMA engine. Each RISC CPU core contains a 64-word register file, sequencer, interrupt handler, arithmetic logic unit, and a floating point unit. The fully memory-mapped architecture allows shared memory access to global off-chip memory and shared non-uniform memory access to the local memory of each core, enabling PGAS programming models. The Epiphany-V processor, shown in Fig. 1, was extended to support 64-bit addressing and floating-point operations. The 1,024-core Epiphany-V processor was fabricated by DARPA at 16 nm. The architecture is supported by the open source GNU compiler collection.

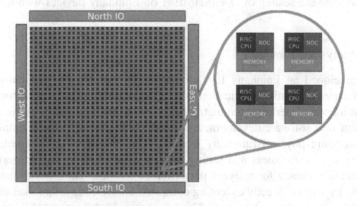

Fig. 1. The Epiphany-V RISC array architecture. A tiled array of 64-bit RISC cores are connected through a 2D mesh NoC for signaling and data transfer. Communication latency between cores is low, and the amount of addressable data contained on a mesh node is low (64 KB). Three on-chip 136-bit mesh networks enable on-chip read transactions, on-chip write transactions, and off-chip memory transactions.

Combining the preference for SPMD execution, PGAS programming models, and full support for the C programming language, the ARL OpenSHMEM for Epiphany implementation was developed to provide a standardized interface and device-level programming model for the Epiphany processor [9]. With the exception of some of the more recent multi-threading support added in the OpenSHMEM 1.4 specification, the OpenSHMEM interface suits the Epiphany architecture well. The 2D mesh network-on-chip is analogous to the network connecting nodes within an HPC cluster. However, the Epiphany network is trivially used so remote reads and writes correspond to load and store instructions to memory-mapped scratchpad memory. This compares very favorably against the complexity required in the Linux operating system, network interface driver software stacks, and networking hardware found in modern clusters. The full ARL OpenSHMEM implementation presently compiles to a library with less than 90 KB of binary code and no required external libraries. Typically, a small subset of the library is used within a device kernel code (approximately 2–5 KB).

3 Approach

Our approach for the development and testing of the OpenSHMEM software stack for future processors based on the Epiphany architecture employs an emulator used to create virtual Epiphany devices that may be integrated directly into the software stack used for physical coprocessor devices. This approach allows for development and testing in advance of the fabrication of physical devices and can be used for the co-design of future devices by evaluating the impact of architecture modifications within a real software stack that does not differ from that which would be employed for a real platform. In this section we provide an overview of this approach as it applies to our efforts to evaluate the scaling of OpenSHMEM on Epiphany devices with up to 1,024 cores.

3.1 Epiphany ISA Emulator

We have developed an Epiphany ISA emulator that enables fast emulation of real compiled binaries for testing application code. This is used to provide virtual devices operating at a level of performance that, albeit slower than real hardware, is amenable to integration into software development workflows identical to those employed for development using physical Epiphany devices. The objective of the emulator is to provide functional correctness and timing accuracy sufficient to predict performance with reasonable accuracy for relevant performance metrics. Thus, performance modeling is done by way of directly executing compiled binary code rather than employing theoretical models of the architecture. The advantage of this approach is that it will simultaneously provide a natural software development environment for proposed architectures and architecture changes without the need for physical devices. The software development and execution environment does not differ between emulation and execution on physical devices.

The design and implementation of an emulator for the Epiphany architecture is initially focused on the 32-bit architecture since physical devices are readily available for testing. The more recent extension of the ISA to support 64-bit instructions will be addressed in future work. The design uses an instruction decoder based on an indirect threaded dispatch model. The emulator for the 32-bit Epiphany architecture is implemented as a modular C++ class, in order to support the rapid composition and variation of specific devices for testing and software development. Implementing the emulator directly in C++, and without the use of additional tools or languages, avoids unnecessary complexity and facilitates modifications and experimentation. In addition, the direct implementation of the emulator in C++ will allow for the highest levels of performance to be achieved through low-level optimization. The emulator class is primarily comprised of an instruction dispatch method and implementations of the instructions forming the ISA. The emulator supports the Epiphany architecture special registers, dual DMA engines, and interrupt handler. The DMA engines and interrupt support are based on a direct implementation of the behaviors defined in the Epiphany architecture reference, and are controlled by the relevant special registers. Additional details can be found in Ref. [10].

The instruction dispatch design will allow for any instruction to stall in order to support more realistic behaviors. Memory and network interfaces are implemented as separate abstractions to allow for different memory and network models. The Open-SHMEM testing relies upon inter-core SRAM memory access mediated by the 2D Network on Chip. A simple memory model is used to incorporate the delay in reads and write instructions based on the distance between cores. In general, the delay for a transaction is modeled as,

$$\tau = 1.5 \times (|r - r_0| + |c - c_0|)$$

where r (c) and r0 (c0) are the row (column) of the remote and local cores, respectively. For read and test-set operations, instruction execution must stall until the transaction is complete and the result is received by the executing core. Data is sampled or written, after a delay of τ clock cycles corresponding to the forward transaction, and then delayed an additional τ clock cycles for the returning transaction. In the case of a write operation, the only delay is in the write transaction itself, whereas the instruction execution is not stalled.

The emulator does not operate as an isolated tool. Instead, it is used to create virtual Epiphany devices using a Linux shared memory segment that appears identical to the memory mapped interface of physical Epiphany co-processors found on Parallella platforms. The result is that the emulated virtual device appears indistinguishable from a physical device to applications targeting an Epiphany coprocessor using the COPRTHR-2 software stack [11]. Moreover, the emulator for the virtual devices is completely decoupled, operating independently from an application. All interaction between application and emulator occurs through the memory mapped signaling just like a physical device. The emulator is used to compose a device of the correct number of cores and topology, and then run "on top" of this shared memory region. By this, it is meant that the emulator core will have mapped its interfacing of registers, local SRAM, and external DRAM to specific segments of the shared memory region. By simply redirecting the COPRTHR API to map/dev/shm/e32 rather than /dev/epiphany/mesh0, user applications executing on the host see no difference in functionality between a physical and virtual Epiphany device. When the user executes a host application that utilizes the Epiphany coprocessor, it will find the virtual device to be active and running, just as it would find a physical device. The decoupling of the emulator and user application replicates realistic conditions and provides visibility into state initialization that was previously only indirectly known or guessed at during early software development.

It is worth emphasizing the transparency and utility of these virtual Epiphany devices. The Epiphany GCC and COPRTHR tool chains are easily installed on an x86 platform, and with which Epiphany application code can be cross-compiled. By simply installing and running the emudevd daemon on the same x86 platform, it is possible to then execute the cross-compiled code directly on the x86 platform. The result is a software development and testing environment equivalent to that of a Parallella development board. Furthermore, the virtual device is configurable in terms of the number of cores and other architectural parameters. It is also possible to install multiple virtual devices appearing as separate shared memory device special files under/dev/shm. Finally, through modifications to the (open-source) Epiphany emulator, researchers can explore "what-if" architecture design modifications. At the same time, the user application code is compiled and executed just as it would be on a Parallella development board with a physical device.

This transparency allows the ARL OpenSHMEM implementation to be tested on virtual Epiphany devices with differing core counts and architecture changes in a manner that does not differ from its use with real physical devices. The design creates a platform for experimenting with OpenSHMEM on virtual MPPA devices using a real software stack, where experiments can be investigated more rapidly than would otherwise be possible without this virtualization.

3.2   OpenSHMEM Scaling Tests

For testing we use the OpenSHMEM test programs originally used to evaluate the ARL OpenSHMEM implementation on a 16-core Epiphany-III coprocessor. Each test is compiled once using the standard workflow provided by the COPRTHR-2 SDK, and then executed on a virtual Epiphany device with up to 1,024 cores. The entire OpenSHMEM test suite was executed, but only interesting results appear below. The shmem_putmem routine is an example of an uninteresting result, where performance scales with the number of cores because all remote stores complete within a single clock regardless of the location on the network.

4   Results

The performance measurements represent an emulated device like Epiphany-III, with 32 KB of local scratchpad and a nominal clock rate. The results are used to identify any scaling issues and to correlate performance of the emulator on the ARL OpenSHMEM code base and new physical devices, independent of final clock rates. The results are executed on virtual Epiphany devices with 16, 64, 256, and 1,024 cores. A line plotted within a figure represents the predicted performance, across various workload sizes, for a device with one of those core counts. As an example of the architecture limitations, the shmem_alltoall64 routine is predicted to achieve high scaling performance for high core counts, but is fundamentally limited by the message size in the available scratchpad. The results in Fig. 2 represent scaling performance for the allocation of two 8 KB source and destination arrays across emulated devices with four different core counts.

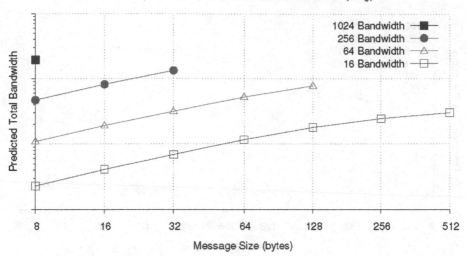

Fig. 2. OpenSHMEM shmem_alltoall64 predicted bandwidth scaling

The shmem_barrier routine showed logarithmic scaling with the number of cores (Fig. 3). There is a small amount of increasing overhead as the size of the emulated device increases.

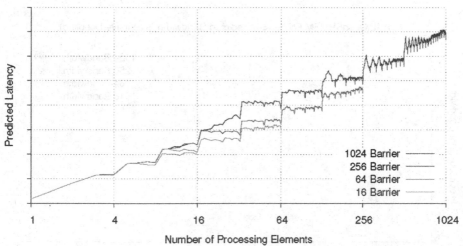

Fig. 3. OpenSHMEM shmem_barrier predicted performance scaling

The shmem_broadcast64 total bandwidth is expected to scale linearly with the number of cores (Fig. 4).

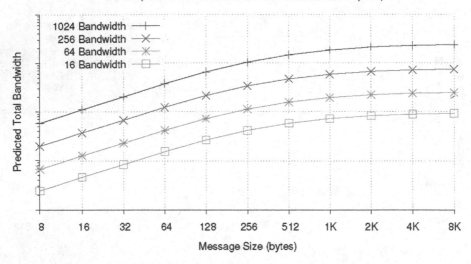

Fig. 4. OpenSHMEM shmem_broadcast64 predicted performance scaling

The shmem_fcollect64 routine has linear performance scaling, but cannot support larger message sizes at high core counts due to scratchpad limitations (Fig. 5).

The shmem_getmem benchmark fetches data from the neighboring core (Fig. 6). With the exception of an increased latency for cores at the end of the row, which have increased latency, the performance scaling is nearly linear with core count. It is

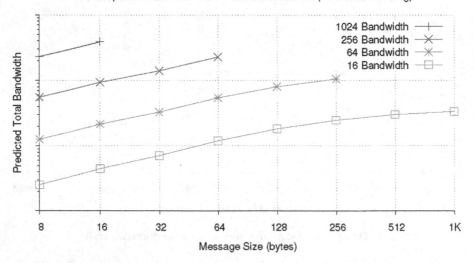

Fig. 5. ARL OpenSHMEM shmem_fcollet64 predicted performance scaling

expected that some network congestion will appear for unfavorable communication patterns, but it has not been modelled in this work.

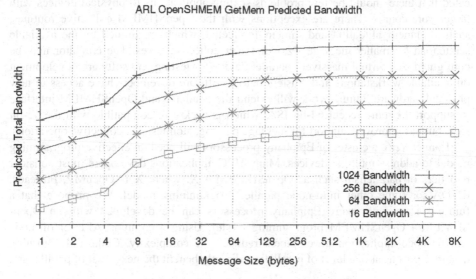

Fig. 6. ARL OpenSHMEM shmem_getmem predicted performance scaling

The predicted performance scaling of global reduction operations appears to have minimal loss in throughput as the number of cores increases (Fig. 7).

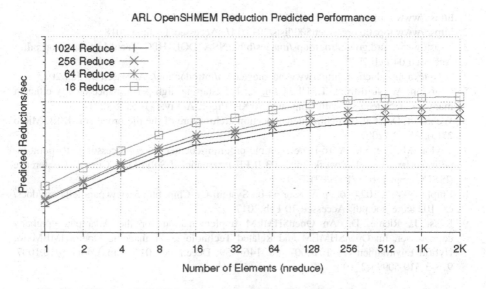

Fig. 7. ARL OpenSHMEM shmem_int_sum_to_all predicted performance scaling

5 Conclusion and Future Work

The performance scaling results of the ARL OpenSHMEM for Epiphany have indicated that there should be few problems scaling applications to physical devices with larger core counts. There are exceptions with the OpenSHMEM collective routines, such as shmem_alltoall64 and shmem_fcollect64, which are limited by the available scratchpad to smaller message sizes or fewer collective cores. The emulator may be configured as a virtual massively parallel device for testing and software development on available workstations and clusters before software developers have access to new physical hardware. Future work will extend the emulator and OpenSHMEM interface to support the more recent 64-bit ISA, which is backward compatible with the 32-bit ISA, but has improved support for message passing, atomics, and collective operations.

Longer-term, a cluster of Epiphany processors will need an effective programming model to address multiple devices. Many HPC applications developers must consider two tiers of parallelism such as OpenSHMEM + X, where X is OpenMP, Pthreads, CUDA, or some other intra-node parallel programming model. We propose that a future system with many Epiphany processors can be developed with an OpenSHMEM + OpenSHMEM programming model. Using a common API for off-node and on-node application development reduces the complexity. Code and algorithm design decisions at one level of parallelism directly benefit the next level of parallelism.

Acknowledgements. This work was supported by the U.S. Army Research Laboratory. Without the relative openness of the Adapteva Epiphany architecture and ISA, this work would have been more difficult.

References

1. https://www.top500.org/lists/2017/11/. Accessed 18 June 2018
2. https://www.top500.org/green500/lists/2017/11/. Accessed 18 June 2018
3. https://www.nitrd.gov/nitrdgroups/images/b/b4/NSA_DOE_HPC_TechMeetingReport.pdf. Accessed 04 Feb 2018
4. Adapteva introduction. http://www.adapteva.com/introduction/. Accessed 08 Jan 2015
5. Olofsson, A., Nordström, T., Ul-Abdin, Z.: Kickstarting high-performance energy-efficient manycore architectures with Epiphany. ArXiv Prepr. ArXiv:14125538 (2014)
6. Wentzlaff, D., et al.: On-chip interconnection architecture of the tile processor. IEEE Micro **27**(5), 15–31 (2007)
7. Taylor, M.B., et al.: A 16-issue multiple-program-counter microprocessor with point-to-point scalar operand network. In: 2003 IEEE International Solid-State Circuits Conference (ISSCC), pp. 170–171 (2003)
8. Epiphany-V: A 1024-core processor 64-bit System-On-Chip. http://www.parallella.org/docs/e5_1024core_soc.pdf. Accessed 10 Feb 2017
9. Ross, J., Richie, D.: An OpenSHMEM implementation for the Adapteva epiphany coprocessor. In: OpenSHMEM and Related Technologies. Enhancing OpenSHMEM for Hybrid Environments, vol. 10007, pp. 146–159, December 2016. https://doi.org/10.1007/978-3-319-50995-2_10

10. Richie, D., Ross, J.: Architecture emulation and simulation of future many-core epiphany RISC array processors. In: International Conference on Computational Science, ICCS 2018, Wuxi, China, 11–13 June 2018
11. Richie, D., Ross, J.: Advances in run-time performance and interoperability for the Adapteva epiphany coprocessor. Procedia Comput. Sci. **80** (2016). https://doi.org/10.1016/j.procs. 2016.05.47

Designing High-Performance In-Memory Key-Value Operations with Persistent GPU Kernels and OpenSHMEM

Ching-Hsiang Chu[1]([⊠]), Sreeram Potluri[2], Anshuman Goswami[2],
Manjunath Gorentla Venkata[3], Neena Imam[3], and Chris J. Newburn[2]

[1] Department of Computer Science and Engineering, The Ohio State University,
Columbus, OH 43202, USA
`chu.368@osu.edu`
[2] NVIDIA Corporation, Santa Clara, CA 95051, USA
{`spotluri,agoswami,cnewburn`}`@nvidia.com`
[3] Computer Science and Mathematics Division, Oak Ridge National Laboratory,
Oak Ridge, TN 37830, USA
{`manjugv,imamn`}`@ornl.gov`

Abstract. Graphics Processing Units (GPUs) are popular for their massive parallelism and high bandwidth memory and are being increasingly used in data-intensive applications. In this context, GPU-based In-Memory Key-Value (G-IMKV) Stores have been proposed to take advantage of GPUs' capability to achieve high-throughput indexing operations. The state-of-the-art implementations batch requests on the CPU at the server before launching a compute kernel to process operations on the GPU. They also require explicit data movement operations between the CPU and GPU. However, the startup overhead of compute kernel launches and memory copies limit the throughput of these frameworks unless operations are batched into large groups.

In this paper, we propose the use of persistent GPU compute kernels and of OpenSHMEM to maximize GPU and network utilization with smaller batch sizes. This also helps improve the response time observed by clients while still achieving high throughput at the server. Specifically, clients and servers use OpenSHMEM primitives to move data between CPU and GPU by avoiding copies, and the server interacts with

This work was sponsored by the U.S. Department of Energy's Office of Advanced Scientific Computing Research. This manuscript has been authored by UT-Battelle, LLC under Contract No. DE-AC05-00OR22725 with the U.S. Department of Energy. The United States Government retains and the publisher, by accepting the article for publication, acknowledges that the United States Government retains a non-exclusive, paid-up, irrevocable, world-wide license to publish or reproduce the published form of this manuscript, or allow others to do so, for United States Government purposes. The Department of Energy will provide public access to these results of federally sponsored research in accordance with the DOE Public Access Plan (http://energy.gov/downloads/doe-public-access-plan). This research was supported by the United States Department of Defense (DoD) and Computational Research and Development Programs at Oak Ridge National Laboratory.

S. Pophale et al. (Eds.): OpenSHMEM 2018, LNCS 11283, pp. 148–164, 2019.
https://doi.org/10.1007/978-3-030-04918-8_10

a persistently running compute kernel on the GPU to delegate various key-value store operations efficiently to streaming multi-processors. The experimental results show up to 4.8x speedup compared to the existing G-IMKV framework for a small batch of 1000 keys.

Keywords: OpenSHMEM · GPU · GPUDirect RDMA · In-Memory Key-Value Store

1   Introduction

In-Memory Key-Value (IMKV) stores like Memcached [13] and Redis [8] have become a critical part of many Internet service systems such as Facebook, YouTube and Twitter. IMKV stores act as caches in these systems to enable low latency and high throughput in the presence of an ever-increasing number of active users and exploding amount of online data. IMKV stores are highly data-intensive workloads and processing cores are usually blocked on pending data loads. Hence, high-throughput IMKV servers with a quick response time are highly desirable for these systems to serve more clients promptly.

Streaming Multi-processors (SM) on Graphics Processing Units (GPUs) are designed for highly data-parallel computation, and the memory subsystems on the GPU are designed for high-bandwidth data access. Compute Unified Device Architecture (CUDA) [4] is the *de facto* programming model for NVIDIA GPUs. Compute work is submitted to the GPU as CUDA kernels. Data movement between the CPU and GPU memories is accomplished using CUDA memory copy APIs, e.g., *cudaMemcpyAsync*, which typically trigger the Direct Memory Access (DMA) engines on the GPU.

Earlier research efforts have shown significantly higher throughput using GPUs in IMKV when compared to using CPUs [18,33]. Increasingly-powerful GPUs and advanced dense-server configurations with larger GPU counts per node enable IMKV stores to be supported with much less cluster infrastructure. This results in savings of both infrastructure cost and energy.

2   Motivation

In a KV store system, clients send queries and updates to key-value servers. First, the request is passed to the server with the input keys. Each server contains key-value pairs stored in memory. Upon receiving a request, a server executes KV operations that can be any typical database operations such as *insert, search or delete*, and the server responds to the client, as required. With a large number of clients each issuing many requests, key-value operations are highly data-parallel. This can be realized by multiple CPU threads or by offloading the operations onto accelerators such as GPUs.

In this section, we provide a detailed performance analysis of the state-of-the-art GPU-based IMKV stores, in particular, Mega-KV [33]. We identify the major performance issues that motivate the designs proposed in this paper. The state-of-the-art GPU-based IMKV design batches requests on the CPU, *i.e.*, system memory, at the server before launching a CUDA kernel to process the batch of operations on the GPU [33]. Explicit copy operations are used to move data between CPU and GPU memories. Multiple CUDA streams are used to pipeline compute kernels and copies so that the execution of copies and compute kernels are overlapped.

There are two limiters to performance in existing designs for GPU-based IMKV (G-IMKV): the **startup overhead** of compute kernel launches and memory copies. These factors limit the throughput of G-IMKV frameworks unless operations are batched into large groups. However, as GPUs get wider with more SMs, the batch size has to be larger to saturate the GPU with a single kernel launch. Unfortunately, this batching results in longer response times to the clients. In such scenarios, there is a trade-off between amortizing kernel launch overheads and higher response times.

Figure 1 shows visual profiles of runs using small and large batches of search operations in Mega-KV [33] on an NVIDIA Tesla P100 GPU. Note that a large batch means that all GPU threads are active to process the batch of keys in parallel. With the small batches of Fig. 1(a), we see that kernel and copy launch overheads dominate the runtime and show up as idle time on the GPU. Using several CUDA streams does not help overlap for the same reason. On the other hand, the profile with larger batches in Fig. 1(b) shows the overlap between launch overheads, memory copies, and compute kernels. However, this results in longer response times.

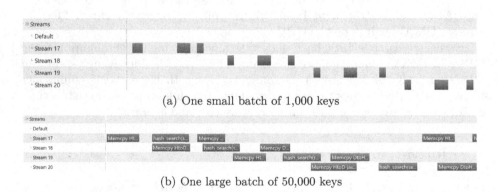

(a) One small batch of 1,000 keys

(b) One large batch of 50,000 keys

Fig. 1. A visual profile of the existing GPU-based search process for small and large batches. One batch is equally distributed into 4 CUDA streams to execute. Timelines are horizontal. Each row represents a CUDA stream executing search kernels and two data movement calls, *i.e.*, *cudaMemcpyAsync*.

In this paper, we propose the use of a persistent GPU compute kernel to amortize the overheads of repeated kernel launches and to improve GPU utilization. This also enables the use of smaller batch sizes, which improves the response time observed by clients. This work enables OpenSHMEM primitives for data movement in the GPU-based IMKV to significantly reduce synchronization overheads and to avoid additional copies. We leverage technologies like GPUDirect RDMA to achieve this. In the proposed designs, clients and servers use OpenSHMEM primitives to move data by preventing copies, and the server interacts with a persistently running compute kernel on its GPU to delegate various key-value store operations efficiently to streaming multi-processors. In this paper, we make the following key contributions:

- We demonstrate the use of persistent CUDA kernels to improve utilization of GPUs in IMKV and, in general, streaming applications.
- We demonstrate the use of an OpenSHMEM implementation equipped with GPUDirect RDMA to optimize data movement in IMKV stores.
- We present a detailed performance evaluation of the proposed designs.

3   Background

This section describes the necessary background knowledge related to this work.

3.1   NVIDIA GPU, CUDA and GPUDirect Technology

Graphics Processing Units (GPUs) have recently become the most popular accelerator for general-purpose computing due to their massive parallelism and high bandwidth memory (HBM). The NVIDIA Volta GPU architecture offers 900 GB/s HBM2, can achieve 14 TFLOPs of single precision, and is connected over Peripheral Component Interconnect Express (PCIe). As can be witnessed in [9], High-Performance Computing (HPC) systems are rapidly adopting GPU to accelerate not only traditional scientific applications but also machine learning and artificial intelligence applications.

CUDA [4] is the standard programming model for NVIDIA GPUs. It provides various APIs and libraries for developers to leverage the computing power of NVIDIA GPU hardware efficiently. In particular, GPUDirect technology [5] is a crucial component for developing high-performance applications. It has offered features such as peer-to-peer transfers and Remote Direct Memory Access (RDMA) since CUDA 5. Specifically, GPUDirect RDMA (GDR) enables third-party PCIe devices such as Network Interface Controllers (NICs) to directly access GPU memory without involving the CPU to reduce latency and to improve bandwidth significantly. As a result, designing high-performance GPU-Aware communication schemes with CUDA and GPUDirect technology has been widely discussed in the literature [11,29,31] and adopted by many communication libraries such like OpenMPI [6] and MVAPICH2-GDR [3].

3.2   GPU-Centric OpenSHMEM

OpenSHMEM is a partitioned global address space (PGAS) library specification, and many implementations such as Cray SHMEM and Sandia OpenSH-MEM are available [7]. It also has been integrated into Message Passing Interface (MPI) libraries such as OpenMPI [6] and MVAPICH2-X [3]. Furthermore, many advanced designs have been proposed to support GPU memory usage on heterogeneous clusters [16,27]. NVSHMEM takes a step further to enable GPU-initiated communication to leverage high-throughput NVIDIA GPUs and RDMA-enabled NICs [28,30]. Currently, OpenSHMEM only supports symmetric or homogeneous memory placement, which means that memory allocations and operations through OpenSHMEM (or NVSHMEM for GPU) must be all on either system or GPU memory, and not span both memory kinds.

3.3 In-Memory Key-Value Stores

As commodity memory has become cheaper in recent years, deployment of huge-memory servers has become common to improve the performance of data- and I/O-intensive workloads. Key-Value Stores (KVS) take advantage of low-cost memory to achieve in-memory caching, so-called In-Memory KV (IMKV) stores, which have become popular due to their low latency access to data. Although GPUs are ideal for data-intensive IMKV workloads, it is practically impossible to store an entire database in GPU memory, since the memory of single GPU is relatively much smaller than system memory (e.g., 32 GB vs. 256 GB). In [33], the authors propose to only offload *indexing* data structure and corresponding operations such as *search, deletion, and insertion* to GPUs. Specifically, small hash tables (typically a few GigaBytes), which contain keys and corresponding location IDs, are stored in GPU memory. Upon receiving requests from clients, the CPU is responsible for batching requests and issuing GPU kernels, which are in turn responsible for searching and returning location IDs based on the keys provided. CPUs can then use location IDs to retrieve or update *values* stored in system memory, and they respond back to clients as required.

4   Proposed Designs

In this section, we first present the use of OpenSHMEM primitives to support CPU-to-GPU one-sided communication. Next, we investigate the optimization opportunities for the existing G-IMKV design. Last, we describe the different design considerations to realize a high-performance key-value server that utilizes persistent GPU kernels.

4.1   Extending OpenSHMEM Primitives

As mentioned in Sect. 3.2, the current OpenSHMEM standard only supports a single symmetric heap. Therefore, one performance blocker for G-IMKV with OpenSHMEM is that an additional data copy is inevitable from CPU to GPU, at the server. Note that the clients of a KVS are usually light-weight machines without GPUs. In [26], Namashivayam *et al.* proposed multiple symmetric partitions in OpenSHMEM. We take a similar approach but with the flexibility to specify the location of each partition at each PE. Communication operations are allowed from/to/between memory allocations from any of the partitions. These extensions allow the use of OpenSHMEM primitives for direct CPU-GPU data movement between client and server on the proposed G-IMKV framework. We leverage NVIDIA GPUDirect RDMA feature with Mellanox InfiniBand to implement data movement primitives in OpenSHMEM as single-copy operations.

Figure 2 depicts the change in control and data flow from using standard OpenSHMEM primitives to using the extensions mentioned above. The four steps involved are as follows: (1) Client sends a request to the server. We depict this as two parts: data and signal, (2) Server copies the request into the GPU and signals the GPU, by launching a CUDA kernel, (3) GPU processes the request and a response is copied back onto the CPU, and (4) Server sends the response back to the client (this will also be a data and signal, but the detail is not shown). Figure 2(b) depicts the proposed approach using OpenSHMEM, the data path of Step 1 is directly written to GPU, and the data copy in Step 2 is avoided. The copy to system memory (SysMem) in Step 3 cannot be prevented as the CPU has to prepare the response by assembling the values as described in Sect. 3.3.

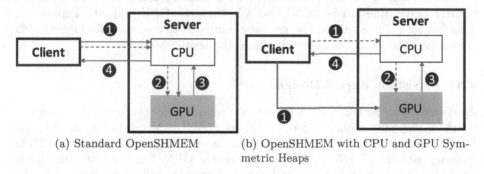

(a) Standard OpenSHMEM   (b) OpenSHMEM with CPU and GPU Symmetric Heaps

Fig. 2. Design space of GPU-based IMKV with OpenSHMEM. Bold and dashed lines represent data and control paths, respectively.

4.2 Data Placement Strategies

In a CUDA program, kernels are most performant when accessing data placed in GPU device memory due to the high memory bandwidth as mentioned in Sect. 3.1. In contrast, the PCIe bandwidth lags behind significantly. For PCIe generations 1, 2 and 3, the bandwidth has scaled from 3 to 6 to 12 GB/s over the same period.

Given the above considerations, it is common that data accessed by CUDA kernels are placed in GPU memory [33]. However, in existing G-IMKV system, requests and responses between clients and servers are typically exchanged over the network on SysMem. In this context, memory copies (e.g., *cudaMemcpyAsync*) are required before and after the CUDA kernels to move the data between SysMem and GPU memory (DevMem). In this work, we explore two other design choices for data placement.

NIC-to-Pinned-SysMem: First, we consider data placement on CUDA zero-copy memory. In a KVS operation, when the number of keys in a batch is small the required memory bandwidth is low. As a result, the PCIe bandwidth limit is not reached and there is no significant benefit from higher bandwidth to GPU memory. In such cases, the execution time of the CUDA kernel is similar between accessing data on pinned SysMem or GPU memory. More importantly, there is a fixed overhead to perform memory copies. Hence, for small batch sizes, the memory copy overhead is a limiting factor, and there is a threshold on batch size for efficient acceleration on the GPU. Zero-copy support, introduced in CUDA 2.0, allocates page-locked memory in SysMem that can be directly accessed by CUDA kernels. CUDA kernels can directly access pointers to such allocations over PCIe. This can potentially help to process small batch size, where the slower bandwidth to SysMem over PCIe does not matter since the peak bandwidth is not reached.

NIC-to-DevMem: Second, the batch of keys received over the network as input to the KVS can be directly placed in the GPU memory using GPUDirect RDMA (GDR) as described in Sects. 3.1 and 4.1 when the GPU and NIC support it. This further reduces the data access time compared to zero-copy for larger batch sizes where the PCIe bandwidth becomes the bottleneck.

4.3   Persistent Kernel Designs

As discussed in Sect. 2, CUDA kernels are launched by the server to process a batch of incoming requests from clients as Step 2 depicted in Fig. 2. Multiple CUDA streams are used to overlap data movement in and out of the GPU memory with the CUDA kernel execution on the GPU. For large batches, this is efficient because the overhead of CUDA API calls is negligible compared to the speedup due to GPU acceleration. However, when the batch size is small, the cost of CUDA API calls limits the throughput of KV operations processed on GPU. To deal with this problem, we adopt the persistent kernel approach similar to CPU KVS where persistent CPU threads wait to service client requests.

Persistent kernels present challenges as they stretch beyond the normal usage of the CUDA programming model. CUDA restricts GPU-NIC consistency at kernel launch boundaries. This restriction is bypassed for persistent kernels to receive requests from the client directly into GPU memory and then signal threads of an already-running CUDA kernel as shown in Fig. 2(b). In the context of x86 servers where the NIC and GPU are connected over PCIe, this consistency can be enforced by issuing a PCIe read to GPU memory (through GPU BAR) that is ordered after the NIC writes data to GPU. The read flushes the previous data writes to consistency on the GPU. In our implementation, the server thread on the CPU issues this consistency-enforcing read once it receives a signal from the client. The signal is ordered with respect to the data over the network (for example, issued on the same RC QP over InfiniBand). In this work, we propose two ways to mitigate the overhead of signaling CTAs (cooperative thread arrays, also known as a thread block): (1) Utilizing GDRcopy [1] to achieve low-latency data movement of signal flags. (2) Use data structures with padding for memory alignment, to enable multiple read operations performed in parallel over PCIe. These schemes can achieve smaller overhead compared to the regular kernel launch as will be evaluated in Sect. 5.4.

Moving data in and out of the GPU is accomplished using CUDA APIs in the non-persistent approach as in [33]. In a persistent kernel, this translates to a reverse offload where GPU threads signal CPU threads to invoke the CUDA API calls for data movement. It is possible that the data movement operation is queued behind the persistent kernel creating a circular dependency, which in turn leads to a deadlock. Due to this deadlock possibility, there are two alternatives to bypass the call to CUDA APIs for data copy. Either the persistent kernel has to read and write data using allocations on pinned SysMem or the persistent kernel needs to include the copies in a prolog and epilog to the kernel. Explicit copy regions at the beginning and end of the kernel can give better performance compared to random in-line accesses because of better coalescing of contiguous memory accesses on the GPU. We also experiment with copies using CPU-side CUDA APIs to show the potential benefit of using GPU's DMA engines. However, this may have the risk of deadlock in the current architectures, as explained above.

5   Evaluation

In this section, we present the evaluation results with IMKV workloads to demonstrate the performance improvement of the proposed designs. Specifically, we focus on the throughput of *Search* operation because it is one of the most critical indexing operations in IMKV [33].

5.1   Experimental Environment

The experiments were carried out on a cluster at NVIDIA. Each node is equipped with an Intel dual-socket 16-core E5-2698 v3 (Haswell) at 2.30 GHz, 256 GB host memory, NVIDIA Tesla P100 GPUs connected with PCIe Gen 3, and a Mellanox FDR InfiniBand host control adapter. Specifically, one NVIDIA Tesla P100 GPU has 16 GB DDR5 memory, 56 SMs and 3584 cores running at 1.33 GHz. The operating system is CentOS 7.5 with Linux kernel 3.10.0-862.2.3. We used CUDA toolkit 9.0.176 and NVIDIA driver 396.26.

The advanced data placement discussed in Sect. 4.2 and persistent kernel designs presented in Sect. 4.3 were implemented on top of Mega-KV [2,33]. We used MVAPICH2-X 2.3b [3] for CPU-CPU data movement. To achieve the CPU-to-GPU OpenSHMEM primitives, we extended NVSHMEM [28] over Infini-Band. In the data flows shown in Fig. 2(b), we used NVSHMEM for Step 1 and MVAPICH2-X for the others. We modified benchmarks from [2] to mimic real Client-Server behavior of IMKV system, where a 100% hit ratio of search is used, and report throughput as Million search Operations Per Second (MOPS). Here, we used one machine continuously issuing requests to emulate multiple clients. There are two major steps evaluated in this paper.

- **Request:** The client sends a request which contains a batch of keys with hash values to the server using OpenSHMEM's *shmem_put* API, followed by *shmem_fence* and *shmem_int_p* to indicate the completion of the put operation. In Sect. 5.3, we examined two variants of data placement on the remote server: (1) put a request into the SysMem, or (2) put request directly to DevMem using proposed primitives that bypass the CPU.
- **Search:** Once the server detects a new request coming it can either (1) repeatedly launch the search kernels as Mega-KV does, or (2) signal a pre-configured persistent kernel to perform search operations as proposed in Sect. 4.3. Moreover, depending on the data placement strategy, a search kernel can either access pinned SysMem directly without explicitly copy or move data from SysMem to DevMem. When a search kernel completes, an array of location IDs will be generated and copied from DevMem back to SysMem.

5.2   Baseline

To build a proper baseline, we evaluated Mega-KV with varying number of CUDA streams and batch sizes on our experimental environment. Figure 3(a) shows that a single CUDA stream yields the highest throughput until the batch size is larger than 9,000. Figure 3(b) indicates that 2 and 4 CUDA streams offer best performance as batch size is increased. This is because more overlap is possible when kernel execution and copy times of kernels are longer, at large batch sizes.

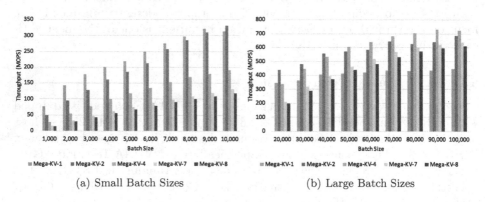

(a) Small Batch Sizes   (b) Large Batch Sizes

Fig. 3. Impact of number of CUDA streams on throughput of search operations in Mega-KV [33]. Number of CUDA streams is varying from 1, 2, 4, 7, and 8.

5.3   Data Placement

As discussed in Sect. 4.2, data in pinned buffers can be placed in DevMem or SysMem. We first present the evaluation of different data placement strategies and their impact on performance. There are three approaches. (1) SysMem with explicit data movements and 4 CUDA streams (**Mega-KV-4**): The request is received and stored in SysMem, and there is one copy (*i.e., cud-aMemcpyAsyn*) from SysMem to DevMem. This is the state-of-the-art proposed in [33]. (2) SysMem with implicitly data movement (**G-IMKV-SysMem**): This is equivalent to **Mega-KV** except that the search kernel accesses pinned Sys-Mem. Thus the GPU kernel can directly access it and perform the search operation in a load/store fashion to avoid issuing explicit copy calls from CPU. (3) DevMem without copies (**G-IMKV-GDR-CE**): The request is received and stored directly to DevMem using GDR-enabled OpenSHMEM primitives as shown in Fig. 2(b). Note that the results are still copied back to SysMem for CPU to prepare a response. Here, we used 4 CUDA streams for **Mega-KV**, *i.e., Mega-KV-4*, as it yields highest peak throughput as shown in Fig. 3. For **G-IMKV-SysMem** and **G-IMKV-GDR-CE**, we only used one CUDA stream for higher peak throughput since a higher number of CUDA streams shows no improvement as zero and low overlap between data transfer and kernel.

In Fig. 4, we compare the three approaches mentioned above. **G-IMKV-GDR-CE** yields the highest throughput for all batch sizes due to the elimination of extra data movement from SysMem to DevMem. The peak throughput of **G-IMKV-GDR-CE** (888 MOPS) is 1.2x and 4.6x higher than **Mega-KV** (729 MOPS) and **G-IMKV-SysMem** (191 MOPS), respectively. For processing smaller batches as shown in Fig. 4(a), the **G-IMKV-SysMem** is up to 3.6x faster than **Mega-KV-4** for batches smaller than 9,000 keys. However, **G-IMKV-SysMem** soon saturates PCIe bandwidth due to the many random accesses to pinned SysMem across the PCIe bus, which has limited bandwidth compared to GPU memory. For larger batch sizes, shown in Fig. 4(b), **Mega-KV-4** reaches peak through (729 MOPS) for the batch size of 90,000 keys. Note that this is higher than the peak throughput, *i.e.*, 303 MOPS, reported in [33] because the newer hardware architectures are used in our experiments (e.g., NVIDIA Kepler vs. Pascal GPU architectures).

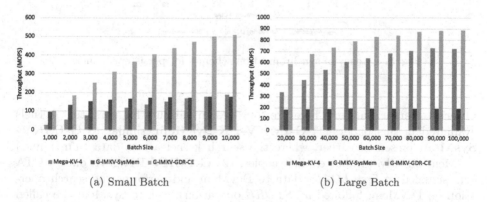

(a) Small Batch   (b) Large Batch

Fig. 4. Performance comparison of search operations among different data placement strategies

5.4   Persistent Kernel

In this section, we present the performance of the proposed persistent kernel designs as described in Sect. 4.3. We first examine the overhead of signaling persistent kernel. Next, we show the performance of search operations using different variants.

Signaling Overhead: We evaluated the signaling overhead for up to 112 CTAs, which is the maximum occupancy of the kernel on NVIDIA Pascal GPUs used in this paper. Figure 5 shows the latency of different approaches. Using the padding approach for SysMem yields latency as low as 4–5 μs, which stays nearly flat as the number of CTAs is increased. Similarly, using one-shot GDRCopy provides 2.6–5.7 μS across 1 to 112 CTAs, but latency grows faster than the padding approach. Kernel launch has a constant overhead, which is around 5 μs as of CUDA toolkit 9.0.176. Hence, the proposed persistent kernel designs have similar or lower synchronization cost compared to non-persistent kernel designs. However, unlike kernel launches which have a serialization effect at the GPU level, as shown in Sect. 2, the synchronization in the persistent kernel is done at a CTA granularity and hence can be pipelined more efficiently for small batch sizes. In the experiments presented in the rest of the paper, we used a padding approach to perform signaling between the CPU and the GPU.

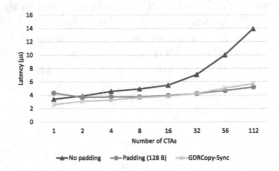

Fig. 5. Latency of synchronization schemes for persistent kernels

Overall Performance: There are four design variants for persistent kernels evaluated in this paper: (1) **G-IMKV-PK-SysMem**: similar to **G-IMKV-SysMem** presented earlier, where the search kernel access data from pinned SysMem directly without explicit copies, (2) **G-IMKV-PK-SM**: once a CTA gets signaled, it first *LOADs* data to DevMem and performs the search operation on DevMem, followed by *STORE* operations back to SysMem, we called it *SM-based copy* in the paper. (3) **G-IMKV-PK-GDR-SM**: with the proposed GDR-enabled OpenSHMEM primitives, the kernel can perform search operations immediately since data is ready on DevMem, followed by a *SM-based* *copy* of results back to SysMem, (4) **G-IMKV-PK-GDR-CE**: similar to **G-IMKV-PK-GDR-SM**, however, the use of Copy Engine performs copies to further utilize GPU hardware resources.

Figure 6 shows the performance comparisons among the four persistent kernel variants. Similar to **G-IMKV-SysMem** shown in Fig. 4, **G-IMKV-PK-SysMem** suffers from limited PCIe bandwidth (peak throughput is 198 MOPS). Although **G-IMKV-PK-SM** does not access SysMem directly during search operations, it suffers from PCIe bandwidth limitations as well when performing SM-based copies between SysMem and DevMem. However, better memory coalescing access makes **G-IMKV-PK-SM** significantly outperform (up to 2x faster) **G-IMKV-PK-SysMem**. On the other hand, GDR-enabled designs achieve much higher throughput. For the batch size of 1,000 as depicted in Fig. 6(a), with a memory-coalesced SM-based copy, **G-IMKV-PK-GDR-SM** achieves 2.7x higher throughput than **G-IMKV-PK-GDR-CE**, which has additional driver overhead to issue copies via the copy engines. However, for the batch size larger than 4,000, the driver overhead of **G-IMKV-PK-GDR-CE** becomes insignificant and lets **G-IMKV-PK-GDR-CE** achieve up to **848 MOPS**, which is 1.5x higher than **G-IMKV-PK-GDR-SM**. These results demonstrate the benefit of the proposed GDR-enabled OpenSHMEM primitives for IMKV.

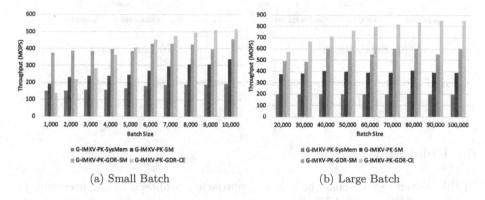

(a) Small Batch   (b) Large Batch

Fig. 6. Performance comparison among different persistent kernel-based designs

5.5   Persistent Versus Non-persistent Kernel Designs

One last question to answer is how persistent kernel designs compare with non-persistent kernel ones. Figure 7 presents the comparison between the state-of-the-art GPU-based IMKV (**Mega-KV-TUNED**. Which is tuned based on results in Fig. 3), and proposed **G-IMKV-GDR-CE**, and **G-IMKV-PK-GDR-OPT**, which is a tuned version between **G-IMKV-PK-GDR** and **G-IMKV-PK-GDR-CE** to obtain the highest throughput across all batch sizes. The proposed GDR-enabled designs significantly outperform **Mega-KV-TUNED** for all batch sizes by a factor of 1.2x to 4.8x. More importantly, the persistent kernel variant **G-IMKV-PK-GDR-OPT** can quickly achieve high throughput due to the low driver and synchronization overhead. For a sample batch size of 1,000, as shown in Fig. 7(a), **G-IMKV-PK-GDR-OPT** can easily get **373 MOPS**, which is 3.6x and 4.8x higher throughput than **G-IMKV-GDR-CE** and **Mega-KV-TUNED**, respectively. For large batch sizes, shown in Fig. 7(b), the peak throughput of **G-IMKV-GDR-CE** is **888 MOPS**, which is 1.04x and 1.23x higher than **G-IMKV-PK-GDR-CE** and **Mega-KV-TUNED**, respectively. It is worth noting that the proposed persistent kernel designs achieve comparable peak throughput to non-persistent kernel designs yet significant higher throughput for small batch sizes.

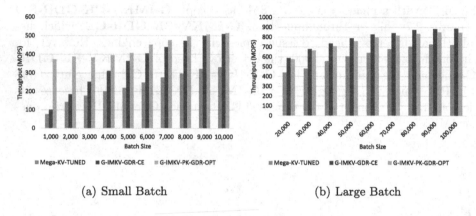

(a) Small Batch   (b) Large Batch

Fig. 7. Performance comparison between proposed designs and state-of-the-art

6   Related Work

In this section, we discuss the various approaches proposed in the literature to accelerate KVS and IMKVS. These approaches can be roughly categorized into three aspects: (1) Communication acceleration, e.g., RDMA-based, [12,14,15, 23–25,32], (2) Memory access acceleration, e.g., GPU-based, [17,18,20,22,33], and (3) Specialized programmable hardware, e.g., FPGA-based, [10,19,21].

Lu *et al.* propose the *RDMA-Memcached* library to leverage RDMA-enabled InfiniBand and high-performance SSD to achieve low latency and high throughput for distributed KVS [24]. Mitchell *et al.* propose *Pilaf* to allow clients to read server memory via RDMA primitives for fast KVS get and put operations [25]. DrTM-KV exploits advanced hardware features such as RDMA and Hardware Transactional Memory (HTM) to improve the performance of KVS [32]. MICA is optimized for multi-core architectures by data partitioning and new data structures for KVS, and achieve high throughput and low latency operations through bypassing the kernel with a light-weight networking stack [23]. SHMEMCache is the first attempt to leverage OpenSHMEM primitives to accelerate request and response times for distributed KVS on HPC systems [14,15]. In [17,18], Hetherington *et al.* characterize and design a scalable GPU-based KVS called MemchachedGPU [18]. Mega-KV strongly demonstrates the capability of GPU for high-performance and energy-efficient IMKV, showing 623 key-value operations per second with eight CPUs and eight Nvidia K40 GPUs [33]. Li *et al.* conduct a cross-layer system characterization to provide insights into leveraging essential software and hardware features for high-performance KVS systems [22]. It shows 120 million requests per second on a commodity dual-socket KVS system. NetCache leverages high-speed programmable switches for high-performance distributed KVS [19]. Blott *et al.* propose a Field Programmable Gate Array (FPGA)-based dataflow architecture to outperform traditional x86 servers for KVS operations [10]. KV-Direct leverages the FPGA programmable NICs to provide extended RDMA primitives for remote direct key-value access to accelerate IMKV operations [21].

Table 1. Summary of the proposed solutions compared to the state-of-the-art

Baseline	Bottleneck	Proposed solution	Result name	Speedup	Batch size
Mega-KV [33]	Copy engine overhead	Pinned SysMem	**G-IMKV-SysMem**	3.6x	1,000
G-IMKV-SysMem	SysMem to DevMem copies	GPUDirect RDMA	**G-IMKV-GDR-CE**	4.6x	100,000
G-IMKV-GDR-CE	Kernel launch overhead	Persistent Kernels	**G-IMKV-PK-GDR-SM**	3.7x	1,000
G-IMKV-PK-GDR-SM	SM-based Copy Inefficiency	Copy Engine for large batch	**G-IMKV-PK-GDR-CE**	1.5x	90,000

7   Concluding Remarks and Future Work

In this paper, we propose advanced designs of persistent CUDA kernel and GPUDirect RDMA-enabled OpenSHMEM primitives to provide low-latency and high-bandwidth memory and network access. As a result, high-throughput GPU-based In-Memory Key-Value (G-IMKV) Stores for all batch sizes become possible compared to the state-of-the-art as summarized in Table 1. The fundamental contributions of this paper are highlighted as follows.

– We identify that GPU kernel launches, explicit data copies, and PCIe bandwidth limitations are bottlenecks in the state-of-the-art G-IKMV.
– We demonstrate the use of persistent CUDA kernels to hide driver overhead and improve utilization of GPUs.
– We demonstrate the use of an OpenSHMEM implementation equipped with GPUDirect RDMA to optimize data movement: G-IMKV-GDR obtained 3.83x the peak throughput of Mega-KV.

– The proposed G-IMKV-GDR design achieves 888 MOPS, which is 1.23x
the peak of Mega-KV, and the proposed G-IMKV-GDR-OPT has 4.8x the
throughput of Mega-KV-4 at a batch size of 1,000.

Future work includes implementing all indexing operations, further exploring optimization techniques with persistent CUDA kernels and evaluating the
proposed designs using benchmarks and applications in various aspects.

References

1. A fast GPU memory copy library based on NVIDIA GPUDirect RDMA technology.
   https://github.com/NVIDIA/gdrcopy. Accessed 9 Sept 2018
2. Mega-KV: A GPU-Based In-Memory Key-Value Store. http://kay21s.github.io/
   megakv/. Accessed 9 Sept 2018
3. MVAPICH: MPI over InfiniBand, Omni-Path, Ethernet/iWARP, and RoCE.
   http://mvapich.cse.ohio-state.edu/. Accessed 9 Sept 2018
4. NVIDIA CUDA. http://docs.nvidia.com/cuda. Accessed 9 Sept 2018
5. NVIDIA GPUDirect. https://developer.nvidia.com/gpudirect. Accessed 9 Sept
   2018
6. OpenMPI: Open Source High Performance Computing. http://www.open-mpi.
   org/. Accessed 9 Sept 2018
7. OpenSHMEM.org. http://www.openshmem.org/site/. Accessed 9 Sept 2018
8. Redis. https://redis.io/. Accessed 9 Sept 2018
9. Top 500 Supercomputer sites. http://www.top500.org/. Accessed 9 Sept 2018
10. Blott, M., Karras, K., Liu, L., Vissers, K., Bär, J., István, Z.: Achieving 10Gbps
    line-rate key-value stores with FPGAs. In: Presented as Part of the 5th USENIX
    Workshop on Hot Topics in Cloud Computing, San Jose, CA. USENIX (2013)
11. Chu, C.H., Hamidouche, K., Venkatesh, A., Awan, A.A., Panda, D.K.: CUDA
    kernel based collective reduction operations on large-scale GPU clusters. In: 2016
    16th IEEE/ACM International Symposium on Cluster, Cloud and Grid Computing
    (CCGrid), pp. 726–735, May 2016
12. Dragojević, A., Narayanan, D., Castro, M., Hodson, O.: FaRM: fast remote mem-
    ory. In: 11th USENIX Symposium on Networked Systems Design and Implemen-
    tation (NSDI 14), Seattle, WA, pp. 401–414. USENIX Association (2014)
13. Fitzpatrick, B.: Distributed caching with memcached. Linux J. **2004**(124), 5 (2004)
14. Fu, H., Venkata, M.G., Choudhury, A.R., Imam, N., Yu, W.: High-performance key-
    value store on OpenSHMEM. In: 2017 17th IEEE/ACM International Symposium
    on Cluster, Cloud and Grid Computing (CCGRID), pp. 559–568, May 2017
15. Fu, H., SinghaRoy, K., Venkata, M.G., Zhu, Y., Yu, W.: SHMemCache: enabling
    memcached on the OpenSHMEM global address model. In: Gorentla Venkata, M.,
    Imam, N., Pophale, S., Mintz, T.M. (eds.) OpenSHMEM 2016. LNCS, vol. 10007,
    pp. 131–145. Springer, Cham (2016). https://doi.org/10.1007/978-3-319-50995-2_9
16. Hamidouche, K., Venkatesh, A., Awan, A.A., Subramoni, H., Chu, C.H., Panda,
    D.K.: Exploiting GPUDirect RDMA in designing high performance OpenSHMEM
    for NVIDIA GPU clusters. In: 2015 IEEE International Conference on Cluster
    Computing, pp. 78–87, September 2015

17. Hetherington, T.H., Rogers, T.G., Hsu, L., O'Connor, M., Aamodt, T.M.: Characterizing and evaluating a key-value store application on heterogeneous CPU-GPU systems. In: 2012 IEEE International Symposium on Performance Analysis of Systems Software, pp. 88–98, April 2012

18. Hetherington, T.H., O'Connor, M., Aamodt, T.M.: MemcachedGPU: scaling-up scale-out key-value stores. In: Proceedings of the Sixth ACM Symposium on Cloud Computing. SoCC 2015, pp. 43–57. ACM, New York (2015)

19. Jin, X., et al.: NetCache: balancing key-value stores with fast in-network caching. In: Proceedings of the 26th Symposium on Operating Systems Principles, SOSP 2017, pp. 121–136. ACM, New York (2017)

20. Kim, J., Lee, S., Vetter, J.S.: PapyrusKV: a high-performance parallel key-value store for distributed NVM architectures. In: Proceedings of the International Conference for High Performance Computing, Networking, Storage and Analysis, SC 2017, pp. 57:1–57:14. ACM, New York (2017)

21. Li, B., et al.: KV-Direct: high-performance in-memory key-value store with programmable NIC. In: Proceedings of the 26th Symposium on Operating Systems Principles, SOSP 2017, pp. 137–152. ACM, New York (2017)

22. Li, S., et al.: Architecting to achieve a billion requests per second throughput on a single key-value store server platform. In: Proceedings of the 42nd Annual International Symposium on Computer Architecture, ISCA 2015, pp. 476–488, ACM, New York (2015)

23. Lim, H., Han, D., Andersen, D.G., Kaminsky, M.: MICA: a holistic approach to fast in-memory key-value storage. In: 11th USENIX Symposium on Networked Systems Design and Implementation (NSDI 14), Seattle, WA, pp. 429–444. USENIX Association (2014)

24. Lu, X., Shankar, D., Panda, D.K.: Scalable and distributed key-value store-based data management using RDMA-memcached. IEEE Data Eng. Bull. **40**, 50–61 (2017)

25. Mitchell, C., Geng, Y., Li, J.: Using one-sided RDMA reads to build a fast, CPU-efficient key-value store. In: Presented as Part of the 2013 USENIX Annual Technical Conference (USENIX ATC 13), San Jose, CA, pp. 103–114. USENIX (2013)

26. Namashivayam, N., et al.: Symmetric memory partitions in OpenSHMEM: a case study with Intel KNL. In: Gorentla Venkata, M., Imam, N., Pophale, S. (eds.) OpenSHMEM 2017. LNCS, vol. 10679, pp. 3–18. Springer, Cham (2018). https://doi.org/10.1007/978-3-319-73814-7_1

27. Potluri, S., Bureddy, D., Wang, H., Subramoni, H., Panda, D.K.: Extending Open-SHMEM for GPU computing. In: 2013 IEEE 27th International Symposium on Parallel and Distributed Processing, pp. 1001–1012, May 2013

28. Potluri, S., Goswami, A., Rossetti, D., Newburn, C.J., Venkata, M.G., Imam, N.: GPU-Centric communication on NVIDIA GPU clusters with InfiniBand: a case study with OpenSHMEM. In: 2017 IEEE 24th International Conference on High Performance Computing (HiPC), pp. 253–262, December 2017

29. Potluri, S., Hamidouche, K., Venkatesh, A., Bureddy, D., Panda, D.: Efficient Internode MPI communication using GPUDirect RDMA for infiniband clusters with NVIDIA GPUs. In: 2013 42nd International Conference on Parallel Processing (ICPP), pp. 80–89, October 2013

30. Potluri, S., Goswami, A., Venkata, M.G., Imam, N.: Efficient breadth first search on multi-GPU systems using GPU-centric OpenSHMEM. In: Gorentla Venkata, M., Imam, N., Pophale, S. (eds.) OpenSHMEM 2017. LNCS, vol. 10679, pp. 82–96. Springer, Cham (2018). https://doi.org/10.1007/978-3-319-73814-7_6

31. Wang, H., Potluri, S., Bureddy, D., Rosales, C., Panda, D.K.: GPU-aware MPI on RDMA-enabled clusters: design, implementation and evaluation. IEEE Trans. Parallel Distrib. Syst. **25**(10), 2595–2605 (2014). Oct
32. Wei, X., Shi, J., Chen, Y., Chen, R., Chen, H.: Fast in-memory transaction processing using RDMA and HTM. ACM Trans. Comput. Syst. **35**, 3:1–3:37 (2015)
33. Zhang, K., Wang, K., Yuan, Y., Guo, L., Lee, R., Zhang, X.: Mega-KV: a case for GPUs to maximize the throughput of in-memory key-value stores. Proc. VLDB Endow. **8**(11), 1226–1237 (2015). Jul

OpenSHMEM Simulators, Tools, and Benchmarks

Tracking Memory Usage in OpenSHMEM Runtimes with the TAU Performance System

Nicholas Chaimov[1]([✉]), Sameer Shende[1], Allen Malony[1],
Manjunath Gorentla Venkata[2], and Neena Imam[2]

[1] ParaTools, Inc., 2836 Kincaid St., Eugene, OR 97405, USA
{nchaimov,sameer,malony}@paratools.com
[2] Oak Ridge National Laboratory, 1 Bethel Valley Rd, Oak Ridge, TN 37831, USA
{manjugv,imamn}@ornl.gov

Abstract. As the exascale era approaches, it is becoming increasingly important that runtimes be able to scale to very large numbers of processing elements. However, by keeping arrays of sizes proportional to the number of PEs, an OpenSIIMEM implementation may be limited in its scalability to millions of PEs. In this paper, we describe techniques for tracking memory usage by OpenSHMEM runtimes, including attributing memory usage to runtime objects according to type, maintaining data about hierarchical relationships between objects and identification of the source lines on which allocations occur. We implement these techniques in the TAU Performance System using atomic and context events and demonstrate their use in OpenSHMEM applications running within the Open MPI runtime, collecting both profile and trace data. We describe how we will use these tools to identify memory scalability bottlenecks in OpenSHMEM runtimes.

Keywords: Open MPI · TAU · Memory · Scalability

1 Introduction

With the approach of the exascale era, the ability for applications to scale to large numbers of cores becomes increasingly important. While applications themselves must be designed with scalability in mind, even a well-designed application may be limited in its scalability by design decisions made in the underlying runtime used by the application for distributed communications. The scaling behavior of runtime memory usage is of particular concern, since exascale systems are expected to have fewer bytes of memory per core than current HPC systems. Runtimes which keep per-processing-element arrays of sizes proportional to the number of processing elements will be limiting themselves as the number of processing elements scales into the millions. In order to design OpenSHMEM runtimes for exascale systems, it will be necessary to characterize the memory

© Springer Nature Switzerland AG 2019
S. Pophale et al. (Eds.): OpenSHMEM 2018, LNCS 11283, pp. 167–179, 2019.
https://doi.org/10.1007/978-3-030-04918-8_11

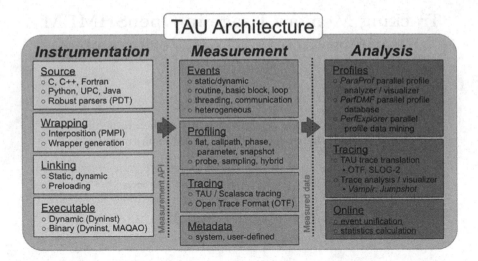

Fig. 1. The architecture of the TAU Performance System. TAU offers multiple mechanisms for application instrumentation, multiple types of measurements, and a suite of tools for analyzing performance data.

scaling behavior of those runtimes. In this paper, we describe our implementation of memory tracking within the TAU Performance System [10].

The TAU Performance System, the architecture of which is shown in Fig. 1 is a powerful and highly versatile profiling and tracing tool ecosystem for performance analysis of parallel programs. Developed over the last twenty years, TAU has evolved with each new generation of HPC systems and presently scales efficiently to hundreds of thousands of cores on the largest machines in the world. TAU can be applied in a portable way to codes written in Fortran, C, C++, Java, and Python, which utilize MPI and/or OpenSHMEM message communication and/or multi-threading (e.g., pthread, OpenMP) for execution across different parallel machines. It can be used through automatic or manual source instrumentation, runtime sampling, binary rewriting, and through library wrapping and interposition. TAU offers native support for performance monitoring of OpenSHMEM applications across several different OpenSHMEM runtimes through automatic generation of library wrappers created by parsing runtime-provided header files [8].

2   Memory Tracking Techniques

2.1   Tracking Allocations with Library Interposition

Our initial approach to monitoring the runtime overhead of OpenSHMEM runtimes was to use TAU's heap tracking support in conjunction with context events to identify the sizes of allocations and to attribute allocations to the application or the underlying runtime. In library interposition, TAU provides alternate implementations for existing library functions which record data about the library call and then call the original implementation of the function. To track heap allocations using library interposition, TAU substitutes its own implementations of `malloc` and `free` and related functions. These record *context events* into the profile or trace being generated. Within TAU, *atomic events* record that an event with a name occurred with a given value; context events record the name and value separately for each callpath along which events of that name occur. Using this approach, we can distinguish between memory allocations that occur inside the runtime (for which an OpenSHMEM API call is on the callpath) and those which occur at the application level (for which no OpenSHMEM API calls are on the callpath).

Name △	Total	NumSamples	MaxValue	MinValue	MeanValue	Std. Dev.
▶ .TAU application						
Decrease in Heap Memory (KB)	0.007	0.188	0.036	0.036	0.036	0
Heap Allocate	59,894,454.571	74,735.352	4,194,304	1	801.421	36,159.707
Heap Free	28,335,073.63	45,649.867	4,194,304	1	620.704	29,656.05
Heap Memory Used (KB)	1,761,526,448.384	125,252.594	30,931.747	0.078	14,063.792	8,228.491
Heap Memory Used (KB) at Entry	8,143,537,888.971	263,345	30,931.747	134.328	30,923.457	159.489
Heap Memory Used (KB) at Exit	8,143,599,224.529	263,345	30,931.747	27,577.029	30,923.69	128.898
Increase in Heap Memory (KB)	61,335.594	5	30,668.419	0.152	12,267.119	13,794.88

Fig. 2. ParaProf's Context Event window showing the top-level memory usage statistics collected for GUPS on 128 PEs, showing overall heap allocations for GUPS on 128 PEs.

	Total	NumSamples	MaxValue	MinValue	MeanValue	Std. Dev.
▼ void shmem_init(void) C						
Heap Memory Used (KB) at Entry	135.609	1	135.609	135.609	135.609	0
Heap Allocate	56,441,752.868	74,058.289	4,194,304	1	762.126	34,251.795
Heap Free	28,185,517.874	45,125.633	4,194,304	1	624.601	29,821.428
Memory Error! Allocation of zero bytes	71.961	71.961	1	1	1	0
Heap Memory Used (KB) at Exit	27,577.03	1	27,577.03	27,577.03	27,577.03	0
Increase in Heap Memory (KB)	27,441.421	1	27,441.421	27,441.421	27,441.421	0

Fig. 3. ParaProf's Context Event window showing the heap allocation statistics which occurred within the `shmem_init` runtime function. Comparing the *Heap Allocate* value here with the top-level timer shows that nearly all of the heap bytes allocated were allocated within `shmem_init`.

Name △	Total	NumSam...	MaxValue	MinValue	MeanValue	Std. Dev.
▼ .TAU application						
Heap Memory Used (KB) at Entry	134.328	1	134.328	134.328	134.328	0
Heap Allocate	132,096	2	131,072	1,024	66,048	65,024
Heap Free	132,608.725	2.016	131,072	1,016.625	65,790.375	64,958.044
Heap Memory Used (KB) at Exit	30,802.747	1	30,802.747	30,802.747	30,802.747	0
Increase in Heap Memory (KB)	30,668.419	1	30,668.419	30,668.419	30,668.419	0

Fig. 4. ParaProf's Context Event window showing the heap allocation statistics which occurred within the `.TAU Application` timer. Since only OpenSHMEM runtime functions were instrumented in this run, this represents application-level allocations.

We demonstrate this approach, as we will with the others described in this paper, using the Giga Updates Per Second (GUPS) benchmark code [5][1] and the Open MPI runtime [4]. We collect heap allocation data, and distinguish between runtime and application events, by using library interposition to wrap memory allocation and OpenSHMEM API calls using an unmodified application and runtime. Figure 2 shows the Context Event window of TAU's ParaProf tool displaying the overall memory usage statistics for GUPS run on 128 PEs on the University of Oregon Talapas system. Context-specific allocation data for the shmem_init function and for uninstrumented (application) functions are shown in Figs. 3 and 4, respectively. The results show that nearly all the heap memory allocated during the run is allocated in the shmem_init function, which allocates both various internal runtime data structures as well as the symmetric heap itself.

Tracking allocations in this way provides a view of the total bytes allocated and deallocated for the application as a whole and per function, but this does not tell us the amount of memory actually consumed by the application (as it may repeatedly allocate and free memory). To provide this data, TAU provides memory footprint tracking, in which the resident set size (VmRSS) and peak memory usage/high-water mark (VmHWM) are periodically sampled.

2.2 Instrumentation of the OpenSHMEM Object System

The allocation tracking approach of recording the sizes passed to calls to malloc and free within different functions allowed us to identify that most allocations were occurring within the call to shmem_init, but does not tell us *what* runtime objects account for the allocations. General approaches to identifying the object *types* associated with allocations are difficult to implement for C code, as the necessary information is not available at runtime. We therefore use an approach of manually instrumenting the Open MPI runtime. The Open MPI runtime's lowest-level layer, OPAL, defines an object system which is used by the higher level ORTE, OMPI, and OSHMEM components, which allows for centralized instrumentation of the allocations of instances of OPAL classes.

Our initial implementation added a public API calls to TAU:

```
void Tau_track_class_allocation(const char * name, size_t size);
```

This call registers an allocation of a particular type (indicated by the name) and size by triggering an atomic or context event within TAU. Adding a single line to the Open MPI runtime code responsible for allocating memory for object instances (opal_obj_new in opal/class/opal_object.h) allows us to record those allocations:

```
static inline opal_object_t *opal_obj_new(opal_class_t * cls)
{
  opal_object_t *object;
  assert(cls->cls_sizeof >= sizeof(opal_object_t));
  Tau_track_class_allocation(cls->cls_name, cls->cls_sizeof);
  [...]
}
```

The initial implementation successfully allowed us to collect data on the memory usage by data type, but did not allow for collection of hierarchical data. Open MPI runtime objects often contain pointers to other objects which are allocated during the initial construction of the first object or shortly thereafter and are properly considered to be owned by the first object. We wished to (1) where possible, *automatically* capture this hierarchical relationship and (2) where not possible, provide a mechanism for manual instrumentation to define the relationship. For our second implementation, we added two new API calls to TAU:

```
void Tau_start_class_allocation(const char * name, size_t size,
   int include_in_parent);
void Tau_stop_class_allocation(const char * name, int record);
```

The `Tau_start_class_allocation` and `Tau_stop_class_allocation` calls are used for recording the sizes of objects, including their child objects. When an allocation region is started, new allocation regions opened *within* the parent region are recorded as *both* a standard atomic event and as a context event indicating, rather than the enclosing *functions*, the the enclosing *allocation regions*. For example,

```
Tau_start_class_allocation("a", 10, 0);
Tau_start_class_allocation("b", 25, 0);
Tau_stop_class_allocation("b", 1);
Tau_stop_class_allocation("a", 1);
Tau_start_class_allocation("b", 10, 0);
Tau_stop_class_allocation("b", 1);
```

will record the atomic events

```
alloc a        10
alloc b        35
alloc b <= a   25
```

which indicates that 10 bytes of a objects were allocated, 35 bytes of b objects were allocated, and 25 bytes of the b objects were child allocations of a objects.

Allocations of most objects in the Open MPI runtime are captured by instrumenting, as before, the `opal_obj_new` function in `opal/class/opal_object.h`, which is called to construct most objects in the OPAL class hierarchy. In this implementation, we wrap the call to the class constructors for the object being instantiated, which automatically captures any child allocations which occur inside the constructor:

```
static inline opal_object_t *opal_obj_new(opal_class_t * cls)
{
    opal_object_t *object;
    assert(cls->cls_sizeof >= sizeof(opal_object_t));

    Tau_start_class_allocation(cls->cls_name, cls->cls_sizeof, 0);

#if OPAL_WANT_MEMCHECKER
    object = (opal_object_t *) calloc(1, cls->cls_sizeof);
#else
    object = (opal_object_t *) malloc(cls->cls_sizeof);
#endif
    if (opal_class_init_epoch != cls->cls_initialized) {
        opal_class_initialize(cls);
    }
    if (NULL != object) {
        object->obj_class = cls;
        object->obj_reference_count = 1;
        opal_obj_run_constructors(object);
    }
    Tau_stop_class_allocation(cls->cls_name, 1);
    return object;
}
```

By using allocation regions, this automatically captures any child allocations that occur within the constructor of the class. For example, the constructor for `orte_rml_posted_recv_t` allocates an object of type `orte_rml_recv_request_t`, and this allocation is recorded as `alloc orte_rml_posted_recv_t <= orte_rml_recv_request_t` in the profile.

This technique does *not* capture any child objects which are allocated *outside* of the constructor for a class. There is no central location where such tracking could be implemented, so any such child allocations are instrumented manually. To do this, *dummy allocation regions* are used to indicate the parent of an allocation without actually recording an atomic event for the parent, which was already record through `opal_obj_new`. To do this, `Tau_start_class_allocation` is called normally, child allocations are recorded, and `Tau_stop_class_allocation` is then called with the `record` parameter set to 0.

A final modification to the Open MPI runtime was to add dummy implementations of the three new TAU API calls which do nothing. These functions are declared with weak linkage, so that another implementation can override the dummy versions. By using this technique, the instrumented Open MPI runtime can be run without TAU with little overhead, and TAU instrumentation can be accomplished by simply linking the application against, or preloading, the TAU library.

We ran GUPS with the TAU memory allocation tracking approach described in this section for 16, 32, 64, 128, 256, 512, and 1,024 processing elements (PEs) on the University of Oregon Talapas system. The results for the subset of objects whose child allocations were manually instrumented is shown in

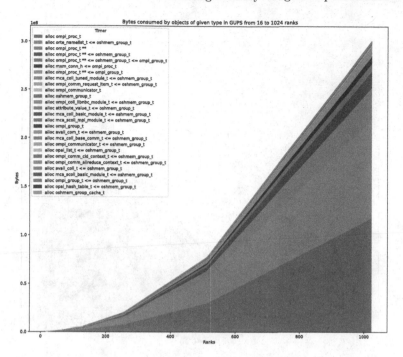

Fig. 5. Total memory allocations in bytes of a subset of OPAL object types during execution of the GUPS benchmark on between 16 and 1,024 processing elements.

Fig. 5. The results show that among the object types inspected, the fastest-growing are ompi_proc_t, which grows to consume 117 MB at 1,024 PEs, and orte_namelist_t as a child of oshmem_group_t, which grows to consume 100 MB at 1,024 PEs. Allocations of these object types will be bottlenecks as the number of PEs increases.

2.3 Memory Allocation Tracing

As with instrumenting malloc and free, profiling memory allocations using instrumentation regions gives us a *total* count for bytes allocated and bytes freed by type, but does not tell us the actual peak memory usage by type. Recording the memory high-water-mark does not help in this case, as the high-water-mark is recorded per-process and not per-type. Figure 6 shows allocations for *all* OPAL data type allocated during runs of GUPS on 16 to 1,024 PEs. While the objects types shown in Fig. 5 are allocated all at once during startup and not deallocated until shmem_finalize, this is not true of OPAL objects in general. Among *all* OPAL object types, opal_value_t objects have by far the most bytes allocated. But we cannot tell from this profile data whether these objects are all allocated *at once*, or are repeatedly allocated and deallocated, with the actual steady-state memory usage much lower. In order to determine this, we use trace data.

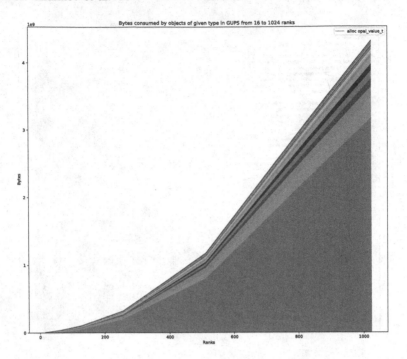

Fig. 6. Total memory allocations in bytes of all OPAL object types during execution of the GUPS benchmark on between 16 and 1,024 processing elements. `opal_value_t` objects account for by far more bytes allocated than any other object type.

In order to generate trace data including OpenSHMEM-specific events such as one-sided communication as well as atomic and context events such as those tracking allocation, we implemented support for native generation of OTF2 format traces [3] of OpenSHMEM applications in TAU. This allows a user to observe detailed information on the execution of an application, including the times and durations of each OpenSHMEM call invoked, as well as the time, source, destination, and size of each communication. These traces are generated by TAU using the `libotf2` 2.1 library. Native OTF2 trace generation provides several advantages over the generation of traditional TAU traces. The OTF2 format provides event types specifically suited for representing OpenSHMEM one-sided communication, which are output by TAU when they are encountered in place of the traditional representation of one-sided communication as if it were two-sided MPI communication. Generating OTF2 files requires communication at runtime in order to create a global mapping of function names to local identifiers; this is implemented in TAU by intercepting the call to `shmem_finalize` and carrying out this communication prior to the actual shutdown of the Open-SHMEM runtime. OTF2 is also highly space-optimized, producing smaller files than equivalent traditional TAU traces. Figure 7 shows a trace visualization of an execution of GUPS on 128 PEs using the Vampir trace visualizer [7].

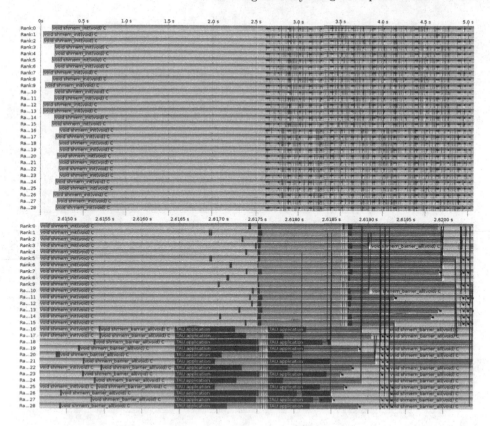

Fig. 7. Example of an OTF2 trace collected for GUPS on 128 PEs as visualized with Vampir. On top, zoomed out to show entire execution. On bottom, zoomed in to display communication events, shown as lines and arrows.

We then implemented API calls in TAU to handle *deallocation regions* analogous to allocation regions but which record when objects are deallocated:

```
void Tau_track_class_deallocation(const char * name, size_t size);
void Tau_start_class_deallocation(const char * name, size_t size,
  int include_in_parent);
void Tau_stop_class_deallocation(const char * name, int record);
```

The OPAL object system in Open MPI uses a reference counting system in which a class destructor is invoked when an object's reference count reaches zero. We instrument the code in the runtime which invokes the destructors, ensuring that we also capture the hierarchical relationship with any child objects that are freed by the destructor of a parent:

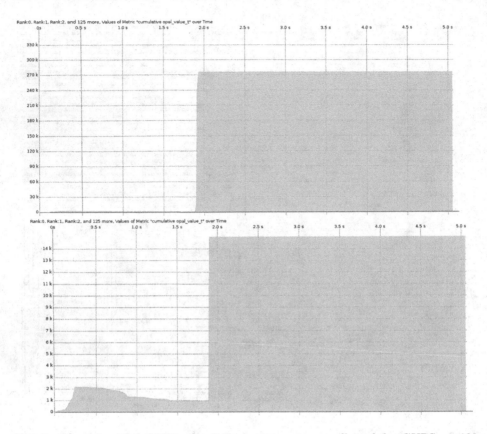

Fig. 8. Example of an OTF2 cumulative memory trace collected for GUPS on 128 PEs as visualized with Vampir for objects of type **opal_value_t**. On top, zoomed out to show the peak cumulative allocation. On bottom, zoomed in to display fluctuation during early parts of **shmem_init**.

```
static inline void opal_obj_run_destructors(opal_object_t * object)
{
    opal_destruct_t* cls_destruct;

    assert(NULL != object->obj_class);

    Tau_start_class_deallocation(object->obj_class->cls_name,object->obj_class->cls_sizeof, 0);
    cls_destruct = object->obj_class->cls_destruct_array;
    while( NULL != *cls_destruct ) {
        (*cls_destruct)(object);
        cls_destruct++;
    }

    Tau_stop_class_deallocation(object->obj_class->cls_name, 1;

}
```

Every instance of an allocation or deallocation of an OPAL object is separately recorded in the OTF2 trace. This allows us to determine, for each PE, the cumulative bytes currently allocated for each OPAL object type. Figure 8 shows the current memory usage of opal_value_t objects over time for a run of GUPS on 128 PEs. Early during shmem_init, there are a large number of small allocations and deallocations, and the total memory usage of these objects fluctuates. As shmem_init completes, large allocations occur which push the current allocation count to 274 kB per PE. The profiling approach described above gives a value of 407 kB of opal_value_t objects per PE – the peak usage is 67% of the total allocated bytes.

3 Related Work

Many general-purpose memory tracking tools have been developed, such as Valgrind's Massiff tool [9], KDE Heaptrack [2], and GNOME MemProf [1]. These tools track heap usage as a function of time and can identify which source lines are responsible for what proportion of the outstanding allocations. However, general-purpose tools like this, when applied to C, lack the ability to attribute memory usage to object *types*, as the TAU features described in this paper can do. Sumimoto et al. have developed a tool for tracking memory usage in Open MPI, DMATP-MPI [11], which distinguishes between runtime and application allocations and identifies the runtime function causing allocations, but which does distinguish allocations based on object type. Janjusic and Kartsaklis have developed a memory tracing tool, Gleipnir [6], which uses Valgrind to instrument memory allocations and attributes allocations to *source files*, but not object types, within the Open MPI runtime.

4 Conclusions and Future Work

In this paper, we have described an approach to tracking memory usage in the Open MPI runtime while executing OpenSHMEM applications, whereby a small amount of manual instrumentation of the Open MPI runtime allows us to distinguish application and runtime allocations, to distinguish allocations by originating function, and, most importantly, to distinguish allocations by *object type*. We implemented these techniques in the TAU Performance System using atomic and context events and demonstrated their use through a test case with the GUPS benchmark. We showed that both profile and trace data can be collected, and that trace data can be used to determine peak memory usage (high-water-mark) for different object types.

We expect to apply the techniques described in this paper to larger-scale analysis of the Open MPI and other runtimes in order to guide the process of optimizing these runtimes for larger numbers of PEs, particularly focused on future exascale systems on which the available bytes per PE will be lower than on currently-existing systems. One potential optimization is to share objects which do not change after initialization between PEs running on the same physical node. To do this, it would be useful to develop an extension of this tool which can identify those objects which are written to after `shmem_init` returns (and which cannot be safely shared) and those which are not written to (and can be safely shared).

Acknowledgments. This work was sponsored by the U.S. Department of Energy's Office of Advanced Scientific Computing Research. This manuscript has been authored by UT-Battelle, LLC under Contract No. DE-AC05-00OR22725 with the U.S. Department of Energy. The United States Government retains and the publisher, by accepting the article for publication, acknowledges that the United States Government retains a non-exclusive, paid-up, irrevocable, world-wide license to publish or reproduce the published form of this manuscript, or allow others to do so, for United States Government purposes. The Department of Energy will provide public access to these results of federally sponsored research in accordance with the DOE Public Access Plan (http://energy.gov/downloads/doe-public-access-plan). This research used resources of the Oak Ridge Leadership Computing Facility at the Oak Ridge National Laboratory, which is supported by the Office of Science of the U.S. Department of Energy under Contract No. DE-AC05-00OR22725. This work used resources of the Performance Research Laboratory at the University of Oregon. This work benefited from access to the University of Oregon high performance computer, Talapas.

References

1. GNOME MemProf. https://wiki.gnome.org/Apps/MemProf. Accessed 27 June 2018
2. KDE HeapTrack. https://github.com/KDE/heaptrack. Accessed 27 June 2018
3. Eschweiler, D., Wagner, M., Geimer, M., Knüpfer, A., Nagel, W.E., Wolf, F.: Open trace format 2: the next generation of scalable trace formats and support libraries. In: PARCO, vol. 22, pp. 481–490 (2011)
4. Gabriel, E., et al.: Open MPI: goals, concept, and design of a next generation mpi implementation. In: Kranzlmüller, D., Kacsuk, P., Dongarra, J. (eds.) EuroPVM/MPI 2004. LNCS, vol. 3241, pp. 97–104. Springer, Heidelberg (2004). https://doi.org/10.1007/978-3-540-30218-6_19
5. Grossman, M., Doyle, J., Dinan, J., Pritchard, H., Seager, K., Sarkar, V.: Implementation and evaluation of OpenSHMEM contexts using OFI libfabric. In: Gorentla Venkata, M., Imam, N., Pophale, S. (eds.) OpenSHMEM 2017. LNCS, vol. 10679, pp. 19–34. Springer, Cham (2018). https://doi.org/10.1007/978-3-319-73814-7_2
6. Janjusic, T., Kartsaklis, C.: Memory scalability and efficiency analysis of parallel codes. Technical report, Oak Ridge National Laboratory (ORNL), Oak Ridge, TN (United States). Oak Ridge Leadership Computing Facility (OLCF) (2015)
7. Knüpfer, A., et al.: The vampir performance analysis tool-set. In: Resch, M., Keller, R., Himmler, V., Krammer, B., Schulz, A. (eds.) Tools for High Performance Computing, pp. 139–155. Springer, Berlin (2008)
8. Linford, J.C., Khuvis, S., Shende, S., Malony, A., Imam, N., Venkata, M.G.: Profiling production OpenSHMEM applications. In: Gorentla Venkata, M., Imam, N., Pophale, S., Mintz, T.M. (eds.) OpenSHMEM 2016. LNCS, vol. 10007, pp. 219–224. Springer, Cham (2016). https://doi.org/10.1007/978-3-319-50995-2_15

9. Nethercote, N., Seward, J.: Valgrind: a framework for heavyweight dynamic binary instrumentation. In: ACM Sigplan Notices, vol. 42, pp. 89–100. ACM (2007)
10. Shende, S., Malony, A.: The TAU parallel performance system. Int. J. High Perform. Comput. Appl. **20**(2), 287–311 (2006)
11. Sumimoto, S., Okamoto, T., Akimoto, H., Adachi, T., Ajima, Y., Miura, K.: Dynamic memory usage analysis of MPI libraries using DMATP-MPI. In: Proceedings of the 20th European MPI Users' Group Meeting, pp. 149–150. ACM (2013)

Lightweight Instrumentation and Analysis Using OpenSHMEM Performance Counters

Md. Wasi-ur- Rahman[1(✉)], David Ozog[2], and James Dinan[2]

[1] Intel Corporation, Austin, TX, USA
md.rahman@intel.com
[2] Intel Corporation, Hudson, MA, USA

Abstract. Partitioned Global Address Space (PGAS) programming models, such as OpenSHMEM, are popular methods of parallel programming; however, performance monitoring and analysis tools for these models have remained elusive. In this work, we propose a performance counter extension to the OpenSHMEM interfaces to expose internal communication state as lightweight performance data to tools. We implement our interface in the open source Sandia OpenSHMEM library and demonstrate its mapping to *libfabric* primitives. Next, we design a simple collector tool to record the behavior of OpenSHMEM processes at execution time. We analyze the Integer Sort (ISx) benchmark and use the resulting data to investigate several common performance issues—including communication schedule, poor overlap, and load imbalance—and visualize the impact of optimizations to correct these issues. Through this study, our tool uncovered a performance bug in this popular benchmark. Finally, by using our tool to guide the application of several pipelining optimizations, we were able to improve the ISx key exchange performance by more than 30%.

1 Introduction

One-sided communication models, such as those provided by OpenSHMEM [19], Unified Parallel C (UPC) [28], the MPI Remote Memory Access (RMA) interface [16], and other Partitioned Global Address Space (PGAS) parallel programming models provide portable, high performance interfaces to high-speed fabrics. These models are especially effective for applications whose performance is dependent upon high-throughput communication patterns [9]; however, because of the scale and high rate at which communication operations are generated, effective performance analysis tools for such models has remained challenging.

Tracing is a common approach to performance profiling of high performance computing (HPC) applications. Tracing typically involves capturing a log of each communication operation for offline analysis and visualization. While this approach has been shown to be effective for a wide variety of applications, it can be challenging for high-throughput usage models that generate large volumes

© Springer Nature Switzerland AG 2019
S. Pophale et al. (Eds.): OpenSHMEM 2018, LNCS 11283, pp. 180–201, 2019.
https://doi.org/10.1007/978-3-030-04918-8_12

of communication. In such scenarios, traces can become extremely large and instrumentation used to record performance information can introduce overheads that impact dynamic behavior and can interfere with performance characteristics of the application under study.

In this work, we propose a performance counter extension to OpenSHMEM that exposes internal one-sided communication state, including the number of posted and completed operations issued by the local process, as well as the number of completed remote access operations that have targeted the given process. In contrast with traditional library interposition profiling approaches, which capture performance data around function invocations, the proposed performance counter interface can be sampled continuously, providing insight into nonblocking communication operations and remote accesses performed asynchronously in the memory of a given process. In addition, the proposed interface can expose completion information that is more detailed than can be gathered using library interposition approaches to profiling. Thus, OpenSHMEM performance counters provide a new and rich source of data for performance analysis that can provide new performance insights.

In this work, we extend the open source Sandia OpenSHMEM (SOS) [23] implementation to support the proposed performance counters API. We observe that the libfabric networking layer used by SOS utilizes event counters, which can enable fine-grain performance tracking at the level of individual OpenSHMEM contexts or operation classes. Next, we create a simple collector tool that runs alongside application processes and samples the performance counters with low overhead. Finally, we evaluate this system using the ISx [9] integer sorting benchmark, which is representative of high-throughput OpenSHMEM applications. By analyzing the performance counter data, we are able to identify and correct several sources of inefficiency in ISx, including such common PGAS performance pitfalls as communication scheduling, load imbalance, and poor overlap. Using the resulting optimized version of ISx, we observed a performance improvement of more than 30% to the ISx key exchange phase in a weak scaling study.

2   Related Work

The topics of communication tracing and analysis have been studied extensively in the context of OpenSHMEM and PGAS models. A number of tools have been developed, including the Cray[1] Performance Analysis Toolkit [6], HPCToolKit (see footnote 1) [1], GASP [26], KOJAK [15], Parallel Performance Wizard [25], Scalasca [11], SCORE-P [12], TAU (see footnote 1) [13,14], VAMPIR (see footnote 1) [17], and others [5]. Tracing and event collection approaches collect highly detailed information; however, these approaches can generate per-operation overheads that may interfere with the application under study. In this work, we use performance counters that can be sampled at varying frequencies, allowing the user to tradeoff accuracy and overhead.

---

[1] Other names and brands may be claimed as the property of others.

Listing 1. Proposed OpenSHMEM performance counter API.

```
/* Retrieve number of issued/completed write operations */
int shmemx_pcntr_get_issued_write(shmem_ctx_t ctx, uint64_t *cntr_value);
int shmemx_pcntr_get_completed_write(shmem_ctx_t ctx, uint64_t *cntr_value);

/* Retrieve number of issued/completed read operations */
int shmemx_pcntr_get_issued_read(shmem_ctx_t ctx, uint64_t *cntr_value);
int shmemx_pcntr_get_completed_read(shmem_ctx_t ctx, uint64_t *cntr_value);

/* Retrieve number of completed target operations */
int shmemx_pcntr_get_completed_target(uint64_t *cntr_value);

/* Retrieve all (issued and completed) operation counters */
int shmemx_pcntr_get_all(shmem_ctx_t ctx, shmemx_pcntr_t *pcntr);
```

Our approach is similar to using hardware performance counters, e.g. with the PAPI Toolkit [4]. Network performance counters have also been used to analyze application-level and system-level performance [3,20,27]; however, they can be challenging to use for application performance analysis since they often do not distinguish between individual processes or jobs. In contrast, our approach allows tools to associate performance information not only to individual processes, but also to individual contexts (e.g. threads) within a process, which is not possible through hardware counter interfaces, such as PAPI. Recently, the Message Passing Interface (MPI) introduced a performance variables interface in MPI 3.1 [16]. MPI supports performance variables that count events; thus, the MPI performance variables interface could also be used to support the performance analysis proposed in this work for the MPI Remote Memory Access (RMA) one-sided communication model.

3   OpenSHMEM Performance Counters

The proposed OpenSHMEM performance counter API is shown in Listing 1. We define counters to be unsigned 64-bit integers that are monotonically increasing over the duration of the program's execution. Counters follow the C language rules for unsigned integer arithmetic; namely, on overflow, they contain the correct result, modulo 2^{64}. The proposed routines can be used to retrieve the number of operations issued and completed for each operation class on a given Open-SHMEM context. In addition, a single query routine is provided to query all counters at once. Querying all counters in a single call can reduce the overheads and skews across counter measurements. In the proposed query-all routine, the caller provides a structure to hold all counters values, which is populated before the routine returns. We further discuss these API usages in Sect. 4.

The design space for a performance counter API is large. In particular, the granularity of operation classes for which counters are provided can range from one for each operation type (e.g. put, get, etc.) to one for all operations. In this work, we propose a simple two-class API where per-context counters are provided for operations that read data from a symmetric object (e.g. get and fetching atomic operations) and operations that write data to a symmetric object (e.g. put and non-fetching atomic operations). Atomic operations (AMOs) are counted either on the read counter pair or the write counter pair, but not both. This two-class partitioning corresponds to the event counting semantics provided by Portals and OFI and used by Sandia OpenSHMEM to track pending operations [24]. Each operation produces zero or more events on the given operation counter. For example, if an implementation fragments a large put operation into multiple smaller puts, the given operation may generate several individual write operations. In addition, if the operation is performed using shared memory, rather than fabric, communication may not be tracked. This last semantic is intended to give implementations the flexibility to expose existing operation tracking counters directly using the proposed API.

3.1   Implementation in Sandia OpenSHMEM

We implement the proposed OpenSHMEM performance counters API in the open source Sandia OpenSHMEM [23,24] (SOS) library. We have implemented the performance counters extension support in both the Portals 4 [21] and Open-Fabrics Interfaces [8] (OFI) transport layers in SOS. Both implementations are similar and take advantage of event counters provided by the low-level networking API. The experiments presented in Sect. 5 utilize OFI; thus, our implementation discussion provides greater detail on the OFI implementation.

Portals 4 and OFI libfabric are two user-level networking APIs that provide user-level access to high-speed fabrics. Both libraries generate events upon completion of a posted operation, allowing the programmer to choose whether the completion generates an event object into a queue and whether it causes an event counter to be incremented. The type of events captured (e.g. local/remote completion) and how they are captured is defined by the object on which the operation is performed, namely a memory descriptor in Portals or an endpoint in OFI.

OpenSHMEM implementations using Portals and OFI typically utilize counting events to track issued operations. Event objects provide a greater amount of information per operation; however, generation of event objects into an event queue incurs additional overhead that can impact small message throughput [2]. Thus, each OpenSHMEM context in SOS utilizes middleware-level counters to track the number of operations issued and fabric-level counters to track the number completed. The difference between the issued and completed counters provides the number of outstanding operations at any given time. SOS divides operations into read and write classes depending upon whether a symmetric object is read from or strictly written to. Performing a shmem_quiet operation generally involves waiting for each counter pair to be equal. Performing a blocking operation involves waiting only for the respective counter pair to be equal. Thus, a blocking fetch-atomic does not involve the completion of nonblocking put operations. Because SOS uses the unordered, reliable datagrams communication model provided by Portals and OFI, only write operations must be completed in a shmem_fence operation, as fetching AMOs issued on the read counter are blocking in the OpenSHMEM 1.4 API and need not be ordered by a fence operation.

In addition to tracking operations that are issued, SOS also tracks the number of fabric operations that have completed in the memory of the local process. In the OFI transport, this is accomplished by enabling the FI_REMOTE_READ and FI_REMOTE_WRITE event types on a libfabric counter, fid_cntr, that is bound to the endpoint exposed for remote access. While all other counters are associated with a particular context, the target counter keeps track of all operations that have targeted the local process.

A particular difference between the Portals 4 and OFI implementations of the counter APIs arises in how each supports threading. Portals 4 and OFI both support a thread safe mode of operation in which middleware-level locking is not needed. In these configurations, fabric-level event counters can be read without synchronization at the OpenSHMEM level. Some OFI providers, namely the Performance Scaled Messaging 2 [22] (PSM2) provider, use the FI_THREAD_COMPLETION model, which requires locking in the OpenSHMEM layer at the level of individual contexts before accessing any of the event counters on the context. For such scenarios, the proposed query-all routine is advantageous since it can reduce the amount of locking required to query the performance counters.

4   Design and Implementation of a Performance Counter Collector

The performance counter APIs presented in Sect. 3.1 can be utilized in a variety of ways. For example, an application may invoke them directly to measure communication progress, or a tool may invoke them to gather additional performance data during profiling. In this work, we present a simple collector tool that creates a thread to run alongside the application and sample the performance counters throughout the execution of the application. In contrast to conventional profiling approaches that capture profiling information during OpenSHMEM function invocations, asynchronous performance counter sampling can provide greater insight into the dynamic behavior of OpenSHMEM communication. For example, sampling can capture information regarding the asynchronous completion of remotely issued operations that targeted a given PE, and it can also capture information regarding completion of nonblocking operations that were issued by the local PE. Relative to detailed profiling at each OpenSHMEM function invocation, sampling-based approaches can also reduce overhead by tuning the sampling frequency. We next present the design of the performance counter collector and we demonstrate its usage for application-level performance analysis in Sect. 5.

Figure 1 illustrates the design of the collector and its usage within an application. It is possible to implement the collector using the profiling interfaces extension that is supported by a number of OpenSHMEM implementations. For simplicity, our implementation relies on manual instrumentation, which involves adding start and stop collection calls to the application, as well as function calls to register OpenSHMEM contexts of interest. The sampling rate of the collector can be controlled via the runtime parameter PCNTR_COLLECTOR_SAMPLING_INTERVAL. This parameter defines the length of the time the collector thread sleeps after each performance counter sample is collected. In this way, the sampling interval can be used to increase the resolution of sampling or reduce the overhead to the application. Samples are timestamped and stored in memory at the collector thread, and dumped out when the collector is stopped. To reduce the number of samples stored, samples are discarded when there has been no change in the counter values since the last collected sample. We use a simple comma-separated format for storing the sample data. However, a more sophisticated tool could report data using Open Trace Format (OTF) [7], allowing it to be imported by existing tools that support this format.

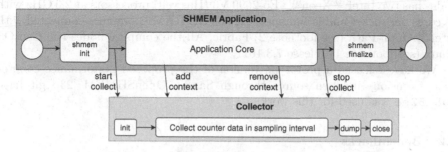

Fig. 1. Design and example usage of the performance counter collector

By default, the collector samples the performance counter data associated with the default context, SHMEM_CTX_DEFAULT, and the target counter. The user may also want to profile additional contexts that are created throughout the application execution. In such cases, the user can add the context to the collector through calls to an add_context routine, which adds the context to the pool of contexts being collected. When the context is destroyed by the application, the user must first remove the context from the collector pool by invoking remove_context. The maximum number of contexts that the collector can sample is controlled via PCNTR_COLLECTOR_MAX_CTX_LIMIT.

Because the collector utilizes a separate thread, it requires the OpenSHMEM library to be initialized in the SHMEM_THREAD_MULTIPLE mode. In addition, contexts to be sampled must also be shareable in order to be sampled asynchronously by the collector thread. Thus, contexts added into the pool of collected contexts must not be created with the SHMEM_CTX_PRIVATE option enabled, as this violates the OpenSHMEM requirement that private contexts be used only by the thread that created them. In addition, contexts added into the pool must not be created with the SHMEM_CTX_SERIALIZED option enabled, since the collector may access the given context in parallel with the application.

5   Experimental Analysis Using Performance Counters

In this section, we present an experimental analysis using the OpenSHMEM performance counters described in Sect. 3.1. We highlight our analyses and observations on four different categories: (1) Functional profiling, (2) Communication schedule, (3) Load balance, and (4) Overlap. At the end, we present a comparative analysis summary among the performance optimization alternatives studied throughout this section. We also analyze the performance overhead associated with our collector implementation.

5.1   Experimental Setup

For our evaluation, we have used a cluster with 14 compute nodes. Each compute nodes has two Intel® Xeon®[2] E5-2699 V3 (Haswell) processors at 2.3 GHz with 18 cores per socket and is equipped with 64 GB RAM. Nodes are connected with Intel® Omni-Path (see footnote 2) Fabric. All the compute nodes run CentOS Linux (see footnote 1) release 7.3.1611.

We have released a prototype version of the proposed performance counter API extensions in open source through Sandia OpenSHMEM [23]; git hash 908682ee was used for this work.

5.2   Benchmarks

Throughout our analysis, we have used Integer Sort (ISx) [10] benchmark version 1.1 and applied several performance optimizations based on our analyses and observations. ISx represents a class of the bucket sort algorithms that perform an all-to-all key exchange communication pattern across all peer processes.

As shown in Listing 2, key exchange involves each PE sending a chunk of data to every other PE. On Line 6, the location where data is written is determined using an atomic fetch-add operation to reserve a segment of the message buffer at the recipient. The subsequent put operation writes data to the destination PE using the fetched offset. The message size used in the put operation depends

---

[2] Intel and Xeon are trademarks of Intel Corporation in the U.S. and/or other countries.

Benchmark results were obtained prior to implementation of recent software patches and firmware updates intended to address exploits referred to as "Spectre" and "Meltdown". Implementation of these updates may make these results inapplicable to your device or system.

Software and workloads used in performance tests may have been optimized for performance only on Intel® microprocessors. Performance tests, such as SYSmark* and MobileMark*, are measured using specific computer systems, components, software, operations and functions. Any change to any of those factors may cause the results to vary. You should consult other information and performance tests to assist you in fully evaluating your contemplated purchases, including the performance of that product when combined with other products.

For more information go to http://www.intel.com/benchmarks.

Listing 2. Key exchange communication loop in ISx.

```
static long long bucket_offset = 0;
static int bucket_keys[BUCKET_SIZE];
...
for (int i = 0; i < shmem_n_pes(); i++) {
    int dest_pe = peers_iter(i);
    long long dest_offset = shmem_longlong_atomic_fetch_add(
                            &bucket_offset, bucket_sizes[dest_pe], dest_pe);
    shmem_int_put(&bucket_keys[dest_offset], ..., dest_pe);
}
```

on the user number of keys per PE benchmark parameter, scaling model, and the total number of PEs.

In addition to ISx, we also use the Stencil kernel from the Parallel Research Kernel (PRK) [29] suite version 2.17 to demonstrate the load balance capabilities, presented in Sect. 5.5. Stencil performs a 9-point stencil operation on a 2-dimensional grid.

5.3 Functional Profiling

We utilize the collector described in Sect. 4 to sample the read, write, and target performance counters with continuous sampling. We first analyze the target counters of all PEs over different execution regions of the application. In this experiment, we run ISx on 8 nodes with 16 processes per node. We run the weak scaling test with the total number of keys per PE set to 64 Mkeys. Figure 2 presents the progression of target counter for all PEs over time. We highlight the progression of the root process (PE 0) as it follows a separate trend compared to the other processes.

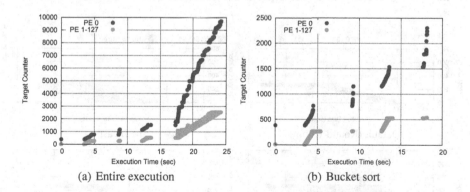

(a) Entire execution   (b) Bucket sort

Fig. 2. Target counter collection for all PEs over different execution regions for ISx

Figure 2(a) presents a scatter plot of the target counter values for all PEs over the entire duration of the execution of ISx. The two disjoint sets of progression lines indicate the difference of the target counter value observed in the root process compared to the other processes from the beginning of the application execution. The high target counter value observed at the root process from the very beginning of the execution is the result of collective operations, such as barrier and symmetric memory allocation, performing their communication operations on the default context. Also, apart from the all-to-all key exchanges across processes, ISx utilizes a number of collective routines for synchronization and collection of timer values that cause the target counters to progress towards the end of the application execution.

Figure 2(b) highlights the regions in Fig. 2(a) where the actual key exchanges take place in ISx across the processes. To isolate the core execution region, we create a separate communication context and use it in the bucket sort routine rather than using the implicit default context, SHMEM_CTX_DEFAULT. We modify our collector to collect the counter values associated with this context and analyze the target counter increments throughout the execution of the bucket sort. The two iterations (one warm-up, one trial) executed in our experiment can be clearly identified (dense regions) based on the target counter values presented in Fig. 2(b).

5.4   Communication Schedule

We next analyze the performance impact of different communication scheduling patterns used during runtime. We use ISx for this analysis and use three different communication schedules it provides: (1) default round-robin, (2) incast, and (3) permute. We run ISx on 8 nodes with 16 processes per node keeping the number of keys per PE to 64 Mkeys. Figure 3 presents this data. To highlight the impact of communication scheduling on the counter value, we focus on the first iteration of the key exchange only. We also divide the total number of PEs into four groups to show the difference in counter progression trends across different PEs.

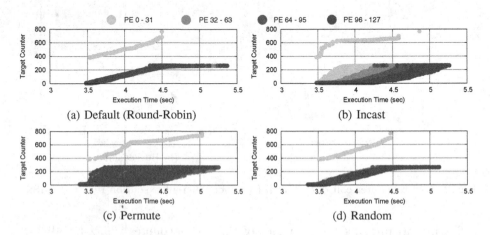

Fig. 3. Target counters for all PEs over time using different communication schedules

The default round-robin communication scheduling is presented in Fig. 3(a). This represents the same data as shown in the first iteration of the ISx execution presented in Fig. 2(b) (starting from 3 sec to 5.5 sec during execution). For key exchange in this communication schedule, the destination PE is selected starting from the next PE based on the current PE's rank and then iterates over the circular array of PEs. The progression of the target counter in this case is quite linear and the flat line at the end indicates different PEs reaching to the maximum of the target value at different times.

Figure 3(b) shows the incast communication pattern where all PEs iterate over a loop of 0 to n^{th} PE. Because of the uniform communication schedule across PEs, the higher ranked PEs receive data later than the lower ranked ones (evident in Fig. 3(b)) and because of this reason, the target counter progression for different PEs starts and ends at different times.

We use the permute communication schedule in ISx and present the result in Fig. 3(c). Although this communication schedule is supposed to randomize the communication pattern, the target counter progression follows a similar trend to the incast pattern (Fig. 3(b)). After analyzing the corresponding code, we have found that the pseudo-random number generator rand() is used without randomizing the seed. Thus, the permute scheduling was generating the same random set of destination PEs at every PE resulting in similar behavior to the incast schedule. However, as shown in Fig. 3(b), it iterates over PEs in a different order rather than sequentially from 0 to n. We updated ISx to seed the random number generator with a different value at each PE, randomizing the order in which each PE sends its messages. The target counter progression for this case is presented in Fig. 3(d). As shown in this figure, the target counters for all PEs start to progress around similar times and reach to the maximum of the target value faster compared to the other communication schedules. This presents an example scenario where performance counters were utilized to detect and correct an existing bug in the application implementation. For the rest of the experiments presented in this section, we use this random communication scheduling for ISx.

5.5   Load Balance

We next analyze how performance counters can be utilized to detect load imbalance across all PEs for ISx and the Stencil kernel. To isolate the application's point-to-point communication operations, we use separate contexts as described in Sect. 5.3. For this experiment, we use 8 nodes with 16 processes per node for both these applications. For ISx, we use 64 Mkeys per PE in the weak scaling test and for stencil, we use a grid size of 1000 and run for 100 iterations.

We present the load distribution for all PEs with ISx in Fig. 4(a). To observe the load characteristics of ISx, we present the final values for completed read, write, and target counters. The write counter represents the put operations from each PE to every other PE, whereas the read counter represents the read operations generated by the atomic_fetch_add. The target counter, on the other hand, represents the operations targeted to this PE. As shown in the figure, ISx

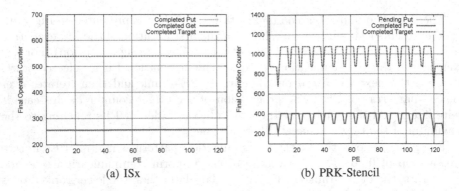

Fig. 4. Load balance through final operation counters across all PEs

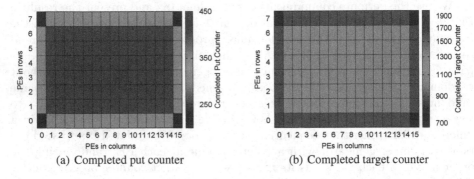

Fig. 5. Load balance using 2D heatmap for Stencil kernel (each tile represents a PE; PE 0 is in bottom left, PE 7 is in top left, PE 120 is in bottom right, and PE 127 is in top right)

maintains a uniform distribution of the data that is evident from the final target counter values across all PEs. Apart from the root process, the target counter values across all PEs are almost identical, representing a perfect load balance.

We also examine the load distribution for the Stencil kernel from the PRK suite and this data is presented in Fig. 4(b). For this benchmark, we present the final counter values for pending and completed write operations with the final target counter. In contrast with ISx, Stencil presents an unbalanced load distribution across all the PEs. Since this experiment was run with a grid of processes of 8 rows and 16 columns, processes on the perimeter of the 2D grid receive less data compared to the inner processes. We validate this by presenting the same data in a 2D heatmap, as shown in Fig. 5. As shown in this figure, the PEs 0, 7, 120, and 127 are at the corners of the grid and have neighbors in two directions. PEs 1–6 and 121–126 form the top and bottom rows and have neighbors in three directions. The remaining PEs form rows, e.g. PE 8 is on the bottom edge with neighbors in three directions, PEs 9–14 are interior PEs with neighbors in all directions, and PE 15 is on the top edge of the grid. As shown in the Fig. 5(a), the inner PEs with higher neighbor count have higher counter values compared to those on the edge. PE 0 also has significantly higher target counter values compared to the rest of the PEs as a result of the setup communication, which is evident in Fig. 5(b).

5.6   Overlap

In this subsection, we analyze the dynamic differences between the posted and the completed operation counters and analyze opportunities introduce communication overlap. For this experiment, we use ISx and apply different optimization strategies based on the counter value differences observed from the issued and completed operations. We use the same experimental environment as used in Sect. 5.4 for ISx.

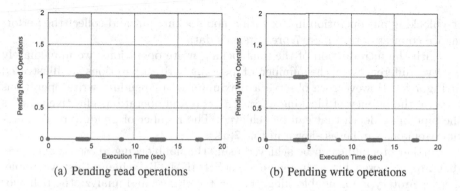

(a) Pending read operations   (b) Pending write operations

Fig. 6. Difference between the completed and posted operations over time across all PEs for ISx

Figure 6 presents the first sets of data analyzing the differences between the posted/issued and completed counters for both read and write operations. We present the data across the entire bucket sort execution corresponding to Fig. 2(b). For each operation, we present the difference between the issued and the completed counter values over time. Figure 6(a) and (b) show the read and write counters, respectively. We observe that the number of pending operations (difference between issued and completed operations) for all PEs are at most 1 throughout the execution. This corresponds to the implementation of ISx where only blocking APIs are used for both write (shmem_put) and read (shmem_fetch_add). Because of the blocking API usage, only one operation is pending at any given time. This clearly illustrates an opportunity to leverage nonblocking communication operations in ISx.

OpenSHMEM 1.3 [18] introduced nonblocking put and get operations that can improve performance by pipelining the iterations of the all-to-all communication loop in ISx. To measure the impact of the nonblocking API, we replace

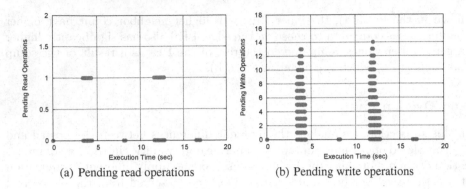

(a) Pending read operations   (b) Pending write operations

Fig. 7. Difference between the completed and posted operations over time across all PEs for ISx with nonblocking put

the blocking put operation in ISx with a nonblocking put and collect the performance counter data. Figure 7 presents this data.

With the introduction of the nonblocking write operations, we immediately observe differences in the number of pending write operations as illustrated in Fig. 7(b). However, we observe a maximum of 14 pending write operations because the latency of blocking `atomic_fetch_add` operations effectively limits the pipelining depth that can be achieved. The number of pending read operations remains similar as shown in Fig. 7(a).

Further pipelining can be achieved using the nonblocking `atomic_fetch_add` that are proposed for inclusion in OpenSHMEM. To achieve this, we implement a prototype for nonblocking `atomic_fetch_add` and analyze the behavior of pending reads and writes for ISx. The output value from the fetch-add operation is stored in a location passed as an extra argument to this routine, which can be read after performing a quiet operation. To maintain the correctness of ISx and increase pipelining between successive reads, we perform a loop fission optimization by breaking the key exchange communication loop into two loops: a first loop to issue nonblocking atomic fetch-add operations and a second loop to issue nonblocking put operations. Put operations have a data dependence on the result of the fetch-add; thus, we introduce a `shmem_quiet` operation between the two loops. Listing 3 presents the corresponding changes in the key exchange loop of ISx presented in Listing 2.

Figure 8 presents the difference between the completed and the posted operations over time across all PEs with the introduction of the nonblocking `atomic_fetch_add` and loop distribution. As demonstrated in Fig. 8(a), the number of pending read operations can be as high as to the number of processes (128 in this experiment) with the addition of nonblocking `atomic_fetch_add`. Because of loop fission, the number of pending write operations can also get increased to the number of processes, which is also the ending value for the loop counter. This clearly represents the maximum number of pending operations obtainable throughout the execution of key exchange routine.

Listing 3. Key exchange loop in ISx with loop fission optimization.

```
static long long bucket_offset = 0;
static int bucket_keys[BUCKET_SIZE];
...
long long dest_offsets = malloc(sizeof(long long) * shmem_n_pes());
for (int i = 0; i < shmem_n_pes(); i++) {
    int dest_pe = peers_iter(i);
    shmem_longlong_atomic_fetch_add_nbi(&bucket_offset, bucket_sizes[dest_pe],
                                        &dest_offsets[dest_pe], dest_pe);
}
shmem_quiet();
for (int i = 0; i < shmem_n_pes(); i++) {
    int dest_pe = peers_iter(i);
    shmem_int_put(&bucket_keys[dest_offsets[dest_pe]], \ldots, dest_pe);
}
```

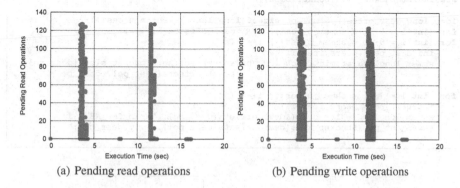

(a) Pending read operations   (b) Pending write operations

Fig. 8. Difference between the completed and posted operations over time across all PEs for ISx with nonblocking put and atomic fetch-add

With the introduction of `shmem_quiet` between the two distributed loops, all outstanding read operations complete before any write operation takes place. This is evident from Fig. 9(a) where we plot posted write operations over completed reads. The two sets of horizontal lines indicate no overlap between reads and writes in both iterations. However, better overlap across these two loops can be achieved by waiting for the result of individual atomic fetch-add operations through `shmem_wait_until` before invoking the corresponding write. This eliminates the need for a quiet operation between the fetch-add and put calls. Listing 4 presents the corresponding changes in the ISx key exchange loop. We implement this modification and plot the posted write operations over completed reads for this implementation in Fig. 9(b). In contrast with Fig. 9(a), we can see overlapping between the two operations towards the end of each iteration for the version that uses the wait-until optimization.

An alternative approach to pipelining the all-to-all exchange in ISx is to distribute loop iterations to multiple threads and launch the threads in parallel. To do this, we use OpenMP parallel threads on the default key-exchange loop (without loop fission) presented in Listing 2 using the nonblocking API for put

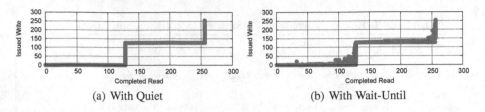

(a) With Quiet   (b) With Wait-Until

Fig. 9. Pipelining between read and write operations for different ISx implementations

Listing 4. Key exchange loop in ISx with loop fission and wait-until optimizations.

```
static long long bucket_offset = 0;
static int bucket_keys[BUCKET_SIZE];
...
long long dest_offsets = malloc(sizeof(long long) * shmem_n_pes());
for (int i = 0; i < shmem_n_pes(); i++) dest_offsets[i] = -1;
for (int i = 0; i < shmem_n_pes(); i++) {
    int dest_pe = peers_iter(i);
    shmem_longlong_atomic_fetch_add_nbi(&bucket_offset, bucket_sizes[dest_pe],
                                        &dest_offsets[dest_pe], dest_pe);
}
for (int i = 0; i < shmem_n_pes(); i++) {
    int dest_pe = peers_iter(i);
    shmem_longlong_wait_until(&dest_offsets[dest_pe], SHMEM_CMP_NE, -1);
    shmem_int_put(&bucket_keys[dest_offsets[dest_pe]], ..., dest_pe);
}
```

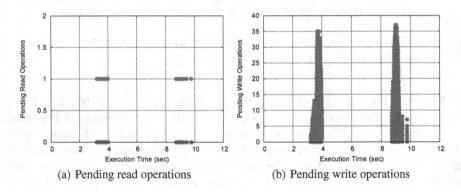

(a) Pending read operations   (b) Pending write operations

Fig. 10. Difference between the completed and posted operations over time across all PEs for threaded ISx (two threads) with nonblocking put

operations and the blocking API for atomic fetch-add operations. We create a separate context for each thread and use that context for invoking SHMEM APIs. This ensures each thread can run independently from one another and thus makes progress of both fetch-add and put operations in parallel. Figure 10 presents the pending operation counts for both read and write operations with this implementation.

For pending read operations presented in Fig. 10(a), we see a similar trend as observed in Fig. 7(a) with the non-threaded ISx implementation. Because the atomic fetch-add operations are blocking, the maximum number of pending read operations does not increase more than one per thread. However, for the pending write operations presented in Fig. 10(b), the threaded ISx implementation achieves a higher number of pending writes compared to that of the non-threaded implementation, presented in Fig. 7(b). This trend shows that with multiple threads, overlapping among different write operations can be increased.

The threaded ISx implementation can also be combined with the nonblocking put and atomic fetch-add APIs using two distributed loops. We implement this design without invoking a quiet operation between the two loops. Both of the loops presented in Listing 4 are made parallel with OpenMP threading annotations. We create an array of contexts based on the number of threads and use the thread id to select the context belonging to each thread. With this implementation, we plot the issued write over completed read to determine the effective level of pipelining. This data is presented in Fig. 11 for two iterations of ISx. Unlike Fig. 9 where the same contexts have been used for both iterations, we create a new set of contexts for each iteration in this implementation. As shown in Fig. 11(a) and (b), in both the warmup and trial iterations, we observe increased pipelining between the fetch-add and put operations compared to the same in Fig. 9.

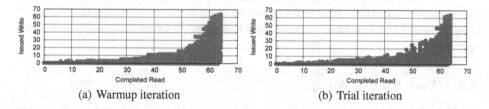

(a) Warmup iteration   (b) Trial iteration

Fig. 11. Pipelining between read and write operations for threaded ISx (two threads) with nonblocking operations and without memory ordering

Each of the optimizations presented so far improves overlap between the fetch-add and put operations in ISx compared to the default implementation. We next analyze the target counter progression for each implementation of ISx in Fig. 12. To compare these with the target counter progression for the default ISx implementation presented in Fig. 3(d), we keep our focus on one iteration of the key exchange routine as before.

Figure 12(a) presents the target counter increments for ISx with the nonblocking put API. Compared to Fig. 3(d), the trend for the target counter increment is similar for most PEs; however, it reaches the end of the iteration execution faster compared to the default one because of the overlapping introduced by nonblocking put. Figure 12(b) presents the ISx implementation with nonblocking APIs for both put and atomic fetch-add without shmem_quiet. We skip presenting

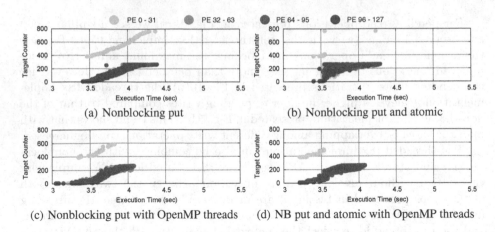

Fig. 12. Target counters for all PEs over time for different optimizations in ISx

here the similar implementation with shmem_quiet as both of these follow similar trends. However, without the quiet operation (Fig. 12(b)), the target counter progression indicates that more PEs reach the maximum of the target counter values faster compared to the case where quiet is used.

The target counter progressions for the threaded implementations of ISx are presented in Fig. 12(c) and (d). Because of the pipelining through threads, these implementations start having target counter increments earlier than the non-threaded implementations and thus reach an effective pipelined state more quickly.

5.7 Weak Scaling Analysis

In this subsection, we present a weak scaling comparison across each performance optimization strategy that we have studied throughout this section. We conduct this experiment from 2 nodes to 14 nodes and run ISx with 16 processes per node in each case. We keep the number of keys per PE to 64 Mkeys and report the average all-to-all time per PE. For each data point, we repeat our experiments at least 10 times and report the best case results. Figure 13 divides the data into two sets of comparison: the optimizations applied to non-threaded implementation of ISx are presented in Fig. 13(a), whereas, the same optimizations applied to threaded implementation of ISx are presented in Fig. 13(b). Table 1 summarizes the optimizations applied for each experiment shown in Fig. 13.

As shown in Fig. 13(a), compared to the Default implementation, NB-Put performs consistently better across different number of processes. With 224 processes on 14 nodes, NB-Put achieves 16.5% improvement compared to the Default. NB-Put-AMO performs significantly better compared to NB-Put for smaller number of processes; however, it performs only as good as NB-Put when the number of processes are increased to 224. With more number of processes, the

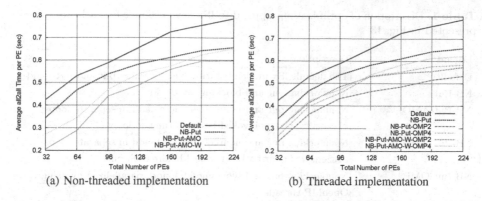

(a) Non-threaded implementation   (b) Threaded implementation

Fig. 13. Weak scaling performance for various optimizations applied to ISx key exchange

overhead of shmem_quiet increases and thus degrades the performance for NB-Put-AMO. NB-Put-AMO-W performs better than NB-Put-AMO as it increases the degree of overlap between the atomic fetch-add and put operations by synchronizing through shmem_wait_until. For 224 processes, NB-Put-AMO-W outperforms NB-Put-AMO by 8.3%.

We present the threaded ISx implementations in Fig. 13(b). For ease of comparison, we keep the performance numbers for Default and NB-Put (single threaded) in this plot as well. We achieve the best performance through NB-Put-OMP2 on 224 processes, obtaining a performance improvement of 32% and 10% compared to the Default and NB-Put-AMO-W (single threaded), respectively. With more OpenMP threads, NB-Put-OMP4 performs worse compared to NB-Put-OMP2 by 9% due to the over-subscription of the number of threads to the system resources available. The NB-Put-AMO-W-OMP2 performs slightly worse compared to NB-Put-OMP2 for small number of processes; however, it presents a good performance trend for larger number of processes achieving the second best performance for 224 processes with a 7.4% performance difference compared to NB-Put-OMP2. NB-Put-AMO-W-OMP4 performs worse compared to NB-Put-AMO-W-OMP2 due to the over-subscription of the number of threads. We plan to investigate performance trend observed between NB-Put-AMO-W-OMP2 and NB-Put-OMP2, as the former provides better overlap than the latter.

5.8 Collector Overhead Analysis

In this subsection, we analyze the overhead imposed by our collector implementation. We use three ISx implementations for this study: the default blocking API implementation (Default), the non-blocking implementation with put and atomic APIs and wait-until (NB-Put-AMO-W), and the threaded implementation with non-blocking put API (NB-Put-OMP2). We choose these three implementations to highlight the overheads associated with different implementation choices studied in Sect. 5.7. We perform this analysis on 8 nodes with 16 PEs

Table 1. Description of optimizations applied to ISx key exchange for each experiment presented in Fig. 13

Legend	Description
Default	The default ISx implementation with blocking put and fetch-add
NB-Put	Nonblocking put and blocking fetch-add
NB-Put-AMO	Nonblocking put and nonblocking fetch-add in separate loops; shmem_quiet is invoked between the two loops
NB-Put-AMO-W	Nonblocking put and nonblocking fetch-add in separate loops; shmem_wait_until is invoked before each put
NB-Put-OMP2	Nonblocking put and blocking fetch-add, parallelized by using two OpenMP threads
NB-Put-OMP4	Nonblocking put and blocking fetch-add; parallelized by using four OpenMP threads
NB-Put-AMO-W-OMP2	Nonblocking put and nonblocking fetch-add in separate loops; shmem_wait_until is invoked before each put; parallellized by using two OpenMP threads per loop
NB-Put-AMO-W-OMP4	Nonblocking put and nonblocking fetch-add in separate loops; shmem_wait_until is invoked before each put; parallellized by using four OpenMP threads per loop

per node and 64 Mkeys per PE. Figure 14 presents these results where the overhead in terms of additional execution times for all-to-all time per PE is shown in Fig. 14(a). The total number of samples collected throughout the analysis is presented in Fig. 14(b). In the x-axis for both of these graphs, we vary the sleep duration for the collector thread using PCNTR_COLLECTOR_SAMPLING_INTERVAL, thereby varying the sampling frequency.

As shown in Fig. 14(a), the overhead associated with the collection of performance counter data is more evident for NB-Put-OMP2 compared to the other implementations. As NB-Put-OMP2 launches additional OpenMP threads during the critical loop execution, the overhead of the collector thread becomes more prominent with the increase in sampling frequency (decrease in sleep duration). The collector overhead almost diminishes as the sampling frequency is decreased. For the Default and NB-Put-AMO-W implementation, the collector overhead ranges from 2 ms to 90 ms and 20 ms to 100 ms with different sampling frequencies, respectively.

We also evaluate the total number of samples collected with different sampling frequency throughout the execution of ISx. As mentioned in Sect. 4, the collector implementation does not record the counter values if there is no change since the previous sample. The total number of samples are presented in Fig. 14(b). As expected, with reduced sampling frequency, all implementations collect almost similar number of samples. However, as we increase the sampling frequency, the number of samples collected is much less for NB-Put-OMP2 compared to the Default and NB-Put-AMO-W because of the thread overheads as well as shorter execution duration.

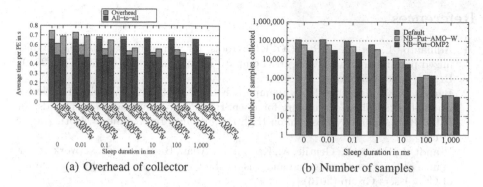

(a) Overhead of collector   (b) Number of samples

Fig. 14. Additional overhead imposed by the collector on different ISx implementations

6 Conclusion

In this paper, we have proposed a performance counter API extension to the OpenSHMEM specification and implemented the open source Sandia OpenSH-MEM library. We have designed and implemented a simple collector tool that can be used to sample the values of these performance counters during the execution of OpenSHMEM applications. Using this tool, we studied the popular ISx sorting benchmark and identified a performance bug in the random communication schedule provided by the benchmark. Next, we used the performance counter data collected by our tool to analyze several optimizations to the ISx key exchange algorithm using recently introduced and currently proposed Open-SHMEM features. Using this data we were able to visualize the effectiveness of each approach at pipelining the key exchange communication. Finally, we conducted a weak scaling study of the optimized ISx benchmark and demonstrated an improvement of over 30% to the all-to-all key exchange phase of ISx. The overhead of the implemented collector tool is also analyzed and can be kept low with a reasonable sampling frequency.

While this work has demonstrated the usefulness of OpenSHMEM performance counters, more investigation is needed to uncover new, automated methods for analyzing performance counter data, which in turn may identify new opportunities for optimization. Of particular interest are analyses that can aid developers of existing OpenSHMEM applications with taking advantage of recently added and proposed extensions to OpenSHMEM. The proposed performance counter APIs may also have applications beyond application-level performance tuning and could be applied at a system level to monitor systems for performance anomalies and identify system-level performance optimization opportunities.

References

1. Adhianto, L., et al.: HPCTOOLKIT: tools for performance analysis of optimized parallel programs. Concurr. Comput.: Pract. Exper. **22**(6), 685–701 (2010). Http://hpctoolkit.Org
2. Barrett, B.W., Brigthwell, R., Hemmert, K.S., Pedretti, K., Wheeler, K., Underwood, K.D.: Enhanced support for openSHMEM communication in portals. In: IEEE 19th Annual Symposium on High Performance Interconnects. HotI, August 2011
3. Brandt, J., Froese, E., Gentile, A., Kaplan, L., Allan, B., Walsh, E.: Network performance counter monitoring and analysis on the Cray XC platform. In: Proceedings of Cray Users Group (2016)
4. Browne, S., Dongarra, J., Garner, N., London, K., Mucci, P.: A scalable cross-platform infrastructure for application performance tuning using hardware counters. In: Proceedings of the 2000 ACM/IEEE Conference on Supercomputing. SC 2000, IEEE Computer Society, Washington, DC, USA (2000)
5. Cong, G., Wen, H., Murata, H., Negishi, Y.: Tool-assisted optimization of shared-memory accesses in UPC applications. In: IEEE International Conference on High Performance Computing and Communication & IEEE International Conference on Embedded Software and Systems, (HPCC-ICESS), pp. 104–111, June 2012
6. DeRose, L., Homer, B., Johnson, D., Kaufmann, S., Poxon, H.: Cray performance analysis tools. In: Resch, M., Keller, R., Himmler, V., Krammer, B., Schulz, A. (eds.) Tools for High Performance Computing, pp. 191–199. Springer, Heidelberg (2008). https://doi.org/10.1007/978-3-540-68564-7_12
7. Eschweiler, D., Wagner, M., Geimer, M., Knpfer, A., Nagel, W., Wolf, F.: Open trace format 2: The next generation of scalable trace formats and support libraries. In: Applications, Tools and Techniques on the Road to Exascale Computing. vol. 22, pp. 481–490, January 2012
8. Grun, P., et al.: A brief introduction to the openfabrics interfaces - a new network API for maximizing high performance application efficiency. In: 2015 IEEE 23rd Annual Symposium on High-Performance Interconnects, pp. 34–39, August 2015
9. Hanebutte, U., Hemstad, J.: ISx: A scalable integer sort for co-design in the exascale era. In: 2015 9th International Conference on Partitioned Global Address Space Programming Models (PGAS), pp. 102–104, September 2015
10. Hanebutte, U., Hemstad, J.: ISx: a scalable integer sort for co-design in the exascale era. In: 9th International Conference on Partitioned Global Address Space Programming Models. pp. 102–104, September 2015
11. Hermanns, M.-A., Geimer, M., Mohr, B., Wolf, F.: Scalable detection of MPI-2 remote memory access inefficiency patterns. In: Ropo, M., Westerholm, J., Dongarra, J. (eds.) EuroPVM/MPI 2009. LNCS, vol. 5759, pp. 31–41. Springer, Heidelberg (2009). https://doi.org/10.1007/978-3-642-03770-2_10
12. Knüpfer, A., et al.: Score-P: a joint performance measurement run-time infrastructure for periscope, scalasca, TAU, and vampir. Tools for High Performance Computing, pp. 79–91. Springer, Heidelberg (2012). https://doi.org/10.1007/978-3-642-31476-6_7
13. Linford, J., Simon, T.A., Shende, S., Malony, A.D.: Profiling non-numeric Open-SHMEM applications with the TAU performance system. In: Poole, S., Hernandez, O., Shamis, P. (eds.) OpenSHMEM 2014. LNCS, vol. 8356, pp. 105–119. Springer, Cham (2014). https://doi.org/10.1007/978-3-319-05215-1_8

14. Linford, J.C., Khuvis, S., Shende, S., Malony, A., Imam, N., Venkata, M.G.: Performance analysis of openSHMEM applications with TAU commander. In: Gorentla Venkata, M., Imam, N., Pophale, S. (eds.) OpenSHMEM 2017. LNCS, vol. 10679, pp. 161–179. Springer, Cham (2018). https://doi.org/10.1007/978-3-319-73814-7_11

15. Mohr, B., Kühnal, A., Hermanns, M., Wolf, F.: Performance analysis of one-sided communication mechanisms. In: Joubert, G.R., Nagel, W.E., Peters, F.J., Plata, O.G., Tirado, P., Zapata, E.L. (eds.) Parallel Computing: Current & Future Issues of High-End Computing, Proceedings of the International Conference ParCo 2005. John von Neumann Institute for Computing Series, 13–16 September 2005, Department of Computer Architecture, University of Malaga, Spain, vol. 33, pp. 885–892. Central Institute for Applied Mathematics, Jülich (2005)

16. MPI Forum: MPI: A message-passing interface standard version 3.1. Technical report, University of Tennessee, Knoxville, June 2015

17. Oeste, S., Knüpfer, A., Ilsche, T.: Towards parallel performance analysis tools for the openSHMEM standard. In: Poole, S., Hernandez, O., Shamis, P. (eds.) OpenSHMEM 2014. LNCS, vol. 8356, pp. 90–104. Springer, Cham (2014). https://doi.org/10.1007/978-3-319-05215-1_7

18. OpenSHMEM application programming interface, version 1.3., February 2016. http://www.openshmem.org

19. OpenSHMEM application programming interface, version 1.4., December 2017. http://www.openshmem.org

20. Pedretti, K., Vaughan, C.T., Barrett, R.F., Devine, K.D., Hemmert, K.S.: Using the Cray Gemini performance counters. In: Proceedings of the Cray Users Group (2013)

21. Portals 4.0. http://www.cs.sandia.gov/Portals/portals4.html

22. Performance Scaled Messaging 2 (PSM2) Programmer's Guide, October 2017. https://intel.ly/2y2uvjb

23. Sandia OpenSHMEM (2018). https://github.com/Sandia-OpenSHMEM/SOS

24. Seager, K., Choi, S.-E., Dinan, J., Pritchard, H., Sur, S.: Design and implementation of openSHMEM using OFI on the aries interconnect. In: Gorentla Venkata, M., Imam, N., Pophale, S., Mintz, T.M. (eds.) OpenSHMEM 2016. LNCS, vol. 10007, pp. 97–113. Springer, Cham (2016). https://doi.org/10.1007/978-3-319-50995-2_7

25. Su, H.H., Billingsley, M., George, A.D.: Parallel performance wizard: a performance system for the analysis of partitioned global-address-space applications. Int. J. High Perform. Comput. Appl. **24**(4), 485–510 (2010)

26. Su, H.-H., Bonachea, D., Leko, A., Sherburne, H., Billingsley, M., George, A.D.: GASP! a standardized performance analysis tool interface for global address space programming models. In: Kågström, B., Elmroth, E., Dongarra, J., Waśniewski, J. (eds.) PARA 2006. LNCS, vol. 4699, pp. 450–459. Springer, Heidelberg (2007). https://doi.org/10.1007/978-3-540-75755-9_54

27. Tallent, N.R., Vishnu, A., Van Dam, H., Daily, J., Kerbyson, D.J., Hoisie, A.: Diagnosing the causes and severity of one-sided message contention. In: Proceedings of the 20th ACM SIGPLAN Symposium on Principles and Practice of Parallel Programming, PPoPP 2015, pp. 130–139. ACM, New York, NY, USA (2015)

28. UPC Consortium: UPC language and library specifications, v1.3. Technical Report LBNL-6623E, Lawrence Berkeley National Lab, November 2013

29. Van der Wijngaart, R.F., et al.: Comparing runtime systems with exascale ambitions using the parallel research Kernels. In: Kunkel, J.M., Balaji, P., Dongarra, J. (eds.) ISC High Performance 2016. LNCS, vol. 9697, pp. 321–339. Springer, Cham (2016). https://doi.org/10.1007/978-3-319-41321-1_17

Oak Ridge OpenSHMEM Benchmark Suite

Thomas Naughton[(✉)], Ferrol Aderholdt, Matt Baker, Swaroop Pophale, Manjunath Gorentla Venkata, and Neena Imam

Computer Science and Mathematics Division, Oak Ridge National Laboratory, Oak Ridge, TN 37831, USA
naughtont@ornl.gov

Abstract. The assessment of application performance is a fundamental task in high-performance computing (HPC). The OpenSHMEM Benchmark (OSB) suite is a collection of micro-benchmarks and mini-applications/compute kernels that have been ported to use OpenSH-MEM. Some, like the NPB OpenSHMEM benchmarks, have been published before while most others have been used for evaluations but never formally introduced or discussed. This suite puts them together and is useful for assessing the performance of different use cases of OpenSH-MEM. This offers system implementers a useful means of measuring performance and assessing the effects of new features as well as implementation strategies. The suite is also useful for application developers to assess the performance of the growing number of OpenSHMEM implementations that are emerging. In this paper, we describe the current set of codes available within the OSB suite, how they are intended to be used, and, where possible, a snapshot of their behavior on one of the OpenSHMEM implementations available to us. We also include detailed descriptions of every benchmark and kernel, focusing on how OpenSH-MEM was used. This includes details on the enhancements we made to the benchmarks to support multithreaded variants. We encourage the OpenSHMEM community to use, review, and provide feedback on the benchmarks.

This work was sponsored by the U.S. Department of Energy's Office of Advanced Scientific Computing Research. This manuscript has been authored by UT-Battelle, LLC under Contract No. DE-AC05-00OR22725 with the U.S. Department of Energy. The United States Government retains and the publisher, by accepting the article for publication, acknowledges that the United States Government retains a non-exclusive, paid-up, irrevocable, world-wide license to publish or reproduce the published form of this manuscript, or allow others to do so, for United States Government purposes. The Department of Energy will provide public access to these results of federally sponsored research in accordance with the DOE Public Access Plan (http://energy.gov/downloads/doe-public-access-plan). This research used resources of the Oak Ridge Leadership Computing Facility at the Oak Ridge National Laboratory, which is supported by the Office of Science of the U.S. Department of Energy under Contract No. DE-AC05-00OR22725.

© Springer Nature Switzerland AG 2019
S. Pophale et al. (Eds.): OpenSHMEM 2018, LNCS 11283, pp. 202–216, 2019.
https://doi.org/10.1007/978-3-030-04918-8_13

1   Introduction

The efficient execution of scientific simulations requires careful development of system software that enables the effective use of high-performance computing (HPC) hardware. A crucial component of this development process is the assessment phase, whereby the application and system software are exercised in a standard and comparable manner (a "benchmark" [9]). In the absence of real world OpenSHMEM code, benchmarks and computation kernels are the only assessments available for the scientific community to compare and analyze the different features and implementations. The OpenSHMEM Benchmark (OSB) suite is one such collection of micro-benchmarks and mini-applications/compute kernels that have been ported to use the OpenSHMEM interface. A compilation of previously published and new benchmarks, this suite is useful for assessing the performance of different use cases of OpenSHMEM and offers system implementers a useful means of measuring performance and assessing the effects of different implementation strategies. The suite is also useful for application developers to assess the performance of the growing number of OpenSHMEM implementations that are emerging. In this paper, we describe the current set of codes available within the OSB suite. We also include information about tests performed with OSB and several OpenSHMEM implementations. This is helpful for users that wish to leverage OSB for performance testing of different Open-SHMEM implementation, and when planning changes to dependent layers of the implementations.

The key contributions of this paper can be summarized as follows:

- A detailed description of every benchmark and kernel with special focus on how OpenSHMEM is used in them.
- Additionally, details are given regarding the enhancements made to extend the OpenSHMEM enabled benchmarks to provide multithreaded variants.
- Usage information for the benchmarks.
- A description of the output from the benchmarks and how to interpret it.
- Sample results using different OpenSHMEM implementations.

The rest of the paper is organized as follows: In Sect. 2, we summarize the current codes included in OSB and, where applicable, the enhancements made to support multithreading. General usage and example output are also included in this section. Section 3 provides concluding remarks.

2   OSB Suite

The OpenSHMEM Benchmark (OSB) suite currently includes five codes, with most including both a single and multithreaded variant. All of the items in the suite have been used in conjunction with prior publications to evaluate enhancements to the OpenSHMEM specification [2,3,6,7,11,13,14]. The suite currently includes the following OpenSHMEM enabled benchmarks.

2.1   Graph 500

The Graph 500 benchmark was designed to represent data intensive workloads, particularly graphs. It implements the Breadth-First Search (BFS) on large undirected graphs. It is characterized by fine-grained communication with sparse spatial and temporal locality. In this benchmark suite, we support both single-thread and multithreaded versions of Graph 500.

The benchmark's functionality can be categorized into three phases. In the first phase, the graph edges are generated using a Kronecker graph generator. The size of the graph is controlled by two parameters $scale\_factor$ and $edge\_factor$. For a given $scale\_factor$ and $edge\_factor$, the number of graph vertices is 2^{scale_factor} and $2 * edge\_factor$. The memory required to store the graph is proportional to the number of vertices, e.g., $2^{scale\_factor} * edge\_factor * 2 * 8$ bytes. In the second phase, the benchmark randomly designates 64 vertices are *root* vertices and builds a tree from the *root* vertex. In the last phase, the BFS is validated for correctness. The time measured by the benchmark includes all three phases, and a figure of merit is the number of edges traversed per second (TEPS).

The OpenSHMEM implementation [6] of the benchmark is adapted from the MPI version [5,16]. The graph is stored in the symmetric heap and partitioned among the PEs. The vertices and edges are accessible to all PEs through the OpenSHMEM interfaces. The implementation uses shmem_putmem and shmem_getmem for accessing the data, and shmem_barrier_all for synchronization. To perform the BFS operations, the implementation uses one predecessor map and two queues. The predecessor map stores the information about the visited and completed, discovered, and undiscovered vertices. The queues are used for the discovered vertices, which are implemented as bitmaps. The queues are updated using shmem_put and atomic memory operations (AMOs), which replaces the MPI_Accumulate operation in the MPI version. A detailed discussion of the Open-SHMEM implementation and an optimized version are given in these papers [6,8].

Multithreading. In this benchmark suite, we extend the Graph 500 benchmark to take advantage of multithreaded semantics introduced in OpenSHMEM 1.4. The benchmark leverages multiple threads to parallelize the workload, particularly during the BFS phase. As vertices are discovered, the vertices are partitioned among the available threads, and each thread continues the execution of the BFS algorithm on the vertices in its partition. Each thread computing BFS on vertices has a separate OpenSHMEM context attached to it, and the threads post the OpenSHMEM operations on that particular context. This straightforward strategy can take advantage of parallelism in compute as well the network.

Usage and Results. The source code for the OpenSHMEM implementation is in the mpi/ directory, along with the MPI based implementations. A make.inc file should be created in the top-level of the Graph500 software tree, and defines the configuration for the build. This must include BUILD_OPENSHMEM=Yes and in the multithreaded case should also enable the OpenMP feature. Also, set the OSHCC variable to the correct compiler instance. There are examples in the make-incs/ directory. Note, there are guards around the OpenSHMEM code paths that allow for an entirely OpenSHMEM build. There is no need to define MPICC nor enable BUILD_MPI if working strictly with the OpenSHMEM variant of Graph500.

```
To compile:
  # Create make.inc in top−level dir
  cd mpi/
  make

To Execute:
  cd mpi/
  oshrun −np 32 ./graph500_shmem_one_sided 24 16
```

Listing 1. Compiling and Executing OpenSHMEM Graph500 Benchmark

```
graph_generation:                 16.875364 s
construction_time:                3.005170 s
Running BFS 0
Time for BFS 0 is 21.030321
Validating BFS 0
Validate time for BFS 0 is 49.637025
TEPS for BFS 0 is 1.27641e+07

... < snip >...

Running BFS 63
Time for BFS 63 is 20.095156
Validating BFS 63
Validate time for BFS 63 is 48.762720
TEPS for BFS 63 is 1.33581e+07
SCALE:                            24
edgefactor:                       16
NBFS:                             64
graph_generation:                 16.8754
num_mpi_processes:                256
construction_time:                3.00517
min_time:                         19.8975
firstquartile_time:               20.6892
median_time:                      21.0218
thirdquartile_time:               21.8296
max_time:                         23.0912
mean_time:                        21.2106
stddev_time:                      0.750554
min_nedge:                        268432547
firstquartile_nedge:              268432547
median_nedge:                     268432547
thirdquartile_nedge:              268432547
max_nedge:                        268432547
mean_nedge:                       268432547
stddev_nedge:                     0
min_TEPS:                         1.16249e+07
firstquartile_TEPS:               1.22967e+07
median_TEPS:                      1.27692e+07
thirdquartile_TEPS:               1.29745e+07
max_TEPS:                         1.34908e+07
harmonic_mean_TEPS:               1.26556e+07
harmonic_stddev_TEPS:             56421.2
min_validate:                     48.3824
firstquartile_validate:           49.7668
median_validate:                  50.2669
thirdquartile_validate:           50.9583
max_validate:                     51.9046
mean_validate:                    50.2551
stddev_validate:                  0.863311
```

Listing 2. Sample Output for OpenSHMEM Graph500 Benchmark

The benchmark runs a validation step after each of the 64 BFS rounds, which is timed and used to calculate the TEPS metric. In the OpenSHMEM version, the valiation step can be disabled by setting the environment variable `SKIP_VALIDATION=1`. Additionally, fewer (8) BFS rounds can be run by setting the environment variable `SHORT_VALIDATION=1`. These options can be helpful when testing to reduce the overall execution time.

A sample of the output from Graph500 is shown in Listing 2. The final portion of the benchmark shows a summary of parameters and statistics (e.g., min,max,mean,std) for the benchmark (Lines 16–49). This particular invocation was run using 256 ranks (Line 20) with *scale_factor* = 24 (Line 16) and *edge_factor* = 16 (Line 17)[1]. When processing the results, a few notable values are the graph generation (`graph_generation`) and construction (`graph_construction`) times and the average time for all BFS rounds (`mean_time`). If the validation phases have not been disabled, the average validation time (`mean_validate`) and harmonic mean TEPS (`harmonic_mean_TEPS`) will also be reported. Figure 1 show the mean time for the BFS using 16 PEs per node, scaling up to 32 nodes. The graph size (scale factor) was also incremented (weak scaling) for each PE increase, respectively (pe:scale): 16:20, 32:21, 64:22, 128:23, 256:24, 512:25.

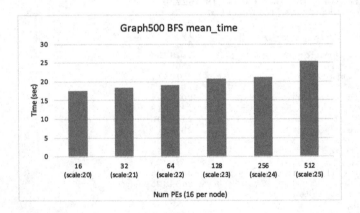

Fig. 1. Graph500 BFS mean-time on Cray XC30 with 16 PEs per node, using up to 32 nodes, with increasing graph scale factor for each step increase.

For additional information on the implementation of Graph500 included in the OSB suite, see the paper by D'Azevedo and Imam [6].

2.2   SSCA1

The Scalable Synthetic Compact Applications 1 (SSCA1) benchmark implements a Smith-Waterman local sequence alignment algorithm with Godah's

---

[1] The test with results shown in Listing 2 was run on a Cray XC30 using command: `aprun -n 256 -S 8 -j 1 ./graph500_shmem_one_sided 24 16`.

improvements for gap scoring [3]. Its value in benchmarking OpenSHMEM libraries is that it can be used to test strategies in managing many small messages with *puts* and *gets* issued in the same inner loop. SSCA1 is implemented as a dynamic programming algorithm where individual characters in a text string are compared and scored. The algorithm uses a similarity matrix meant to simulate DNA codon to protein encoding and scoring the sequence is based on the presence of a gap. The way the benchmark is designed there is an inner loop where the program is doing 5 small *gets* and 3 small *puts*. The *puts* need to be completed before starting an outer loop while the *gets* need to be completed on each inner loop.

The benchmark comes in two versions. One is multithreaded and OpenSH-MEM specific. The other one is single threaded and may be built using either MPI-3 one sided routines or OpenSHMEM routines.

Multithreading. The threaded SSCA1 is in a separate directory from the non-threaded version. The options are the same as the single threaded version, except there is no MPI option. The code was modified to remove the MPI-3 one sided operations and add threaded OpenSHMEM 1.4 extensions. This implementation of SSCA1 is structured such that there is an outer loop that can not be parallelized, and an inner loop that is parallel using OpenMP threads. This can be visualized as the dynamic programming matrix is solved where the outer loop represents solving each anti-diagonal, then the inner parallel loop solves each entry in the anti-diagonal in a loop independent way.

Usage and Results. There is a single runtime option for the benchmark to adjust the size of the input, which is set via an environment variable SCALE (default $= 22$). An input of $SCALE = 22$ should run in half the time as $SCALE = 23$. It should be noted, increasing the number of remote nodes while keeping $SCALE$ the same may result in a slow down. This is because $SCALE$ creates a problem size N, and each node gets M elements for $M = N/n_{ranks}$. Adding more ranks reduces the size of M, resulting in more remote operations to complete the benchmark. Increasing SCALE by 1 when doubling the number of ranks will result in a similar run time in this case. Typically launching SSCA1 with 1 PE per NUMA domain will see performance scaling with each added rank, while launching the threaded SSCA1 to saturate the socket with threads will result in a slow down when adding ranks.

```
1  To compile:
2    make
3
4  To Execute:
5    export SCALE=23
6    oshrun −np 32 ./ssca1
```

Listing 3. Compiling and Executing OpenSHMEM SSCA1 Benchmark

To build the benchmark, edit the Makefile for the respective SSCA1 subdirectory, and set the $COMPILER$ variable to the correct compiler instance, the default is oshcc. There are predefined options for compiling with mpicc, gcc, and Cray cc. The executable produced is ssca1. The C defines −DUSE_SHMEM and -DUSE_MPI3 are used to select between OpenSHMEM or MPI-3 one sided operations, respectively. This benchmark has been tested with Cray compilers using the PGI programming environment for both MPI-3 and SHMEM. GCC has been tested with OpenSHMEM-X and OpenMPI.

An excerpt of output from SSCA1-threaded is shown in Listing 4. This particular invocation was run using 4 ranks with $SCALE = 31^2$. When interpreting the results (Listing 4), *Kernel 1* is the relevant benchmark number (Line 9). The Scalable Data Generator and the Kernel 2 times are informational only. Kernel 2 verifies the results of Kernel 1. The first three results should be, in order, *IDENTICAL*, *MISQRMATCHES*, *STARTGAPMIDST---END*, with scores of 55, 54, and 53 respectively (blue highlight). If the end result is not these values then the underlying implementation of OpenSHMEM is faulty. Verifications below these sequences are based on random chance, however they should still be in order by score. The sort used to arrange these scores is not stable.

```
1  Running with OpenMP, thread count: 8
2  Running with OpenMP, thread count: 8
3  Running with OpenMP, thread count: 8
4  Running with OpenMP, thread count: 8
5  Running with OpenSHMEM, npes = 4
6  ...< snip >...
7  Begining Kernel 1 execution.
8
9    Elapsed time: 0 hour(s), 4 minute(s), 56 second(s), 526 milliseconds
       , 761 micro second(s).
10
11 Begining Kernel 2 execution.
12
13   Elapsed time: 0 hour(s), 0 minute(s), 0 second(s), 39 milliseconds,
       320 micro second(s).
14
15 Found 100 acceptable alignments with scores from 55 to 25.
16
17 Starting    Amino      Codon         Ending
18 position    acids      bases         position
19
20 verifyAlignment 0, succeeded; score 55:
21   26590  *IDENTICAL*  tgaatagacgagaacacgatatgcgcgctgtga      26600
22   29129  *IDENTICAL*  tgaatagacgagaacacgatatgcgcgctgtga      29139
23
24 verifyAlignment 1, succeeded; score 54:
25    1039  *MISQRMATCHES*  tgaatgataagccagagaggatggcgacgtgccacgagagctga
         1052
26   23093  *MISQRMATCHES*  tgaatgataagcaggcagatggcgacgtgccacgagagctga
         23106
27
28 verifyAlignment 2, succeeded; score 53:
29   13839  *STARTGAPMIDST—END*
         tgaagcacggcgaggacgggggcgccgatgatagacagcacg——————gagaacgactga
         13856
30   37081  *STARTGAPMIDST—END*  tgaagcacggcgaggacg————————
         atgatagacagcacggggggcgccggagaacgactga      37098
31
32 ...< snip >...
```

Listing 4. Sample Output for OpenSHMEM SSCA1-threaded Benchmark

---

[2] The test with results shown in Listing 4 was run on a Linux Cluster (Turing) using command: orterun -np 4 --map-by ppr:2:node --bind-to socket --hostfile hosts -x OMP_NUM_THREADS=8 -x SCALE=32 ./ssca1.

Sample results for a $SCALE = 31$ with 256 PEs on a Cray XC30 (EOS) system using Cray-SHMEM v7.7.0 are given in Fig. 2a. Figure 2b shows results from a smaller run on a Linux cluster (Turing) using OpenSHEM-X, also with $SCALE = 31$ with 48 PEs. In Fig. 2, the number of PEs is increased, while keeping the scale fixed ($SCALE = 31$). More detailed results for evaluating implementation of contexts can be found in [3].

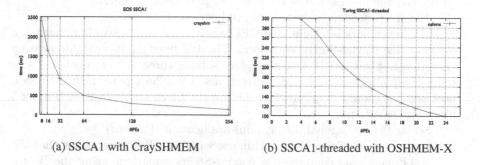

(a) SSCA1 with CraySHMEM   (b) SSCA1-threaded with OSHMEM-X

Fig. 2. SSCA1 run showing elapsed time as number of PEs increases

2.3 NPB

A collection of minimal application kernels that perform simplified instances of commonly occurring algorithms in scientific applications. The NPB [10] tests are implemented in either Fortran or C, with OpenSHMEM variants available for the following (implementation language given in parenthesis) [11] that are adapted from their MPI variants. The OpenSHMEM descriptions for benchmarks taken from [11], where process of arriving at the OpenSHMEM version of these benchmarks is discussed and more detailed comparison across different OpenSHMEM implementations is provided.

- IS: Integer Sort, random memory access (C)
  IS is the bucket sort based integer sorting kernel where each process has a *range* associated with it and sorts the *keys* based on the key range they fall under. Initially each process has a set of randomly generated *keys* which are processed and after finding the correct process depending on the range, the *keys* need to be sent to that process. The OpenSHMEM Specification does not have support for *AlltoAll* and *AlltoAllv* used in the original MPI codes, hence, a combination of OpenSHMEM *put/get* calls is used to simulate *AlltoAll* and *AlltoAllv* to communicate the *keys*.
- MG: Multi-Grid, long/short distance communication, memory intensive (Fortran)

The MG benchmark uses a V-cycle Multi Grid method to compute the solution of a 3D scalar Poisson equation [1]. In the OpenSHMEM MG version the original three sub-routines from the MPI version (*ready*, *take*, and *give*) used to post MPI_irecv requests, wait and then send data respectively, are collapsed into a single sub-routine. This is possible since OpenSHMEM has one sided communication and only requires to synchronize to ensure updates are visible to all PEs. The explicit synchronization through the *shmem_barrier_all* ensures all the process are at the same stage in their execution.

- BT: Block Tri-diagonal solver, mini-application (Fortran)
  The BT benchmark is a simulated CFD application that solves 3-dimensional compressible Navier-Stokes equations. The BT benchmark uses Alternating Direction Implicit (ADI), which involves solving three sets of uncoupled systems of equations in x, y and z directions [12]. The OpenSHMEM version uses *gets* for communication when solving the block tridiagonal with a 5×5 block size equations.

- SP: Scalar Penta-diagonal solver, mini-application (Fortran)
  SP is a variation of the BT benchmark with the difference being that SP solves 3-dimensional compressible Navier-Stokes equations using the Beam-Warming approximate factorization. BT has a higher communication to computation ratio [1] but the SP benchmark facilitates better overlapping of computation with communication in the OpenSHMEM version by issuing communication when the data is ready but only performing synchronization when the communicated data is going to be used.

Usage and Results. To compile the benchmarks, first create a `make.def` file in the `config` directory. Several examples are provided as a template. A `suite.def` file is also provided to compile all the available NAS benchmarks. The default compiler is set to `oshcc`.

```
To Compile:
   make <benchmark-name> NPROCS=<number> CLASS=<class> [SUBTYPE=<type>]

      where <benchmark-name>  is "bt", "cg", "ep", "ft", "is", "lu",
                                 "mg", or "sp"
             <number>          is the number of processes
             <class>           is "S", "W", "A", "B", "C", or "D"
To Execute:
   oshrun -n 256 ./bin/benchmark.class.number
```

Listing 5. Compiling and Executing OpenSHMEM NAS Benchmarks

Sample results for 32 PEs on a Cray XC30 (EOS), which has 8 physical cores per socket and 2 sockets per node with all nodes connected via a Cray Aries interconnect are shown in Listing 6.

```
 1  NAS Parallel Benchmarks 3.2 —— IS Benchmark
 2
 3  Size:   134217728   (class C)
 4  Iterations:   10
 5  Number of processes:      32
 6
 7  ... < snip >...
 8
 9  IS Benchmark Completed
10  Class            =                          C
11  Size             =                  134217728
12  Iterations       =                         10
13  Time in seconds  =                       1.00
14  Total processes  =                         32
15  Compiled procs   =                         32
16  Mop/s total      =                    1342.18
17  Mop/s/process    =                      41.94
18  Operation type   =                keys ranked
19  Verification     =                 SUCCESSFUL
20  Version          =                        3.2
21  Compile date     =                02 Jul 2018
22
23  Compile options:
24     SHMEMCC       = cc
25     CLINK         = $ (SHMEMCC)
26     CSHMEM_LIB    = (none)
27     CSHMEM_INC    = (none)
28     CMPI_LIB      = (none)
29     CMPI_INC      = (none)
30     CFLAGS        = −O3 −g
31     CLINKFLAGS    = −O3 −g
32  ... < snip >...
```

Listing 6. Sample Output for OpenSHMEM IS NPB

The IS NAS benchmark obtained on the Cray XC30 (EOS) using Cray-SHMEM is shown in Fig. 3. The tests used 4 nodes, placing increasing numbers of PEs per node until all (64) physical cores were full.

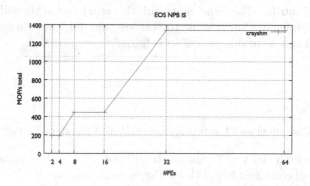

Fig. 3. IS results using OSHMEM-X on EOS

2.4   Random Access Benchmark (GUPs)

The OpenSHMEM versions (single PE and multithreaded) have been adapted from the Random Access Benchmark initially developed by David Koester and Bob Lucas. The Giga UPdates per Second (GUPS) [13,14] is calculated by identifying the number of memory locations that can be randomly updated in one second, divided by 1 billion (1e9). The term "randomly" in this context means that there is little to no relationship between one address to be updated and the next, except that they occur in the space of one half the total system memory. An update is a read-modify-write operation on a table of 64-bit words (HPCC_Table). In the OpenSHMEM version both the address and PE on which the update is to be performed is generated randomly. In absence of atomic xor in the OpenSHMEM Specification (1.3) at the time of implementing the benchmark, the benchmark uses *get* to fetch a remote value and then updates it using a *put* followed by a *quiet* to make the update visible on remote PE. We are aware that the current implementation of the benchmark limits the achievable concurrency and we hope to update it in the near future to match up better with the original benchmark description where the value at an address that is read from memory is modified by an integer operation (add, and, or, xor) with a literal value, and the new value is written back to memory.

Multithreading. The multithreaded version uses the OpenSHMEM context API to map one thread to a single resource context to provide an added level of concurrency. In the multithreaded version using OpenSHMEM contexts the iterations that modify the random locations within the HPCC_Table are split between the threads. More detailed results for evaluating implementation of contexts can be found in [4].

Usage and Results. The benchmark sub-directory has a Makefile. Set CC to the correct compiler within this file to test specific implementations. Default is set to oshcc. The executable produced is 'gups'.

```
1 To compile:
2    make
3
4 To Execute:
5    oshrun −np 32 ./gups
```

Listing 7. Compiling and Executing OpenSHMEM Random Access Benchmark

Sample results for 32 PEs on Turing, an Intel® Xeon® E5 Cluster 2660 processors with 10 physical cores and hyper threading, a Mellanox ConnectX-4 VPI adapter card, EDR IB (100 Gb/s) and 12 GB RAM are shown below:

```
1  Running on 32 processors
2  Total Main table size = 2^26 = 67108864 words
3  PE Main table size = (2^26)/32   = 2097152 words/PE MAX
4  Default number of updates (RECOMMENDED) = 268435456      and actually
       done = 268435456
5  Real time used = 58.660473 seconds
6  0.004576087 Billion(10^9) Updates    per second [GUP/s]
7  0.000143003 Billion(10^9) Updates/PE per second [GUP/s]
```

Listing 8. Sample Output for OpenSHMEM Random Access Benchmark

The GUPs obtained on our test system, Turing, using OSHMEM-X is shown in Fig. 4. There are two ranks per node (one per socket) with 10 OpenMP threads per PE (10 cores per socket).

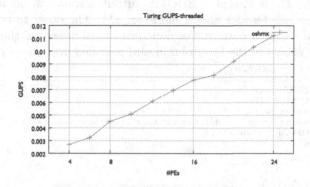

Fig. 4. GUPs results using OSHMEM-X on Turing

2.5   SHOMS

SHOMS is a micro-benchmark suite for testing the OpenSHMEM API [2]. It is based on the UOMS benchmark for UPC micro operations [15]. It is designed to do a minimal test of each function call in the library and report performance numbers. All of the tests will report latencies (min/max/average) and bandwidth when a function does data transfer. All tests are done in a simple manner, each function is setup with preallocated memory and transfers initialized data with the receiving end doing no checks on the data. The intention is to strictly test the performance of the OpenSHMEM, rather than a correctness test. SHOMS also features an affinity mode, where a subset of tests are run on two nodes, SHOMS repeats the tests between all combinations of single cores on each node. This allows SHOMS to identify if a core is favored by OpenSHMEM on a particular node.

Usage and Results. A `Makefile` has been provided in the benchmark directory. Changes to `CFLAGS` is a low value exercise since SHOMS is a network benchmark rather than a code benchmark. If working with a different build system (e.g. Cray) then change the `OSHCC` variable to the compiler that is used to build OpenSHMEM code (e.g. `OSHCC=cc` on Cray). The default compiler is set to `oshcc`.

```
1  To Compile:
2    make
3
4  To Execute:
5    oshrun -np 2 ./shoms --input test_FEATURE.txt
```

Listing 9. Compiling and Executing SHOMS Benchmarks

The SHOMS output is formatted in a consistent manner for all the benchmarks. The columns are labeled and instances where the value does not apply are marked with *N/A*. An excerpt of SHOMS output is shown in Listing 10, which highlights the single test for `shmem_barrier_all`. The other tests are omitted but they follow a similar pattern. For non-zero length messages, the actual number of bytes is shown in the first column and is scaled up to a user controllable maximum size (`--maxsize`).

```
1  Using OpenSHMEM version 1.3
2  Created all test list.
3  Will be running with 128 different tests
4  Will be running with 22 different size configurations
5  Using OpenSHMEM version 1.3
6  Running tests
7
8  ...<snip>...
9
10 #-------------------------------------------------
11 # Benchmarking shmem_barrier_all
12 # #processes = 8
13 #-------------------------------------------------
14        #bytes  #repetitions      t_min[nsec]        t_max[nsec]
       t_avg[nsec]       Bw_aggregated[MB/sec]
15         N/A          1000           12345              43411
       12937.99                  N/A
16 ...<snip>...
```

Listing 10. Sample output for OpenSHMEM SHOMS

Sample output for the SHOMS `shmem_barrier_all` test is shown in Listing 10. Figure 5 shows the results from a scale-up test of the `shmem_barrier_all` test using Cray-SHMEM on a Cray XC30 (EOS). The barrier synchronization was run over an increasing number of PEs (8-256)[3].

3   Conclusion

The collection of micro-benchmarks and mini-applications/kernels that comprise the OpenSHMEM Benchmark (OSB) suite has been described in detail. This included details on how to use the benchmarks and interpret their output. We have also provided demonstrative results from our use of OSB on machines at

---

[3] The test was run using command: `aprun -d 16 -S 1 -n $NPES ./shoms --input barrier.txt --maxsize 8`.

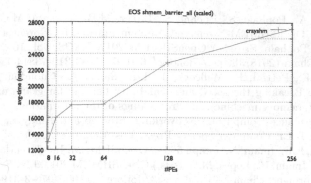

Fig. 5. SHOMS results for `shmem_barrier_all` with CraySHMEM on Cray XC30 (EOS)

ORNL with different implementations of OpenSHMEM. We also highlighted the enhancements required for creating the mulithreaded variants of three benchmarks included in the suite: Graph500, GUPS and SSCA1.

These codes have been developed over a number of years and have been used to evaluate a variety of capabilities using OpenSHMEM [2,3,6,7,11,13,14]. The suite is publicly available at https://github.com/ornl-languages/osb. We encourage the community to use the available codes and provide suggestions for improvement.

Acknowledgements. This research was supported by the United States Department of Defense (DoD) and Computational Research and Development Programs at Oak Ridge National Laboratory. This work was sponsored by the U.S. Department of Energy's Office of Advanced Scientific Computing Research. This research used resources of the Oak Ridge Leadership Computing Facility at the Oak Ridge National Laboratory, which is supported by the Office of Science of the U.S. Department of Energy under Contract No. DE-AC05-00OR22725.

References

1. Bailey, D., et al.: The NAS parallel benchmarks. Technical report RNR-94-007, NASA Ames Research Center, March 1994
2. Baker, M., Aderholdt, F., Venkata, M.G., Shamis, P.: OpenSHMEM-UCX: evaluation of UCX for implementing OpenSHMEM programming model. In: Gorentla Venkata, M., Imam, N., Pophale, S., Mintz, T.M. (eds.) OpenSHMEM 2016. LNCS, vol. 10007, pp. 114–130. Springer, Cham (2016). https://doi.org/10.1007/978-3-319-50995-2_8
3. Baker, M., Welch, A., Gorentla Venkata, M.: Parallelizing the Smith-Waterman algorithm using OpenSHMEM and MPI-3 one-sided interfaces. In: Gorentla Venkata, M., Shamis, P., Imam, N., Lopez, M.G. (eds.) OpenSHMEM 2014. LNCS, vol. 9397, pp. 178–191. Springer, Cham (2015). https://doi.org/10.1007/978-3-319-26428-8_12

4. Bouteiller, A., Pophale, S., Boehm, S., Baker, M.B., Venkata, M.G.: Evaluating contexts in OpenSHMEM-X reference implementation. In: Gorentla Venkata, M., Imam, N., Pophale, S. (eds.) OpenSHMEM 2017. LNCS, vol. 10679, pp. 50–62. Springer, Cham (2018). https://doi.org/10.1007/978-3-319-73814-7_4
5. Checconi, F., Petrini, F., Willcock, J., Lumsdaine, A., Choudhury, A.R., Sabharwal, Y.: Breaking the speed and scalability barriers for graph exploration on distributed-memory machines. In: Proceedings of the International Conference on High Performance Computing, Networking, Storage and Analysis, SC 2012, pp. 13:1–13:12. IEEE Computer Society Press, Los Alamitos (2012)
6. D'Azevedo, E.F., Imam, N.: Graph 500 in OpenSHMEM. In: Gorentla Venkata, M., Shamis, P., Imam, N., Lopez, M.G. (eds.) OpenSHMEM 2014. LNCS, vol. 9397, pp. 154–163. Springer, Cham (2015). https://doi.org/10.1007/978-3-319-26428-8_10
7. Grossman, M., Doyle, J., Dinan, J., Pritchard, H., Seager, K., Sarkar, V.: Implementation and evaluation of OpenSHMEM contexts using OFI libfabric. In: Gorentla Venkata, M., Imam, N., Pophale, S. (eds.) OpenSHMEM 2017. LNCS, vol. 10679, pp. 19–34. Springer, Cham (2018). https://doi.org/10.1007/978-3-319-73814-7_2
8. Grossman, M., Pritchard, H., Budimlić, Z., Sarkar, V.: Graph500 on OpenSHMEM: using a practical survey of past work to motivate novel algorithmic developments. In: Proceedings of the Second Annual PGAS Applications Workshop, PAW 2017, pp. 2:1–2:8. ACM, New York (2017)
9. IEEE Standard Glossary of Software Engineering Terminology: IEEE Std 610.12-1990, pp. 1–84, December 1990. ISBN: 1-55937467-X
10. NAS Parellel Benchmarks. https://www.nas.nasa.gov/publications/npb.html
11. Pophale, S., et al.: OpenSHMEM performance and potential: a NPB experimental study. In: Proceedings of the 6th Conference on Partitioned Global Address Space Programming Models (PGAS 2012), 10–12 October 2012
12. Saphir, W., Van Der Wijngaart, R., Woo, A., Yarrow, M.: New implementations and results for the NAS parallel benchmarks 2. In: 8th SIAM Conference on Parallel Processing for Scientific Computing (1997)
13. Seager, K., Choi, S.-E., Dinan, J., Pritchard, H., Sur, S.: Design and implementation of OpenSHMEM using OFI on the aries interconnect. In: Gorentla Venkata, M., Imam, N., Pophale, S., Mintz, T.M. (eds.) OpenSHMEM 2016. LNCS, vol. 10007, pp. 97–113. Springer, Cham (2016). https://doi.org/10.1007/978-3-319-50995-2_7
14. Shamis, P., Venkata, M.G., Poole, S., Welch, A., Curtis, T.: Designing a high performance OpenSHMEM implementation using universal common communication substrate as a communication middleware. In: Poole, S., Hernandez, O., Shamis, P. (eds.) OpenSHMEM 2014. LNCS, vol. 8356, pp. 1–13. Springer, Cham (2014). https://doi.org/10.1007/978-3-319-05215-1_1
15. Taboada, G.L., Mallon, D.A.: UPC Operations Microbenchmarking Suite 1.1 User's manual. CESGA Alliance (2010). http://forge.cesga.es/projects/uoms
16. Willcock, J., Lumsdaine, A.: Graph500 Benchmark: MPI Reference Implementation. https://github.com/graph500/graph500/blob/v2-spec/mpi/README

Author Index

Printed in the United States
By Bookmasters